ENVIRONMENTAL ETHICS

Science Action Coalition is a nonprofit research organization located in Washington, D.C., that investigates public-interest issues, including energy, environmental protection, consumer safety, and other health-related topics. Albert J. Fritsch, S.J., Ph.D., is a director of SAC and an organic chemist. He has been particularly involved in areas concerning environmental protection and resource conservation. As former co-director of the Center for Science in the Public Interest, he authored *99 Ways to a Simple Lifestyle* and *The Household Pollutants Guide*, both published by Anchor Press/Doubleday.

ENVIRONMENTAL ETHICS

Choices for Concerned Citizens

by Science Action Coalition
with Albert J. Fritsch, S.J., Ph.D.

Contributors:
Gerard McMahon
Alan Okagaki
William Millerd, S.J.

Anchor Books
Anchor Press/Doubleday
Garden City, New York
1980

We gratefully acknowledge permission to reprint excerpts from *The Jerusalem Bible*, copyright © 1966 by Darton, Longman & Todd, Ltd., and Doubleday & Company, Inc. Used by permission of the publisher.

Library of Congress Cataloging in Publication Data
Science Action Coalition.
    Environmental ethics.

    Includes index.
    1. Environmental policy—Moral and religious aspects. 2. Environmental protection—Moral and religious aspects. I. Fritsch, Albert J. II. Title.
HC79.E5S3   1979   301.31
ISBN 0-385-14880-1
Library of Congress Catalog Card Number: 78-14701

ACKNOWLEDGMENTS

We owe to the large number of citizens who are concerned about our environment sincere thanks for the environmental work they have done. Their efforts helped make this book possible.

In the effort to acknowledge all the persons who aided us in special ways, we always run a risk of leaving someone out. Nonetheless we will try. First, we are especially grateful to Dick Marchand, who assembled the preliminary materials during the summer of 1976. We are also thankful to Ann Pierotti, Ken Bossong, and Dennis Darcey, who read our preliminary drafts, and to the Jesuit Council on Theological Reflection for initial funding of the project. Special credit is due to Marge Oldfield for endangered species information; to the National Council of Churches Energy Taskforce Committee for allowing two of us to participate in their proceedings; to Tom Conry and Art Purcell for hazardous-chemical discussion; to David Fry, who offered many points on the book, especially in the lifestyle section; to Drew Christianson for his overview and highly professional insights, to Maureen Flynn McCoy and Bob Schemel for reading the entire manuscript; to Angela Iadavaia-Cox for her many fine editorial comments, general impressions, and patience; and to Gerry Munley for proofing parts of the text.

We dedicate this book to the late Dick Marchand, who symbolized in his struggle against cancer the essence of the environmental battle.

CONTENTS

V VIII HS(A)

Looks good book inclusive

ENVIRONMENTAL ETHICS

TOWARD AN ENVIRONMENTAL
ETHICS

From the ominous note sounded almost two decades ago in Rachel Carson's *Silent Spring* to the current controversies of endangered species preservation, nuclear power, strip mining, and hazardous chemicals, we are surrounded by evidence that environmental deterioration is often a companion of modern lifestyles.

This book is not intended as an effort to heighten environmental consciousness, or to pinpoint blame. Much has been written about the causes, symptoms, and detection of environmental deterioration, and the references at the end of the first four chapters provide ample aid in ecological consciousness raising. Instead, we are attempting to explore the values that underlie this environmental degradation and the sets of principles that citizens must apply to remedy the situation. "Ecological brushfire fighting" is outdated. The dash from one crisis to another is successful in stirring public awareness, curbing blatant polluters, and developing and passing good legislation. Such ad hoc attempts, however, obscure the environmental and social injustice threatening to engulf both nonhuman and human systems. A remedial impasse is not surprising given the lack of understanding and consensus on how and why we value our environment. We need a set of ethical principles—analogous to ones developed in medicine, business, law, and other professions—to direct proper environmental action.

Several factors contribute to our current ecological crisis. While not exhaustive, the following list does indicate obvious problem areas. One evident factor is the disregard for life in all its forms, extending beyond the human sphere to include plant and animal life as well. Worse yet, it is the failure to define our humanity by other creatures around us, to perceive the unity of the various forms of life, to break with self-interests and consider the needs of other creatures. Various cultural and technological developments have promoted the dualism of "man and nature," and in the resulting alienation the interdependence between human beings and other creatures has been obscured.

Another factor is the uncontrolled condition of modern technology. We have yet to cope with the alluring qualities of the scientific revolution and, instead, are duped by the axiom "What can be done must be done." We have welcomed every advance in the generation and distribution of energy, weapons, communication, and other "necessities," while neglecting their total impact on our lives and communities. We give little time and effort to developing safeguards to control technology, to assessing total resource demand to operate it, and to limiting our use to where technology is authentically needed.

A third factor is an attitude among many that there is an unlimited supply of global resources, whether they be energy, raw materials, or financing. While the earth's resources are sufficient for basic human needs, they are not so for human greed. Our modern habits require immense expenditures of these resources, and, as might be expected, we have extracted the more easily accessible mineral and fossil fuel reserves, thus making it more difficult for the Third World or future generations to obtain a proper share.

It follows that a fourth factor is the large-scale use and waste of materials by consumers, whether corporate or individual. From an ecological viewpoint, this is more acute in the area of synthetic chemical use. The volume of these chemicals now consumed is beyond what the environment can safely absorb and neutralize. Some remain for centuries before decomposing into harmless by-products. Harmful chemicals are now found in even remote reaches of the planet.

Looking more deeply into the underlying causes of resource depletion and overconsumption, we find that our economic system does not grant an intrinsic value to often unquantifiable environmental components. There's no price tag on a breath of air—fresh or otherwise—or a view of a wild river. This has led to burdening the environment and yet not paying for this burden. Economic growth that neglects environmental deterioration is hardly growth.

The sixth factor is an exaggerated sense of freedom to choose any individual or collective lifestyle that suits our fancy, with little thought to consequences. Is one really free to be extravagant in a finite world with many human needs?

The final factor is a shortsighted focus on the present moment and little care about the future, about keeping the earth at least as good as we found it, about respect for unborn generations, and about thoughtful planning.

This book will not illustrate the history and development of these factors, but rather present them as motivating forces in our—the authors'—lives. As public-interest workers, we do not view environmental ethics as a mathematical or deductive system, nor as a set of self-evident principles, nor as a refuge from activism for ivory tower dwellers. Such views do not convey our experience and urgency. On the other hand, we know that unreflecting environmental action is counterproductive; it makes mistakes; it arrives at limited and incomplete solutions; often it dwells on nonessentials; its advocates lose enthusiasm. Environmentalists are gradually coming to a consensus about environmental needs. But our understanding needs development.

AN ENVIRONMENTAL CONSCIOUSNESS

The environmental crisis has triggered a new awareness among many of us that can be stated in the following seven ways:

1. *Everything Is Related to Everything Else*

An ecosystem encompasses living organisms and nonliving substances interacting to produce an exchange of materials between the living and nonliving parts. Included are populations of species, as well as their natural habitats. The basic insight of ecology is that all living things exist in interrelated systems; nothing exists in isolation. The world system is weblike; to pluck one strand is to cause all to vibrate; whatever happens to one part has ramifications for all the rest. Our actions are not individual but social; they reverberate throughout the whole ecosystem.

Homo sapiens stands at the summit of an ecological pyramid, with soil organisms at the base, then vegetation in many forms, then herbivores, and up to carnivores. The continued health of the entire structure depends on the richness of the base, the number of levels, the diversity of forms, and the complexity and activity of living beings at the top. The depletion of resources and pollution threaten both us and many other species vital to the well-being of the entire ecosystem. We enrich ourselves when enriching other inhabitants of this earth.

2. Not Everything That Can Be Done Should Be Done

With the explosion of scientific knowledge, and its handmaiden technology, many think that almost anything can be accomplished. Astronauts walk on the moon; modern medicine keeps us alive and well; electricity operates a hundred convenience items in our lives. But technology can be both a promise and a peril. Unprincipled use of technological power is autonomous and sterile; it soon controls our lives while we cling to the illusion that it serves us.

The master-servant roles in a high-technology society are dramatized through the film *2001*, when the spaceship is commandeered by its computer, HAL 9000, which resists when the pilot tries to regain control. A mechanical mutiny develops, serving as a metaphorical warning to our society. A technological mirage can seduce and control as thoroughly as HAL 9000, whether disguised as the automobile, electric appliance, or computer. Awareness is increasing that technology must be responsibly controlled and certain forms of innovation restricted.

3. This Earth Has Only Limited Resources

The Arab oil embargo gave the industrial West a rude awakening. A sense that we could always turn somewhere else when in need died suddenly. Before our modern appetite for goods, the earth seemed uncrowded, the ocean and air infinite receptacles of wastes, and the resources there for the grabbing. Individual exploiters of forests and soil were mavericks. Now we observe fossil fuel reserves dwindling, living space increasingly at a premium, oceans and atmosphere growing dirty, and animals becoming endangered. It even takes resources to clean up the environment, and these are costly and not readily available. The truth is inescapable: this earth is finite.

4. *Chemicals Can Pollute Our Environment and Harm Us*

People throughout the ages have discovered and protected themselves from poisons. With the advent of modern technology, we now face literally thousands of new chemicals in the home, in consumer products, in foods, in agriculture and industry. Many of these chemicals are dispersed globally via air and water. Awareness of the dangers of chemical pollutants has become a major source of environmental concern. But overpublicizing chemical mishaps can confuse citizens who do not have knowledge of how to use certain chemicals prudently. They often seek some form of official approval or disapproval and forget that proper handling requires training and experience. What is missing is a genuine respect for all chemicals, not just the most harmful ones.

5. *If We Have to Grow, Let's Do It Properly*

Economist E. J. Mishan, who popularized the term *growthmania*, says that societies have a predilection for a "cornucopia of burgeoning indices." This tendency is nurtured by conventional economics and modern business preaching the maximization of gross national product (GNP) —a value index measuring the flow of annual production. By equating well-being with the size index, social improvement is soon linked with GNP growth. However, social and economic problems arise with continued GNP growth. There is a limit to the capacity of the environment to service this growth, both in providing raw materials and in assimilating by-product wastes due to consumption. The largesse of technology can only postpone or disguise the inevitable.

Thoughtful people perceive that growth in some form is a psychological need of human beings and part of our teleological and spiritual nature. When growth is equated with material improvement or acquisition, then an ecological cancer results. Alternative growth practices that require fewer resources are needed, but the implementation of these calls for a fundamental rethinking of our social, political, and economic systems.

6. It's Good to Simplify Our Lives

We are children of a culture that glorifies the modern. Food is fast, overpackaged, tasteless, and full of chemicals; clothes are cheap, poorly fashioned, and quickly discarded; homes are hastily constructed, poorly ventilated, and high energy users; vehicles are expensive, individualized, and in need of constant attention. All is not lost, however; those living simply are starting to speak out, but their power to publicize is minuscule compared to that of the mass media, which depend on complex living habits for their livelihood.

7. We Are Agents of This Earth's Future

To be human is to exist in history, to make one's own history, to create oneself. In earlier ages the world was perceived as possessing a fixed and somewhat static order, and all creatures accepted their place in that order. Each person became an actor in a drama of personal salvation. Very little thought was directed toward interaction between and within the various strata that underlay the order.

We now have a better sense of creating ourselves, our society, and our world. Unjust social structures are not preordained metaphysical necessities; they result from narrow, selfish human choices. The days of passivity are past; we are responsible. We sense both our power and our fragile position in this ecosystem. We both create and are dependent on the world around us. While directing history we can also destroy nature. The works of Teilhard de Chardin and Rachel Carson can be coupled.

Past human awareness of shaping history was never strong because change came more gradually. We are the fruit of rapid technological innovation; we see an earth changing around us—especially dramatic in strip-mining regions—sometimes for better and sometimes for worse. Evolution becomes personalized and is transferred out of the realm of relatively haphazard impersonal laws of mutation, adaptation, and chance survival into the conscious control of human beings. We are in charge of the world's future.

TOWARD AN ENVIRONMENTAL ETHICS

Merely concentrating on environmental crisis factors and growth of consciousness is insufficient, because the picture is not solely black or white but includes the shaded areas where values compete and clash. Underlying each of the human factors leading to environmental crisis are values both helpful and detrimental to the environment. It is important to unravel these values and discover where conflicting values are present and where they demand resolution (see chart at end of Introduction). Environmentalists are generally open to attitudinal changes, which are often contingent on understanding the values we use to justify our environmental actions.

Each of the chapters of this book highlights pairs of value conflicts that we have found in our public-interest work in the respective areas discussed. From our constant work with both citizen groups and technical people we see the struggle that a broad spectrum of environmentalists engage in to resolve some of these conflicts. As public-interest persons with ethical concerns and training, we approach the subject in a different way from that of some professional ethicists. Our method is inductive; our audience is one of concerned citizens; our tools are not teeming references, quotations, and charts but results from experience in the field; our method is not academic but public interest–oriented; our goals are more perfect environmental activities.

The first four chapters deal with more specific problem areas (endangered species, nuclear safety, coal problems, and chemical pollution), but each has related problem areas where the working principles evolved may apply:

First: plant, animal, and ocean ecology, wetlands use, animal rights, use of animals for experimentation, agricultural practices;

Second: hazardous waste disposal, international environmental controls, weapons proliferation, technological limitations, sabotage, radiation pollution;

Third: gas and oil extraction, land disturbances and reclamation, power plant siting and problems, automotive pollution, vibrational pollution;

Fourth: food additives, drugs, pesticides, fertilizers, occupational health, industrial chemical disposal and transportation, consumer products.

The underlying values of each chapter are not exclusive to that problem area, but are given an emphasis due to the nature of the matter:

Survival is implied in the continued process of all life and not just the fittest forms. Should all living species be allowed to exist? Should we not make an effort to preserve them when they are threatened by economic or special interests? Is there an overconcern about particular plants and animals? Is not the attitude that endangers a species the same that fosters social injustice?

Technological optimism conveys the attitude that human beings can be rescued from any difficulty through the power of technology. This attitude led to the "peacetime" use of the atom. But will not a worldwide proliferation of nuclear power plants require us to review nuclear production, containment, and waste disposal risks? Should the risks be justified or should a moratorium be declared until sufficient safeguards are found?

Ecojustice means an exercise of balance in utilizing natural resources and dealing with ecosystems. It is required for the development of any energy policy. Should not energy alternatives be used that have less ecological and human health impact? Should not the local inhabitants control energy production and use in their area?

Prudence refers here to the use of products only to the degree necessary. There is special need in the area of hazardous chemicals, which are produced, transported and used, and eventually disposed of in unprecedented quantities. Are the various constituencies (workers, consumers, regulators, industrialists, scientists) even aware of particular rights and responsibilities? Is there a need to enforce existing laws to a greater degree?

Human fulfillment involves an orientation toward spiritual, intellectual, artistic, and cultural growth. Is there not a temptation to define human fulfillment in terms of acquisition of

Chapter Topics	Factors Leading to Environmental Crisis	Awareness	Underlying Values	Conflicting Values
1. Endangered Species	Disrespect for plant and animal life	Interrelatedness of all species	Survival	Human rights and needs versus plant and animal welfare
2. Nuclear Safety	Uncontrolled modern technology	Limits to technological application	Technological optimism	Faith in human abilities versus caution about human error
3. Coal Extraction	Attitude of having unlimited resources	Limits to resources	Ecojustice	Economic fuel needs versus environmental concerns
4. Hazardous Chemicals	Overconsumption of material goods	Chemicals cause pollution	Prudence	Availability of consumer products versus safety controls for citizens
5. Qualitative Growth	Economics does not grant intrinsic ecological value	Growth need not be quantitative	Human fulfillment	Psychological need to grow versus conservation
6. Lifestyle Choices	Exaggerated freedom of lifestyle choice	Simple lifestyles have merit	Communality	Individual freedom versus collective restraint and decision-making
7. Theological Reflections	Activity for the present moment only	Agents of the earth's future.	Stewardship	Passive acceptance of nature versus preserving and improving nature
8. Environmental Action Criteria	—	Need for critical reflection	Ecological wisdom	Activity versus reflection

material products? Do we simply give lip service to conservation of resources while countering by evoking the specter of unemployment, economic stagnation, and loss of world economic leadership? Is not the challenge to develop ethically based alternatives that restrict material growth among the affluent and open the way to sharing among the world's poor?

Communality means the joining of diverse elements in dynamic cooperation while respecting and fostering the growth of individuals. This can be done by directing the drive toward interior growth into simpler, less consumptive lifestyles. This requires profound attitudinal changes by individuals and communities. Is not some form of social restraint required, since voluntarism by itself has such a poor track record? Is not the challenge to preserve the greatest possible personal freedom while at the same time curbing lifestyle extravagances?

Stewardship is a conscientious assumption of responsibility to preserve and improve the environment. Is it enough that we treat nature with such awe and respect that we leave it untouched and undeveloped? Are we faithful to our Western traditions if we fail to practice some form of control over the forces of this earth? Cannot responsible activity help recreate a better environment?

Ecological wisdom creates within the concerned individual a balance between reflection and proper environmental action. It is not enough to reflect on a series of environmental problems and conflicting values, for values are not exclusive and conflicts not isolated. Wisdom moves one to action that is better informed and directed. Thus our concluding chapter sets up some criteria for environmental action, which will make us better prepared to meet new environmental challenges.

SUGGESTED GENERAL READING

I. G. Barbour, ed. *Earth Might Be Fair: Reflections on Ethics, Religion, and Ecology.* Englewood Cliffs, N.J.: Prentice-Hall, Inc. 1972.

R. Dubos. *So Human an Animal.* New York: Charles Scribner's Sons, 1968.

G. T. Miller, Jr. *Living in the Environment: Concepts, Problems and Alternatives.* Belmont, Calif.: Wadsworth Publishing Company, 1975.

B. Ward. *Spaceship Earth.* New York: Columbia University Press, 1966.

I

WHY FAREWELL TO PLANTS AND ANIMALS?

When the buffalo are all slaughtered, the wild horses all tamed, the secret corners of the forest heavy with the scent of many men, and the view of the ripe hills blotted by talking wires, where is the thicket? Gone. Where is the eagle? Gone. And what is it to say good-by to the swift and the hunt, the end of living and the beginning of survival?

> "This Earth Is Sacred,"
> Letter from Chief Sealth
> to President Franklin Pierce
> (1855)

Since the seas spawned the first simple unicellular organisms about 2 billion years ago, some 350,000 plant species and perhaps 1 million species of animals have evolved on this planet. However, since humanity learned to profoundly change this natural world, the ecosystems have been increasingly disturbed. Development projects with massive environmental implications have been undertaken with little scientific understanding of their impact.

In the last two hundred years, and especially over the last fifty years, a tremendous increase in the number of extinct species has occurred. Of the over one hundred recorded animal extinctions, about half are since 1900. At least one hundred plant species have been lost in the last hundred years, including some of extreme beauty. Nearly one thousand species of birds, fish, and mammals are now listed as "endangered"—i.e., faced with immediate extinction—and still more are classified as "threatened" or could become extinct without positive preservation measures. The U. S. Federal Office of Endangered Species is wading through petitions requesting that an additional 23,000 species of plants and animals be designated either endangered or threatened. Some estimate that 10 percent of the world's plant and animal life is now believed to be endangered.

George M. Woodwell, a noted ecologist, says the earth is in the throes of a series of unprecedented biotic changes caused by human beings that at best can be described as a "biotic impoverishment."[1] S. Dillon Ripley of the Smithsonian Institution predicts that the majority of the nation's animals could be extinct by the year 2000.[2] According to economist Kenneth Boulding, it may become economically impossible to maintain any nondomesticated animals outside of zoos by the next generation.[3]

Human beings are the cause of most of the recent recorded extinctions. Many species of birds and animals have been shot, trapped, or hunted into oblivion: the North American passenger pigeon, Eastern elk, Carolina parakeet, heath hen, Merriam elk, Badlands bighorn, Eastern timber wolf, and Eastern cougar, among others. Wilderness habitats and forests have given way to farms and pastures; river valleys are dammed; nesting sites are disturbed by resort developments; fertilizers, pesticides, and other chemicals contaminate water systems and damage even remote ecosystems. Rare plant species have suffered an analogous fate from overzealous collectors and profiteers.

The serious problem has sparked public concern. Forty nations participated in a three-week conference in 1973 to hammer out an international treaty restricting the export and import of endangered plants and animals. The U. S. Endangered Species Act of 1973 protects rare and vanishing forms of life, but its implementation has been problematic. Citizens sued the Tennessee Valley Authority (TVA) under provisions of the act and halted construction on a $100 million dam because it would exterminate the snail darter, an endangered fish. Fearing other such threats to development projects, business interests are lobbying Congress to repeal the act.

Underlying the preservation movement is the unfolding notion that we have ethical responsibilities to other living beings on Earth. This flies in the face of *homocentric* (human-centered) Western thought, since it is *ecocentric* and focuses on the natural world. A host of questions arise: Are there limits to what we can ethically do to alter the environment on behalf of our vested interests? Do rare animals and plants have a right to continued existence? Is there not an intrinsic good, which is not economic- or human-oriented, that endangered species possess? The answers are worthy of extended public discussion.

RATIONALE FOR PRESERVATION

Several writers have suggested that an environmental ethics is a logical and inevitable step in the development of Western ethics. The nineteenth-century author Victor Hugo once wrote:

> In the relations of man, with the animals, with the flowers, with the objects of creation, there is a great ethic, scarcely perceived as yet, which will at length break forth into the light and which will be the corollary and complement to human ethics.[4]

Other thinkers, from Charles Darwin to the American naturalist Aldo Leopold, have traced the broadening of ethical concerns from narrow self-interest to a more expansive consideration of the rights and welfare of all people. In his book *Sand County Almanac,* Leopold describes the progress of Western ethics as a kind of "spiraling out" from the individual, to the society, and to all of humanity. While the first ethics dealt with the individual, later ethics defined relations between people in society and then between individuals and society in general. Leopold believed a further extension of ethics to encompass "the land and the animals which grow upon it" was both an "evolutionary possibility and an ecological necessity."[5] Surveying the damage wrought by humans upon the biosphere, Leopold concluded that the health of the natural world could be preserved only through an ethics that defined and prohibited unacceptable actions. The insight of Leopold and the biological sciences is that the activities of human society do take place within the larger community of the biosphere. Given the extent of the human/nature interdependencies, it is imperative that all people affirm a set of ethical principles that protects the biosphere, including the rare and endangered species that are integral parts of the natural world.

The development of an ethics of endangered species has been linked to our growing understanding of ecological principles. As the biological sciences have progressed, we have become much more aware of our dependencies upon the species of plants and animals comprising the natural world. Species function in interconnected, interrelated fashion within the biosphere, and all species play roles that contribute to the health of the total ecosystem. Through the process of evolution, organisms are continually adapting vis-à-vis the physical environment and the other organisms within the ecosystem. The physical characteristics of species and size of species populations respond to changes in the environment. In a sense, the ecosystem is driven by a logic that manipulates the number and characteristics of organisms within the system so that the ecosystem as a whole can make most efficient use of available resources. As a result, there are never any "vestigial" life forms within an ecosystem. Since each species does play a role, the ecosystem becomes weaker every time we cause the extinction of any form of life.

Although we may not understand what precise roles each species performs within the ecosystem, our studies have taught us that species diversity is both an indication of and a contributing factor to the strengths of ecosystems. Our relative ignorance about the processes and relationships within the ecosystem suggests that we should be cautious in the ways we alter the natural environment. We can almost never state with certainty (1) a particular species' place in the biological complex; (2) its relationships with other species; and (3) the effect on the ecosystem if it were to be artificially brought to extinction. We do know that when a species becomes extinct its ecological niche is sooner or later filled by another species. But whether this replacement species will be benign or harmful, or how it will affect the character of the ecosystem, is far beyond our powers of prediction.

We simply must confess to not knowing detrimental consequences that follow extinction of rare species. The lack of known consequences may reflect more upon our ignorance than on the true impacts upon the environment. However, we can cite many examples where human tampering has affected ecosystems. Species of birds, plants, and mammals have been introduced into new ecosystems and, lacking predators or other controls, have reproduced to huge populations and wrought terrible damage on the environment. The introduction of the cotton culture into the southeastern United

States brought about considerable reduction of many plant and animal populations. The boll weevil invasion followed. In the case of a single rare species, perhaps the change from only a few members to none would have little impact on the ecosystem as a whole. But one has to wonder how many times this argument can be repeated and still be valid. Although the loss of one, two, or perhaps a dozen species would little affect the biosphere, naturalists estimate that over 200,000 plant and animal species are either endangered or will become endangered in the near future. One has to doubt how well the biosphere can endure rapid wholesale extinction of species that took millions of years to evolve.

The diversity of species is probably even more important to the long-term future of the biosphere than it is to its present viability. The ecologist Eugene P. Odum has stated:

> The advantage of a diversity of species, that is the survival value of its [ecological] community lies in increased stability. The more species present, the greater the possibilities for adapting to changing conditions.[6]

Every living species has a unique composition of genes which represent an important resource that can never be replaced if the species were to become extinct. The environment is not static: climatic, biological, chemical, and geological factors will change in the future, and ecosystems and the organisms within the ecosystems will have to adapt accordingly. With a large and diverse gene pool, the ecosystem has greater overall flexibility to adapt to a wider range of new conditions. Since rare species are often adapted to unusual or harsh habitats, their genetic material is likewise unique and especially valuable. The Devil's Hole pupfish that survives in but one pool of water in Death Valley is known to have an extraordinary tolerance for temperature variations. Many rare plants grow in difficult habitats—islands, ocean and estuary shorelines, mountaintops, rock faces, deserts, bogs, and so on —and contain potentially valuable genetic material. When conditions change in the future, today's rare species could be uniquely suited to the new environment and become dominant species.

The size of the gene pool is equally relevant to agriculture. Cultivated plants have been bred for special purposes and qualities, often to the point where they are totally dependent upon human care and heavy inputs of chemical fertilizers, pesticides, and water. Over thousands of years, a very small number of plants have been selected for food crops. In the industrialized nations, genetic specialization is taking place within each kind of crop as well. The National Academy of Sciences' study *Genetic Vulnerability of Major Crops* found that 70 percent of the United States corn production came from six different species and 50 percent of the wheat crop from just nine species, and that there were similarly narrow bases for other major crops.[7] Genetic specialization makes food crops extremely vulnerable to a new pathogenic disease, a new biotype of insect pest, or other kind of environmental stress. The Irish potato crop had a very narrow genetic base and fell to the fungus *Phytophthora infestans* in the 1840s. Wide-scale planting of T-cytoplasm in the United States opened the way to the corn blight of 1970.

Special efforts have to be made to preserve the progenitors of our current food crops. More and more races of food crops are being lost as Western-style agriculture with its genetically specific crops supplants older and more traditional methods of agriculture. By preserving the progenitors, plant breeders can draw upon the genetic resources within the pool that are resistant to new pests and diseases. Crossbreeding and hybridizing with wild species can also bring out greater productivity under different soil and climate conditions. But it is essential that the agricultural genetic base no longer be allowed to diminish as it has in recent years.[8]

As we learn more about the properties of rare organisms, species that have no present commercial uses can suddenly become invaluable. Individual species have unique biological and chemical characteristics that can suit them for different purposes. It has been estimated that another 50,000 new chemicals could be discovered in plants, many of which will have medical, scientific, or commercial applications, and many of which could be lost if wholesale extinction of plant life does occur. History has shown some of the most important discoveries coming from the most unlikely sources. The

South American cinchona tree was thought to be worthless until quinine's antimalarial properties were discovered. The fungus *Penicillium* became the chemical base for the antibiotic penicillin. Certain lawn fungi can clean carbon monoxide from the air.[9] Many mollusks produce a chemical substance called mercenene that shows promise as an anti-cancer drug.[10] The manatee, an endangered species, can control the water hyacinths that clog inland waterways more effectively than mechanical or chemical methods.[11] Plants produce biologically active chemicals, including some that can be synthesized into safe insecticides. This list could go on indefinitely; the future worth of rare species is incalculable.

The study of endangered species could provide insight into the workings of ecosystems. Research pertaining to rare species in their habitats will lead us to a greater understanding of evolution, the adaptation within ecosystems, and the strengths and stability of ecosystems. With the proliferation of artificial human-controlled environments, natural ecosystems must be preserved to act as "norms" for research: i.e., to let us see how the laws of nature operate in settings unaltered by humans. For example, comparisons between wild species in their native habitats and domestic crops will, we hope, explain the declining performance of cultivated plants and lead us to an agriculture that sustains the soil rather than depleting it. Learning why species become extinct—especially when their demise is related to air or water pollution or human-induced chemicals in the environment—could teach us how to modify our activities to become more benign toward the ecosphere. The ascendance and the decline of species are themselves indicators of the health of ecosystems that we should monitor more closely.

Out of habitat, individual species have been tools in other spheres of biological research. The fruit fly has been the "guinea pig" in countless genetic experiments. Monkeys were invaluable in developing vaccinations for poliomyelitis, the fox squirrel provides an animal model for the study of certain hereditary diseases, and armadillos are being tested in leprosy research. Medical researchers are studying the desert pupfish, a relative of the Devil's Hole pupfish, because it has extraordinarily efficient kidneys. While the field of comparative medicine is still very underdeveloped, we can be certain that many rare species are potentially very important.

Equally important, endangered species should be preserved because they are part of our heritage. Endangered species include some of the world's most beautiful and unusual inhabitants. The whooping crane is the most majestic bird in the United States, the bald eagle is probably the most important national symbol, and the California condor is the nation's largest native bird. The grizzly bear is the most fearsome carnivore in the continental United States; the blue whale is the largest creature ever to live on Earth; the dolphin, though not endangered, has been killed off at a shocking rate and is possibly one of the most intelligent animals. Huge seagoing turtles, the American crocodile, the wolf (which is such a large part of American folklore), the elusive bighorn sheep, and the pronghorn antelope are all endangered. Many beautiful species of plants, especially cacti and orchids, are likewise endangered. The state with the richest and most exotic wildlife, Hawaii, has suffered by far the most natural devastation. About half of Hawaii's 1,729 native species of plants are endangered; the state's only two endemic mammals—the Hawaiian monk seal and the Hawaiian hoary bat—have declined alarmingly; 23 of the 67 known species and subspecies of native birds are already extinct, and of the remaining 44 kinds of birds, 29 are listed as endangered.[12] Wildlife species, especially rare and endangered organisms, are our environmental heritage, the end products of millions of years of evolution. They should be preserved just as we preserve Egyptian temples and classical art and historic buildings as links to ages past.

These are compelling cases for the protection of rare organisms: history has shown that rare species often have unexpected and irreplaceable utility, and the biological sciences have demonstrated that our livelihood is tied to the health of the ecosphere. And yet, despite the persuasiveness of this rationale, the movement for preservation of endangered species draws its strength primarily from a more subjective, intuitive value placed on vanishing wildlife by society. This subjective value is based on emotion and empathy. It arises, not from logically derived principles or from consideration of human self-interest, but from a deeper, perhaps primordial, sympathy for the well-being of nature and its creatures.

In *The Descent of Man*, Charles Darwin spoke of the progressive extensions in human social instincts and sympathies —from the individual, to a small surrounding circle, and finally to the human race—that Leopold was to write about many years later. But Darwin phrased the extension in terms of "sympathies becoming more tender and widely diffused, extending to men of all races, to the senile, maimed, and other useless members of society, and finally to the lower animals. . . ."[13] In his use of the words "sympathies" and "tender" and his references to the senile, maimed, and useless, Darwin alludes to a motivation that is qualitatively different from rational homocentric self-interest. As Darwin suggests, people do feel a kinship with fellow living beings in the world. Although our civilization has widened the distance between a person and nature, each of us remains a biological being with inexplicable ties to the natural world that transcend the ideology of rational self-interest. The experience of the ties is not rational but in some sense mystical or almost spiritual.

Although empathy with nature is usually suppressed by a culture grounded in homocentric thought, it surfaces repeatedly in the writings and the actions of certain individuals. A succession of American writers has expressed this empathy with nature and with endangered species. Thus George Catlin, writing from Fort Pierce, South Dakota, in 1832, could see the buffalo as a "noble animal in all its pride and glory" and deplore "that its species is soon to be extinguished and with it the peace and happiness of the Indians who are joint tenants with them in the occupying of this vast and idle Plains."[14] Nearly 130 years later, the novelist Wallace Stegner could write:

Something will have gone out of us as a people if we ever let the remaining wilderness be destroyed; if we permit the last virgin forests to be turned into comic books and plastic cigarette cases; if we drive the few remaining members of the wild species into zoos or to extinction; if we pollute the last clear air and dirty the last clean streams and push our paved roads through the last of the silence. . . .[15]

Henry David Thoreau could feel consoling powers of nature for man trapped in the noise and pace of human society. And naturalist John Muir could argue in favor of preserving areas of outstanding scenic beauty, likening them through his imagery to "a sacred place where human beings can transcend the limitations of everyday experience and become renewed through contact with the power of creation."[16] Although the life experiences of these and other authors differ, they have all shared some kind of emotionally rooted attachment to nature that is decidedly not homocentric. They accord nature an intrinsic worth apart from the basic homocentric concerns of human survival, human culture, and human utility.

The "enduring intuition that sustains the movement"[17] is apparent in many human interests and actions. It is manifest in our curiosity and interest in endangered species. People want to be able to experience endangered species; they want to see whooping cranes or rare orchids or bighorn sheep and they want their children to be able to see them also. But beyond normal curiosity, people who never see an endangered species in their lives are nevertheless moved when they learn that the blue whale or the grizzly bear or the whooping crane could go the way of the passenger pigeon. America's early experiences with extinction, the near-extermination of the buffalo and the extinction of the passenger pigeon, drew a powerful visceral response from a populous unaware of the scientific rationales that crystallized later. The death of Martha, the last passenger pigeon on earth, made the front pages of American newspapers dominated by stories about World War I. Over thirty years later, her stuffed and preserved remains were at the center of a conference exclusively in memory of the passenger pigeon. The subjective value is also apparent in reviewing congressional testimony for the 1966 and 1969 Endangered Species acts. Nor can the extremes to which the more militant elements of the preservation movement have taken their cause be understood under any rational scheme of scientifically enlightened self-interest. Members of the Greenpeace movement rowed in front of herds of whales to stop them from being harpooned and bodily protected baby seals in Newfoundland from hunters armed with clubs. Other people have devoted time, effort, and resources to preservation far beyond what homocentric rationales would justify.

There is a powerful rationale for preserving endangered species. The rationale is unusual because it draws from science and subjective experience and fuses homocentric self-interest with empathy with other beings. The ethics of endangered species preservation is both a guide to actions that are in the best interest of human society and an affirmation of the ties between human beings and nature. But its practical worth does not merely lie in intellectual acceptance; it depends upon its application to the actions and decisions of a people, and here is where problems occur.

THE HISTORY AND POLITICS OF ENDANGERED SPECIES

Though the rationale for saving endangered species may be convincing, our track record of preservation has been very poor and our future prospects are even more bleak. Why? The problem is clarified by understanding how our concern for endangered species evolved, the ways in which this stance has been incorporated into societal decision-making, and the interactions and conflicts between this preservation value and other commonly accepted social values. These facets can best be understood by looking into the past and present politics of endangered species.

The slaughter of the buffalo for decades culminating in the 1880s made Americans understand species extinction. The immense herds of buffalo personified the vast frontier, just as their decline later echoed the conquered American wilderness and the subdued native American tribes. No one knows how many buffalo there actually were (most estimates fall between 60 and 125 million), but before white people came to North America they roamed from Canada to Mexico and from New York State to Oregon. The buffalo was thought to be inexhaustible, just as the frontier was thought to be limitless. Yet the buffalo was hunted, relentlessly and often for no purpose, until only a handful remained by the mid-1880s.

Although wiping out so populous a species might be sardonic tribute to human perseverance, the profligate and senseless waste in their slaughter was nothing but appalling. The Plains Indians made use of the whole buffalo: hides were fashioned into tepees, moccasins, and robes; the bones became tools; and buffalo chips were burned for fuel. The white people were not so judicious. Of the millions of buffalo killed by whites, some were killed for hides and a few were killed for meat. Others were shot to clear away farmland. Many were killed for the joy of killing. Train passengers would gun down buffalo from their car windows. Sportsmen shot buffalo by the hundreds, leaving the carcasses to rot on the Plains. In prairie states, so many skeletons lay bleached in the sun that, from a distance, the land seemed drifted with snow. Knowing how dependent the Indians were on the beast, the federal government unofficially encouraged the extermination of the buffalo as a way to subdue native Americans.[18]

By 1880 the buffalo had been reduced to one herd, numbering about one million and ranging from the lower Yellowstone River into Canada. When the railroad reached Montana in the early 1880s, the fate of the last herd was sealed. Professional hunters and skinners descended on the last herd in droves. In 1882, 14,000 hides were shipped East. By 1884 only 2,500 hides went East, and by the next year there were none. In 1889, when Congress ordered the Great Plains surveyed for buffalo, search parties found but 85 survivors, which were later given refuge in Yellowstone National Park. When President Cleveland signed a bill in 1893 outlawing the killing of animals in national parks, the buffalo slaughter officially ended. That act was the first significant legislation passed protecting wildlife.

Congress initially considered legislation for the general protection of wildlife in the early 1900s. But it took thirty years for the first meaningful legislation, the 1934 Fish and Wildlife Coordination Act, to be passed. This law required only that any federal agency constructing a dam consult with the predecessor of the U. S. Fish and Wildlife Service concerning the use of fish migration aids. Under subsequent legislation, this provision was broadened so that agencies engaged in any activity (not just dams) affecting waterways must consult with the U. S. Fish and Wildlife Service to see if wildlife losses could be avoided and if it would be possible to strengthen wildlife populations as a part of the project. In addition, these laws stated that the wildlife aspects of the project must be given "equal consideration" with other factors such as flood control, power generation, and irrigation.

The Endangered Species Preservation Act (1966) was the first legislation expressly concerned with endangered species and with the Endangered Species Conservation Act (1969) and the Endangered Species Act (1973) formed a very potent body of law. The 1966 act created an official list of "endangered" species and authorized expenditure of funds to acquire their habitats. The 1969 act banned the importation and sale of wildlife threatened with worldwide extinction. The major weaknesses of the first two acts were: they applied only to vertebrate animals; they gave no protection to species which, though not endangered, were declining and would be threatened by extinction in the near future; and they provided no absolute protections against major federal projects (such as dams) that could exterminate a species overnight.

The deficiencies of the 1966 and 1969 acts were rectified in the 1973 Endangered Species Act. The stated purpose of this act was to "provide a means whereby the ecosystems upon which endangered species and threatened species depend may be conserved, [and] to provide a program for conservation of such endangered species. . . ."[19] All plants and animals, except insects determined to be pests, came under the provisions of this statute. It established a list of "threatened" species (those likely to become endangered in the future) and granted them protections also. Private citizens and citizen groups could petition to have a species they believed to be endangered reviewed. The act recognized the relationship between a species and its environment by requiring the Department of the Interior to determine the "critical habitats" of endangered and threatened species. Most important, Section 7 of the act prohibits federal agencies from authorizing, funding, or carrying out actions that will jeopardize the continued existence of endangered or threatened species or result in the destruction or modification of their critical habitat.

Most of the functions of the 1973 act are carried out through the Office of Endangered Species (OES) within the U. S. Fish and Wildlife Service. The OES screens and approves additions and deletions to the endangered and threatened species lists; determines critical habitats for endangered species; develops and implements recovery plans for their restoration; engages in joint programs with other federal, state, and private organizations for the protection of endangered species; acquires habitat lands and waters; and enforces the protection of endangered species.[20] The office has had its successes and problems. Since OES began operations in 1975, several species have come back sufficiently to be taken off the endangered list. Numerous species have been screened by the office, and it has appointed some sixty recovery teams to try to restore endangered species. Thousands of acres of habitat have been acquired. OES-supported research has made great strides in breeding rare animals in captivity and transplanting them to the wild. Through 1977, the office had engaged in about ten thousand consultations with other agencies concerning possible conflicts between federal projects and the livelihood of a species.[21]

Unfortunately, the program's successes have been dwarfed by the magnitude of the endangered species problem. OES has received thirteen petitions from groups to list, delist, or reclassify a total of 23,810 species of plants and animals.[22] Since it takes about thirty-six professional person-days and five clerical person-days just to list a species, the present-size staff would need hundreds of years just to review the nearly 24,000 species plus time to implement recovery plans. Despite criminal penalties and enforcement measures, the problem of illegal taking or killing of endangered species, especially for profit, continues. Funding allocated for habitat acquisition helps only a fraction of the unprotected species, and the scarcity of resources generally raises the question: Which species do we save?

But the largest controversies centered on the Section 7

provision that prohibited any federal agency from acting to threaten or destroy the habitat of a species. The Oregon Bureau of Land Management has stopped a timber sales contract because it would destroy the nesting sites of the northern spotted owl. Interstate highway construction in Mississippi landed in court because it would destroy the nesting area of the forty surviving Mississippi sandhill cranes. A Hawaii program that supported feral goats and pigs for sport hunting was denied funding because the animals were tearing up the critical habitat of the palila, an endangered species of honeycreeper. The California condor, the Yuma clapper rail, the peregrine falcon, the grizzly bear, the whooping crane, the bald eagle, the pine marten, and other species have also figured in the fate of development projects.[23]

A head-to-head confrontation between a species and a development project can be and usually is avoided. Projects can be altered to accommodate the needs of the rare species rather than sacrificed. The Fish and Wildlife Service reports that among the 4,500 cases reviewed through the end of 1976, only 3 conflicts were unresolvable within the framework of the act. All three ended in court. Two were resolved fairly quickly. But the final case, the snail darter versus the Tellico Dam, was appealed all the way to the Supreme Court and was the focal point of the entire endangered species protection controversy.

The Tellico project, approved in 1966, would dam the Little Tennessee River in eastern Tennessee, creating a thirty-mile-long recreational and industrial reservoir covering 16,500 acres. Thirty-eight thousand acres of valley land were condemned and purchased by the Tennessee Valley Authority (TVA) and construction began in March 1967. As of February 1977, the TVA had spent $103 million of the projected $116 million total cost and the dam was nearly complete. The finished project was expected to provide recreation, attract industrial development to the region, and enhance flood protection downstream. However, if the dam gates were ever closed, the reservoir behind the dam would destroy the critical habitat of the snail darter, a three-inch fish that lives in the gravel shoals of the Little Tennessee.

The snail darter was discovered in August 1973 by Dr.

David Etnier, an ichthyologist at the University of Tennessee, when the Tellico project was about 50 percent complete. It was placed on the endangered species list in 1975, and the following year a seventeen-mile portion of the Little Tennessee was designated the snail darter's critical habitat.

A law professor and two of his students filed suit in February 1976 to permanently enjoin the closing of the Tellico Dam on the grounds that destruction of the snail darter's critical habitat violated Section 7 of the Endangered Species Act. The district court concluded that closure of the dam would "significantly reduce if not completely extirpate" the only known population of snail darters. However, in weighing the value of preserving the species against the benefits of the Tellico project, the court sided with the TVA and dismissed the case.

Environmentalists immediately filed an appeal. On January 31, 1977, the Sixth District Court of Appeals in Cincinnati ruled unanimously to overturn the lower court decision and permanently enjoin closing of the Tellico Dam. The court of appeals decision was in turn appealed by the TVA to the Supreme Court. The Supreme Court upheld the ruling of the Sixth District Court. But while the decision was outwardly a clear-cut victory for environmentalists, the Supreme Court's supporting arguments were too narrow to legitimize endangered species preservation as an ethic or a societal value. In its deliberations, the Supreme Court did not concern itself with the "rightness" of the Endangered Species Act, or the relative values of dams and snail darters. Instead, the high court merely examined the wording and legislative history of Section 7 and concluded that it was intended to stop all agency actions that threaten an endangered species, no matter what the circumstances or consequences. Furthermore, the Court asserted that deciding the relative priorities between legislatively mandated programs and projects is the exclusive province of Congress and that the Court's responsibility was to interpret the meaning of Congress and no more. As the decision itself states:

We [the Supreme Court] have no expert knowledge on the subject of endangered species, much less do we have a mandate from the people to strike a balance of equities on the side of the Tellico Dam. Congress has spoken in the plainest of words, making it abundantly clear that the balance has been struck in favor of affording endangered species the highest of priorities. . . .[24]

In other words, the Supreme Court ruled in favor of the snail darter because to do otherwise would be a violation of the Constitution's separation of powers doctrine. Within the structure of the federal government, establishing society's values and priorities belonged to Congress.

Congress responded to the Supreme Court decision by changing the law. Under the Endangered Species Act Amendments of 1978, exemptions to Section 7 can now be granted if a conflict between an endangered species and an agency action is not resolved through the normal consultation process. The final decision rests with a seven-member Endangered Species Committee consisting mostly of the heads of different federal agencies. An exemption can be granted if five members of the committee agree that:

(1) There are no "reasonable and prudent" alternatives to the agency action; (2) the benefits of the agency action clearly outweigh the benefits of alternative course of action consistent with conserving the species or its critical habitat, and that such action is in the public interest; and (3) the action is of national or regional significance.[25]

In assessing the benefits of the agency action, the committee is asked to consider the aesthetic, ecological, educational, historical, recreational, and scientific value of any endangered or threatened species as well as the economic benefits. The basic intent of the amendments is to give the law more "flexibility" to achieve a balance between the protection of species and competing economic values. The Tellico Dam case was decided on January 23, 1979, under these provisions by the Endangered Species Committee. The Committee voted unanimously to kill Tellico and save the fish. But six days later Senator Baker introduced a bill to abolish the committee. The battle goes on.

The politics surrounding endangered species preservation have grown complex and emotional. However, virtually all of the political issues reduce to a single question: How much is an endangered species worth, and why? In our relations with endangered species, we have tacitly affirmed the value we see in them and in wildlife generally. From the late stages of the buffalo slaughter to the Endangered Species Act of 1973, these species progressed from having no value to having absolute value. Now, with the Supreme Court decision and the 1978 amendments, the value of endangered species has become uncertain. The Supreme Court refused to compare the value of the snail darter with the value of the Tellico Dam and based its ruling solely on legal arguments. In legislating its new exemption procedure, Congress may have solved the most obvious political problem, but it completely avoided its broader ethical responsibility of establishing priorities: i.e., of determining value.

By interpreting the 1973 act as favoring the species over the development project in all cases, one essentially confers infinite value upon the endangered species. The value of the species was so high that it could not be exceeded by the benefits from any development. Such a position is untenable. The ethical principle of saving endangered species is a high one, but it is not absolute. There are higher values that must take precedence over endangered species preservation. The ethic of endangered species preservation must be given a place within the hierarchy of all societal values.

ECONOMICS OF ENDANGERED SPECIES

Society has several different ways to assign values to entities, but the problems of resolving competing goals and values have increasingly fallen within the realm of economics. In the United States, the market system is supposed to allocate scarce resources toward fulfilling the needs society values most. In cases where a major decision must be made, a cost-benefit analysis is often performed. In a cost-benefit analysis, the future social benefits and future social costs associated with a decision or a project are predicted and then compared.[26] In other words, the benefits that will accrue from a project are quantified and compared with total costs. Projects where benefits clearly exceed costs are pursued.

The TVA performed a cost-benefit analysis in 1968 for the Tellico Dam. In the analysis, the TVA stated that the Tellico Dam project would yield direct benefits of $3,760,000 per year.[27] Secondary benefits, arising from the additional jobs created through industrial development around the Tellico reservoir, were valued at $3,650,000 annually. The direct benefits calculated by the TVA are:

Recreation	$1,440,000
Shoreline Development	710,000
Flood Control	505,000
Navigation	400,000
Power	400,000
Fish and Wildlife	220,000
Water Supply	70,000
Redevelopment	15,000

The TVA claims a total (direct and secondary benefits included) benefit-to-cost ratio of 3 to 1, and claims the Tellico project is economically justified. A coalition of environmentalists, including the Tennessee Endangered Species Committee (TESC), a citizens' group concerned with education and public information in the snail darter controversy, disagrees sharply with the TVA and proposes that the public good would be best served by allowing the river to run free. TESC notes that 15,500 acres of the 38,000-acre project are highest-quality agricultural lands and that another 10,000 acres could be very productive crop, grazing, or timber lands.[28] Intensive farming of the 15,500 prime acres alone would yield an estimated $27 million annually while creating 300 to 350 jobs, and would allow resettlement of the area by the land's former owners. Conversely, industry is not moving into the Tennessee Valley as rapidly as predicted. Recent TVA projects have not attracted the industrial development anticipated and there are no guarantees that land set aside for industrial growth will be utilized.

In the eyes of TESC, the agricultural benefits alone justify maintaining the Tellico area as a river valley. But TESC does cite other reasons to abandon the TVA development. Since there are already twenty-two reservoirs within a fifty-mile radius of the Tellico Dam, it maintains that the Little Tennessee has greater recreational value as a free-flowing river park. While the TVA has emphasized the need for expanded energy production as a rationale for Tellico, TESC claims that the Tellico Dam will increase system generating capacity by only 0.1 percent at a cost several times greater per kilowatt than elsewhere in the TVA system. And finally, the river valley has many historical and archaeological sites, including burial grounds and former town sites of the Cherokee nation dating back ten thousand years. Although TESC has not performed a formal cost-benefit analysis, it concludes that the most promising use of the area would be to return the agricultural lands to farming and to develop a free-flowing river park facility.[29]

The discrepancies between the conclusions of the TVA and TESC show the generic weakness of cost-benefit analysis: that they reflect the biases and values of the people doing the analysis. A methodologically sound analysis can arrive at a decision that is not in the public good. TESC's more intuitive arguments, while not necessarily invalidating the TVA analysis, account for values that the TVA analysis does not, and perhaps cannot, quantify.

A more profound problem is that traditional economics has been insensitive to the contributions natural ecosystems make to our livelihood. In looking at preservation alternatives, we seldom, if ever, accurately account for all the benefits we derive from undeveloped land or untouched ecosystems. Within the scheme of traditional economics, there are no ecosystems: there is "developable" land. Land itself is valueless; its economic value is usually equated to its development potential. If land can be developed for agriculture, it will have a certain value. If land holds minerals that can be extracted, it will have a different value. If it can be developed for industrial, commercial, or residential purposes, the land will have other value.

Although we place little value on undeveloped land, the facts remain that such acreage and its ecosystems provide us with services, some of which could not be duplicated at any cost. Natural ecosystems clean and regenerate the air we breathe. They filter our water and return organic wastes and other nutrients to the soil. Their genetic pool is the guarantee that the biosphere can adapt to a changing future. Natural ecosystems affect climate through interactions with the atmosphere, and, by absorbing and utilizing solar energy, they form the base of the energy-use pyramid. Nevertheless, the service values of natural ecosystems are virtually never incorporated into decision-making. The reasons are twofold: it is very difficult to assign a dollar figure to these services, and most decision-makers are unaware that we are actually taking advantage of them.

The ecologist Eugene P. Odum, in conjunction with James Gosselink and R. M. Pope of Louisiana State University, has done some research into the service values of coastal wetland ecosystems. They identified four components that should go into a dollar value calculation for a wetlands area. They are:[30]

1. By-product production—Coastal wetlands are the nursery grounds for many commercial and sport fish. Up to 90 percent of all marine finfish and shellfish spend some part of their life cycle in coastal marshes and estuaries. It is estimated that two thirds of the cash value of species harvested on the Atlantic and Gulf coasts are estuary-dependent. This value was calculated to be $100/acre/year.

2. Waste assimilation—Sewage dumped into a coastal wetland is oxidized and disappears. Wetlands are especially efficient at removing the inorganic content of sewage, mostly nitrogen and phosphorous, and storing and recycling these nutrients through the ecosystem. Since the removal of inorganic nutrients (tertiary sewage treatment) is very expensive (approximately $2/pound) if done artificially, the sewage treatment value of a wetland comes to a return per acre of $2,500/year.

3. Energy flow—Odum and associates assume that energy productivity measures the total services provided by the ecosystem. They list waste treatment, carbon dioxide absorption, oxygen production, support of waterfowl and wildlife, and protection of cities and beaches from storms as examples of

these kinds of service. The total energy productivity of a wetland was determined and divided by 10,000, a round figure representing the number of kilocalories equivalent to one dollar. The general life-support value of a wetland was determined to be $4,100/acre/year. Thus the total value of an acre of wetland, taking into account life-support waste treatment and commercial fishery functions, is $6,700, or in excess of $100,000 if one considers "income-capitalization" value at a 5 percent interest rate.

Although the methodology may be suspect, the concept that natural ecosystems must be valued for the services they provide is valid. With better understanding of the ecologies of natural systems and the mechanics of life-support contributions, the Odum-Gosselink-Pope methodology can be refined to yield more accurate valuations.

Using this methodology, the value of an endangered species would be equal to its contribution to an ecosystem's productivity in providing useful services for human beings. This value would be calculated by taking the difference in the productivity of service of the ecosystem with the species and with the species extinct. But such a calculation would take far more knowledge of ecology than we currently possess.

Another basic problem is that endangered species just do not lend themselves to any kind of economic analysis, regardless of perspective. The genetic, commercial, scientific, and other values of an endangered species are usually speculative. Past experience tells us that, out of the large pool of endangered species, *some* will have special utility. Except in rare instances where a species has an obvious and valuable property (e.g., the highly efficient kidneys of the desert pupfish), we do not know which species these are, or how great the utility will be, or when the benefits will accrue. Similarly, no one can predict how valuable a species' genetic complex will be in the future productivity of the ecosystem. The subjective values associated with endangered species are equally difficult to deal with objectively—e.g., how much, in dollars, would society's experience of nature be lessened if the whooping crane were lost? All of these uncertainties make it impossible to assign a dollar value to the benefit of species preservation.

In the wake of the incompleteness of economic analysis, other guides to decision-making are sought. The only reasonable alternative to our overly heavy reliance on object economic analysis for making value decisions is to devise practical ethical principles. This ethical development should incorporate our knowledge of the rationale for endangered species preservation and evaluate the strength of that rationale in light of rationales for conflicting values.

TOWARD AN ETHICS OF PRESERVATION

Although we can affirm an ethical principle to preserve all animal and plant species, the practical costs of doing so are extremely high. There will continue to be situations where a development project that is truly necessary for human well-being will come into conflict with the existence of species. Given the political and economic reality of limited resources available to the present and future preservation efforts, a priority system must be devised so that the maximum number of species is saved.

Efforts to save some species may be judged too costly or too impractical. An analogy from air pollution is apropos. Environmentalists may argue that all people have a *right* to clean air. Such a right is perfectly defensible and reasonable, for air belongs to all people and each must have it to live. But in practice absolutely clean air is impossible in many developed parts of the world. While the industrial misuse of air as a "free resource" cannot be denied, neither can the need for industrial use of air. To guarantee absolutely clean air may mean heavy curtailment of industry. The same dilemma faces the purist endangered species position. Although we can set a goal and strive for zero human-induced extinctions, our intrusions into the world of endangered species are ongoing and so all-encompassing that we can hardly stop them.

So we must weigh competing values and needs in any program for comprehensive endangered species preservation. Our Western society's reliance on economics must now give way to ethical guidelines that are just, rational, practical, and relevant, but that need not be economically based. Ideally, all human ethical actions should affirm life on this planet, which includes protecting rare and endangered species. In practice, this affirmation needs to be guided by a priority of values that often conflict.

Ecological Value

In giving preservation efforts priority, one criterion is the value of the species in question to its native habitat or, conversely, what the impacts of its extinction will be on the ecosystem. As already noted, in a majority of instances it is not known exactly what roles a rare species plays in the ecosystem as a whole. Nevertheless, our thinking must be oriented toward looking at ecosystems as components contributing to the total strength of the life-support system. One of the steps Odum took in assessing the value of coastal wetlands was to examine the amount of energy (in the form of combustible organic material or biomass) "fixed" by species of plant life, and to assign a dollar value on the basis of prevailing energy rates from traditional organic fuels.[31] This technique, although inexact, does measure one life-support function of a species in its habitat. Further study of ecosystems should better define life-support services and the roles each species plays within these services.

But real decisions must be made before studies are completed. On occasion the impact of species on ecosystems has been predicted with reasonable certainty. In some cases a species might be a predator that keeps the population of a pest under control; for instance, wolves keep the populations of deer and other herbivorous animals from stripping forests. The presumption is always that a species is important to its ecosystem and that the world will suffer from its loss. When economic interests interfere with natural habitats of these species, the burden of proof of its nonimportance should be placed on the intruder.

Species Uniqueness

The uniqueness of the species in question must also be considered. If the species is the only existing member of a family, it should receive a higher priority than if it is one of many members of a given family. We should aim toward preserving a diversity of species, as well as a diversity of habitats. By our placing a high priority on diversity, the gene pool can remain at a maximum size and the biosphere will maintain greater adaptability and flexibility. Diversity is also justified in terms of preserving our ecological heritage as completely and accurately as possible. Furthermore, diversity allows for future scientific, medical, and commercial utility. But the greatest reason for diversity is that it is good for its own sake. The beauty, richness, and glory of a unique species is worth having around, irrespective of its value to people or its usefulness. The creative mandate to increase and multiply includes maintaining diversity. In conclusion, every unique species has a value for its own sake and deserves to be preserved.

Scientific and Medical Value

Assuming that a species is not believed to have great ecological value and that it is closely related to other more numerous species, then its scientific and medical value should be examined. Those species with current or promising biological, medical, or chemical utility should be assigned a higher preservation effort. We must always, however, be wary of becoming too homocentric in such assignments. Species such as the desert pupfish (highly valued for scientific research) or the mollusks that produce mercenene (a chemical substance effective against certain kinds of cancer) should get special priority. Research to determine ways of picking out species with unusual scientific or medical value is obviously needed, so that some form of screening procedure might be possible in assigning priorities. All in all, species that aid us in coming to know the universe and how to conquer disease need special care in preservation efforts.

Commercial Value

Many species are endangered because they are commercially valuable and are being harvested faster than they can reproduce. Ironically, some of these are species used in scientific laboratories. Most of the endangered species of plants in the Southwest are cacti that are being illegally taken and sold. The majority of them could be grown as a cash crop and marketed, undercutting the illegal black market removal of cacti from wilderness areas. In fact, in many cases species could and should be commercially cultivated.

For instance, the large sea turtles are being driven to extinction by hunters who kill the turtles for their leather (for making shoes and handbags), for their oil (an ingredient in cosmetic lotions), and for the calipee (a cartilaginous material lying next to the turtle body shell and used in making clear green turtle soup). Turtle mariculture, where turtles are hatched and reared in captivity, put out to enclosed sea pasture areas, and then harvested, could supply the demand for turtle products without threatening natural populations. Society would perform the dual function of domestically cultivating the species for its own use while preserving the wild population in its native habitat.

It is obvious that no commercial species should ever be allowed to be harvested to extinction. When a natural or synthetic (even petrochemically based) substitute can be found for a necessary endangered species product, it should be promoted and used. Thus synthetic furs are preferable to those from threatened species of animals. Special promotion should be given to products obtained from plentiful but not commercially utilized species that are not destroyed in making the product (leaves, fruit, berries, or nuts of a plant).

Sperm oil from sperm whales was thought to be indispensable in certain industrial lubricants, but, with the depletion of the sperm whale, substitutes were sought. No chemically synthesized substitutes were found acceptable. However, Mexican and United States researchers discovered that oil from the jojoba plant (Simmondsia chinensis) in the North American desert areas was a virtual sperm oil duplicate—and could be used without requiring major reformulation. Where commercialization is unfeasible, all possible efforts to find substitutes for the uses of threatened species should be undertaken.

When substitutes are not found, society must ask itself whether the product made from an endangered or threatened species is truly necessary. Such products are commonly luxury items: leopard-skin coats, crocodile leather shoes, clear green turtle soup. It is quite often the scarcity of the plant or animal species that makes the item produced so sought after.

Game, Recreational, and Observational Values

Obviously, hunting and trapping to extinction are intolerable. But quite often hunters need food or compete for the same land as wildlife. This is especially true in heavily populated parts of Asia and Africa. Wealthier nations can assist these people in growing food and in still preserving natural habitats.

Preservation out of habitat should be permitted only as a last resort. First efforts should be made to transfer or transplant the species within a natural range. Much of the species' value rests with functioning within its habitat—not behind bars in some zoo. While the educational and observational values for human viewers are generally acknowledged, zoological gardens should still follow certain norms: should resemble the habitats of the animals; should not attempt to gather all animal types (some, like badgers, are driven almost mad by wire enclosures, while wild ducks so adapt to zoos that they attract migrating relatives); should be a place of last resort for endangered or threatened species; should enhance the species number, not reduce it.

In conclusion, we should never threaten a species with extinction, but especially not those with, firstly, ecological or unique value and, secondly, scientific and medical value. In the case of commerce, the species should be cultivated commercially or a substitute found; endangered species should be protected from hunting, and placed in captivity as a matter of last resort.

PRESERVATION POLICY IMPLICATIONS

Planning and Land Management

Conflicts between human activities and wildlife arise primarily because past resource and land management decisions ignored the endangered species issue. The fact that only 3 out of 4,500 development activities proved to be irreconcilable demonstrates that we can coexist with the natural world. Alternative sites, special conservation measures, and modified activities do protect delicate habitats. As we learn to coexist better, the number and severity of conflicts should diminish.

* Future population growth, agricultural expansion, and other resource development should be channeled, whenever possible, into areas that have few or no endangered species. Ecosystems, like species, vary in their sensitivity to human intrusion. For instance, a footprint or tire track in high Rocky Mountain elevations remains for decades. Expansion activities in general should be directed into less sensitive ecosystems.

* When development is necessary in an endangered species habitat, it should be so conducted as not to interfere with the species' livelihood. Land use should be restricted to activities that enhance or coexist with, rather than threaten, rare species. In some instances, this kind of restrictiveness could be interpreted as a violation of the "taking only with just compensation" principle. But the restrictions are justifiable, for rare species are a public good that benefits all people and are good in themselves. A "development" activity that causes an extinction is not development at all but a violation of our delicate ecosystem.

* It is the responsibility of a developer who undertakes a project that threatens a species to prove the activity will not harm that species. It is not the duty of a concerned citizenry to do the job. The strength and population of the species should be monitored while the activity is in progress. If it is evident that the species is threatened by the activity of the developer-aggressor, society should have the means to halt the project immediately, and the developer has the responsibility to restore the species to its original status.

Species Pools

Special efforts should be made to preserve plant and animal species that could be used for crossbreeding and hybridization of food crops and domesticated animals. Preservation of the agricultural gene pool is especially important with such a major portion of the earth's surface under cultivation of relatively few crops. If environmental or climatic conditions change and the agricultural gene pool is not diverse enough to adapt, the costs and problems would be astronomical.

Monitoring, Assessment, and Feedback

The rate of extinction should be monitored closely. Research is needed to determine an "upper limit" for the extinction rate, modeled somewhat after air pollution limits and warning systems. Safety margins of extinction beyond which the ecosystem is in serious trouble should be established. When extinctions or threats intensify, more resources should be devoted to preservation efforts and stiffer restrictions on human activities that impede the survival and recovery of endangered species. Ultimately, target extinction rates should be set up, leading to a time when human beings can contribute their superior powers to preserving, not destroying, the species.

Development Versus Preservation Cases

Equity is always to be considered in cases of species versus development—who gains, who loses. For example, wetlands being turned into beach resorts benefit few people: developers, builders, certain vacationers. On the other hand, the construction of the Columbia River dams resulted in cheap electricity for thousands of people. We must remember that a species loss is a total loss to everyone, the ecosystem suffers, and the heritage is depleted. Extinction is never justified for the benefit of a privileged few.

In evaluating species versus development, the intruding activity should be assessed on how it fulfills primary human needs, not luxuries. A Columbia River dam project may be undertaken when people are genuinely in need of cheap, plentiful, environmentally safe energy. Wetlands turned vacation spots are not justifiable when species are threatened in the process. Needs of species are simple and basic: a habitat in which to feed, reproduce, and grow. When human and rare-species needs conflict, the human may prevail; but when human luxuries are at stake, stewardship is violated by endangering the species.

People must ask whether this need is fulfilled only by a threat on a given species. Are there alternatives, and how feasible are they? Is a given dam necessary, or are there other, less threatening ways of deriving energy? Can we delineate justifiable extra costs to save the species? Are the people able to pay? To whom do the benefits accrue? If cost discrepancies are very large, and if practical workable schemes can be implemented, society benefits in the preserved species and thus should bear part of the additional cost of alternatives.

Justifiable Extinctions

Not all species are of equal value. When species are found of unusual ecological, scientific, or commercial worth, they obviously should be preserved. But what about those with little or no known value when the price of preservation is considered too high to bear by society? A species extinction could conceivably be justified if the threatening activity meets five criteria: (a) if the benefits accrue to a large number of persons and not to a privileged few; (b) if the beneficial action is related to genuine human needs and not luxuries; (c) if the preservation costs are too great to be borne by society; (d) if the species is not unique and possesses no known value (such as commercial); and (e) if alternative habitats are not available.

Most activities fail these tests and thus efforts to preserve the species must be made. Such a pest as the smallpox virus (see Appendix I, "Pest Control") is worthy of extinction, and the efforts of the World Health Organization to eradicate it are to be praised. Activities that perhaps come closest when dealing with nonharmful animals are those in East Africa where native peoples compete for land with wild animals. Perhaps the local governments are not able to provide alternative habitats; here the world perspective requires that wealthy people assist in finding alternatives so that at the same time human beings can grow food and cattle and wildlife may be preserved.

Citizen Action

Direct action, such as that of the Greenpeace Foundation on behalf of the whales, is a necessary component of the battle to preserve endangered species. Many conservation groups, however, are insulated from the needs felt by many human disadvantaged, leading some civil rights groups to remark that more attention is paid to migratory birds than to human migrants. Groups advocating environmental and human rights must realize that their constituencies suffer a common oppressor—materialistic growth for private gain. This understanding, coupled with better efforts at mutual education and communication, might lead to a powerful coalition of the forces actively working for environmental and human justice.

46   WHY FAREWELL TO PLANTS AND ANIMALS?

REFERENCES

1. G. M. Woodwell, "The Challenge of Endangered Species," in *Extinction Is Forever: The Status of Threatened and Endangered Plants in America*, G. H. Prance, ed. (Bronx, N.Y.: New York Botanical Garden, 1976), p. 5.
2. As quoted in H. M. Iltis, "Man First? Man Last? The Paradox of Human Ecology," *Bioscience* 22:14 (1972), p. 820.
3. Ibid.
4. As quoted in J. A. Passmore, *Man's Responsibility for Nature: Ecological Problems and Western Traditions* (London: Gerald Duckworth & Co., 1971), p. 3.
5. A. Leopold, *Sand County Almanac* (New York: Ballantine Books, 1966), p. 239.
6. E. Odum, *Ecology* (New York: Holt, Rinehart & Winston, 1963), pp. 34–35.
7. *Genetic Vulnerability of Major Crops*, report of the Committee on Genetic Vulnerability of Major Crops, Division of Biology and Agriculture, the National Research Council (Washington, D.C.: The National Academy of Sciences, 1972), p. 17.
8. D. W. Jenkins and E. S. Ayers, "One-Tenth of our Plant Species May Not Survive," *Smithsonian* 5:10 (1974), p. 94.
9. J. L. Hopson, "A Plea for a Mundane Mollusc," New York *Times Magazine* (Nov. 14, 1976), p. 69.
10. Ibid.
11. "Manatees Urged as Weed Killers: Florida Team Convinced of Value in Clogged Canals," New York *Times Magazine* (Dec. 4, 1976), p. 81.
12. "Recovery Effort Intensifies to Save Hawaii's Endangered Wildlife," *Endangered Species Technical Bulletin* 1:5, Endangered Species Program (Washington, D.C.: U. S. Fish and Wildlife Service, 1976).
13. C. Darwin, *The Descent of Man*, reprinted from 2nd English ed., rev. (New York: A. L. Burt, 1974), pp. 120–21.
14. G. Catlin, letter reprinted in R. Nash, *The American Environment: Readings in the History of Conservation* (Reading, Mass.: Addison-Wesley, 1976), pp. 8–9.
15. W. Stegner, "The Wilderness Idea," reprinted in Nash, op. cit., p. 193.
16. J. Rodman, "Theory and Practice in the Environmental Movement: Notes Toward an Ecology of Experience," unpublished paper presented before Sixth I.C.U.S., San Francisco (Nov. 25–27, 1977), p. 5.
17. J. Rodman, "The Liberation of Nature?," *Inquiry* (Spring 1977), p. 88.
18. A. Stoutenburg, *Animals at Bay: Rare and Rescued American Wildlife* (Garden City, N.Y.: Doubleday & Company, 1968).

19. *The Endangered Species Act of 1973*, Conference Report No. 93-740 (Dec. 19, 1973), section 2b, p. 2.
20. *1976 Annual Report of the Fish and Wildlife Service* (Washington, D.C.: Government Printing Office, 1977), pp. 20-40.
21. Statement by C. Warren, Director of the Council for Environmental Quality, *Oversight Hearings of the Senate Public Works and Environmental Committee on the Endangered Species Act, July 1977* (Washington, D.C.: Government Printing Office, 1978).
22. *Annual Report of the Fish and Wildlife Service*, pp. 20-40.
23. P. Steinhart, "Mighty, Like a Furbish Lousewort," *Audubon Magazine* 79:13 (1977), p. 123.
24. Supreme Court of the United States, *"Tennessee Valley Authority vs. Hill et al."* Docket No. 76-1701, decided June 15, 1978, p. 39.
25. House of Representatives (95th Cong., 2nd sess.), *Endangered Species Act Amendments of 1978: Conference Report*, Report No. 95-1804 (Oct. 15, 1978), Sect. 7(h) (1), p. 8.
26. P. Stralter, "Cost Benefit and Other Problems of Method," in *Political Economy of the Environment: Problems of Method* (Paris: Moulton, 1972), p. 52.
27. *The Tennessee Valley Authority's Tellico Dam Project—Costs, Alternatives and Benefits*, report to the Congress by the Comptroller General of the United States (EMD-77-59) (Oct. 14, 1977), pp. 27-35.
28. S. Grigsby Cook, C. Cook, and D. Gove, "What They Didn't Tell You About the Snail Darter and the Dam," *National Parks and Conservation Magazine* 51:5 (1977), pp. 10-13.
29. Ibid.
30. E. P. Odum, "Pricing the Natural Environment," *Research Reporter* (Fall 1977), University of Georgia, reprinted in *Hearings Before the Committee on Public Works, U.S. Senate, 94th Congress, July 27-28, 1976, Section 404 of the Federal Water Pollution Control Act of 1972* (Washington, D.C.: Government Printing Office, 1976), pp. 467-69.
31. Ibid., p. 467.

II

NUCLEAR PROBLEMS: NO END IN SIGHT

We travel together, passengers on a little spaceship, dependent on its vulnerable resources of air and soil; all committed for our safety to its security and peace; preserved from annihilation only by the care, the work and—I will say—the love we give our fragile craft.

Adlai Stevenson

The Three Mile Island power plant accident during the spring of 1979 made most of us aware that the use of radioactive materials contains a risk to human health. Although these materials have been widely beneficial for medical diagnosis and treatment and in industry, large quantities of radioactive substances are used only for weapons and for electric power generation. National security and supposedly cheap electricity are thus major benefits achieved from the mastery of the atom. But these benefits, and even the use of X rays for medical diagnosis, carry serious risks. The risk of nuclear annihilation makes many people question the arms race and call for mutual disarmament. The cancer risk from medical X rays has resulted in a halt to mass screening for lung disease or frequent mammography for breast cancer.

Similarly, the world is reexamining its electricity needs in the light of nuclear power risks. As economic costs increase and the risks become clearer, questions are arising about the extent of the true need for centrally generated electricity and about alternative modes of supply. People are asking whether most energy needs could not be met *without* electric power and whether needed electric power could not be supplied by a modest use of fossil fuels or, especially, by various forms of solar (or renewable-resource) energy, including hydroelectric resources.

The biological risks from radioactivity and the levels of exposure that can result from commercial nuclear power generation are the prime focus of this chapter. But the acquisition of materials for nuclear weapons from commercial reac-

tor fuels—the so-called nuclear proliferation problem—is also
an issue of major international and environmental concern.
Since the handling of the proliferation problem involves
changes in the commercial nuclear fuel cycle, with its attendant dangers, some aspects of that issue will be discussed in
the section on nuclear waste management.

The hazards of radioactivity are contingent upon both the
biological harm from exposure and the likelihood of exposure. Releases of radioactivity to the environment are of little
consequence if this exposure does little harm. However, the
more numerous the possibilities for routine or accidental
release, the more important accurate knowledge of the biological consequences becomes. Proportionate care can then
be taken to prevent releases.

Clearly, a reliable understanding of the biological damage
from radioactive exposure is of prime importance. Exagger-
ation of harm will unduly limit the possible beneficial uses of
the technology; underestimation can produce excessive risk
to health. Unfortunately, the early development of nuclear
power technology took place at a time when the biological
effects of radiation were underestimated by the scientific
community. Standards of design and operation of nuclear
plants have since had to be made more stringent, with resultant increases in cost. Whether the standards are sufficiently
tight is still controversial, especially since the Three Mile Island mishap.

Similarly, many of the potential failure mechanisms
whereby radioactive materials could be released were not
recognized. As a result, additional backup safety systems
have had to be designed and installed, again at considerable
cost. The effectiveness of these safety systems is also being
seriously questioned today, as are estimates of the probability
of accidents requiring use of the safety systems.

Besides nuclear power plants, other parts of the nuclear
fuel cycle produce exposure to radiation. Some parts of that
cycle, such as uranium mining and processing and waste
reprocessing, can expose workers to severe doses of radiation.
The unusable crushed ore left from mining uranium (tailings) and the numerous wastes from the power, fuel fabrica-
tion, and reprocessing plants are all potential sources of envi-

ronmental pollution and must be properly managed and disposed.

HEALTH HAZARDS OF IONIZING RADIATION

Over the past several years the toxic and tragic effects of radiation have received growing attention from the public and in the media. Cancer victims among military servicemen exposed to atomic blast and fallout, children genetically deformed possibly because of their fathers' exposure to nuclear wastes, leukemias among radiologists—these have put the dangers of radiation into the public spotlight. Assurances that the public—especially the worker—is adequately protected from radiation dangers have been greeted with skepticism and renewed scrutiny. Unfortunately, it took additional "corpses in the morgue" to stir this deepening concern over radiation poisoning.

As a consequence, atomic workers have gone on strike for contractual guarantees that their employers will abide by radiation protection standards. Further limitations on occupational exposure have been recommended. Stricter regulations for medical X-ray exposure are promulgated, and doctors are urged to reduce by half the number of exposures they require of their patients. Nationwide searches for the soldiers exposed to atomic weapons explosions have awakened bureaucratic fears of liability claims and public anger over the unnecessary neglect of the victims. The apparently higher risks from radiation renew concern that the benefits of nuclear power will come at a high cost.

Efforts to impose stricter standards for radiation exposure or to substitute alternative energy strategies can be seen as a threat to special industrial or professional interests. Utility companies are investing billions of dollars in nuclear generating equipment. Westinghouse, General Electric, Babcock & Wilcox, Exxon, Gulf Oil, and hundreds of financial institutions have other billions invested in manufacturing capability and uranium resources. Physicians prescribe diagnostic X rays for their patients' welfare as well as to protect themselves against liability for misdiagnosis. Again, the need for these technologies and the standards controlling them are subject to intense scrutiny and emotion.

By some estimates, the dangers of radiation are not as serious as those of coal mining and burning, or those of the oil refining and chemical industries. Much of the nuclear industry has made expensive efforts to reduce exposure to the workers and the public. Nuclear proponents make claims to a safety record better than those of many other industries. Yet in the wake of Three Mile Island the evidence will probably require that the nuclear industry, like all other dangerous industries, be even more carefully controlled, or perhaps replaced by less-risky technologies.

Health damage from radioactive materials is generally similar to damage from many organic chemicals in producing genetic mutations, cancer, and other forms of ill health or death, but other properties of radioactive materials make them significantly different from ordinary chemical pollutants, whose toxicity is for the most part determined by the structure of the chemical molecule. In contrast, the toxic effect of the radioactive element can be independent of the molecule on which it is bound. Relatively harmless carbon dioxide becomes radiotoxic if the carbon in the molecule is radioactive carbon 14. Steel, concrete, even water and steam can become radioactive through fission processes. Iodine also, which is needed for healthy thyroid activity, can when radioactive become a threat to the thyroid gland. Thus steam, small losses of iodine compounds, and other releases from a nuclear plant must be carefully controlled in ways not needed in other technologies.

The chemical makeup of radioactive molecules determines how they enter the body (such as by inhalation, ingestion, or contact); they also determine how long the radioactive material resides in and thereby threatens various parts of the body. The chemical properties determine whether the whole body or only particular organs (lung, thyroid, intestines, for example) are irradiated. The body's reaction to the chemical properties can force the radioactive poison out quickly or, in other cases, allow it to remain a threat for a long time.

While the toxicity of many dangerous chemicals can be reduced by their reaction with other chemicals, radioactive poisons cannot be neutralized. Conversion of radioactive chemicals to others does not reduce the radioactivity as such.

In other words, the total radioactivity remains the same despite the chemical reaction. At best, chemical reactions may "immobilize" the radioactive material or limit its contact with living organisms. For example, a radioactive material may be encased in a polymer or glass where it will not get into the atmosphere or water system. Other chemical reactions—even unavoidable ones—may, however, free immobilized materials and allow contact with living systems.

Although radioactivity cannot be chemically neutralized, it does not last indefinitely. Each radioactive isotope has an average half-life over which one half of the radioactive element decays and radioactivity is thus reduced. Fortunately, many of the radioactive materials produced by nuclear technology have half-lives of a few minutes or less. Except in sudden accidental releases, these poisons will not exist long enough to endanger a biological system.

Other radioactive elements, however, have half-lives ranging from several days to tens or hundreds of thousands of years. The longer-lived of these radioactive elements (or radionuclides), such as plutonium and iodine 129, will have a long history of interactions with the environment, changing chemical form, passing from one biological system to another. All the while they retain their capability of delivering a toxic radiation dose. The long-lived radioactive poisons remain dangerous for hundreds of human generations after the generation for whose advantage they are produced.

The decay of a radioactive material does not guarantee a harmless product. While this is true of some chemical substances, we know that many organic substances break down into such simple molecules as carbon dioxide and water. However, the parent radioactive element may decay into a "daughter" element that is frequently radioactive also but with a different half-life and chemistry from those of the parent. For example, radon, a radioactive gas, decays into nongaseous polonium, which clings to dust particles. As a gas, radon can escape from the ground or ore piles; after its decay, its daughter element polonium, residing on the dust particle, is easily inhaled and causes intense radiation of the lungs in which the particle is implanted. Predictions of behavior of radioactive materials must take into account that of possible decay products.

Despite complicated decay processes, the basic mechanisms whereby radioactive materials damage living organisms are simple. As the radioactive element decays, the energetic particles emitted pass through living cells like tiny bullets, breaking the bonds that hold vital molecules together. This process transfers energy to the cell, and a measure of this per gram of tissue is a *rad*, or *r*adiation *a*bsorbed *d*ose. When rads are multiplied by a quality factor that varies with the type of radiation (X ray, beta ray, alpha ray, or neutron radiation) one obtains the term *rem*, which is what we find radiation health doses measured in. Alphas and neutrons have more impact on the biological system, and use of the rem unit takes this increased impact into account.

The cell's and the body's reactions to the molecular damage determine the ultimate effects of the assault. Some cells die; others are repaired, but frequently with misarranged chromosomes. Radiation damage results in various cancers, genetic mutations, and other illnesses and debilitation through mechanisms that are poorly understood. High doses of radiation cause severe breakdown in many bodily functions resulting in acute radiation sickness or death.

There is little controversy about the severe illness or death that arises from doses of a hundred or more rems. Considerable, and at times heated, disagreement among scientists arises, however, about how hazardous low doses of perhaps a few rems or less may be.

Hazards of Low Doses: Early Estimates

Statistical difficulties in distinguishing radiation-induced cancers from those caused by other carcinogens, uncertainties in applying observations from animal experimentation to humans, and presently incomplete understanding of the mechanisms that cause cancer and degenerative diseases lead to inevitable disagreements among investigators. It is becoming clear, however, that earlier studies of the effects of low-level radiation seriously underestimated cancer risks. As a consequence, many current standards, engineering designs, and

NUCLEAR PROBLEMS: NO END IN SIGHT   57

operational procedures for technologies using radiation may not adequately protect workers or public from these risks.

The control of radiation risks has been hampered by the early, and now somewhat ingrained, underestimation of risks. Genetic changes in insects were an indication of the dangers of genetic damage from radiation. Cancer deaths among pioneers in radiation research and among radium workers made clear there was some risk of cancer. Yet early theories of how radiation damages living tissues and the lack of experimental evidence led to mistakes in evaluating the risks. Even today many scientists (in nonradiation specialties), doctors, radiologists, and other radiation workers judge radiation risks on now-disproven hypotheses.

In an analogy with many toxic chemicals, it was assumed in the beginning years of radiation work that a threshold dose of radiation existed below which exposure was harmless. Even though a single high dose might be harmful, the same total dose received as a series of small doses spread over a period of time appeared to be less dangerous or not harmful at all. For example, in the military services in the late 1940s and early 1950s, it was taken for granted that a person could receive as much as one-tenth rem per day without harmful effect.

The body has mechanisms for repairing broken chromosomes provided the breaks are not too numerous. According to early theories of radiation effects, high doses produce too many breaks to allow repairs and frequent low doses do not allow time for the repair mechanisms to operate. Thus many cells die, bodily functions are impaired, and illness or death follows. In contrast, infrequent low doses would produce relatively few chromosomal breaks and allow enough time for repairs. Excessive cell deaths and the resultant bodily disfunctions would be prevented.

The repaired chromosomes, however, would frequently have somewhat altered genetic information. If this occurred in cells involved in the reproductive process, the result could be genetically deformed children. In nonreproductive organs, the disordered chromosomes would allow normal cell functioning, but in some cases lead eventually to cancer. The early analysis concluded that genetic defects were the most serious effect of low doses. Such a viewpoint has held that in nonreproductive organs low doses could cause cancer, but even here doses below a certain threshold would be harmless.

In addition, those holding the "threshold" position cited the presence of radiation in the natural environment and concluded that human beings have survived and even flourished despite the hazard. Background radiation from cosmic rays and from the release of radon gas from the ground exposes the United States population to an average yearly dose of 0.102 rem, with doses varying from 0.05 rem in Florida to as much as 0.24 rem in Colorado. Some radioactive potassium occurs naturally in the human body. The conclusion is easily drawn that such low doses are below a threshold level for damage to human beings.

Early evaluations of the biological risks of radiation therefore focused on damage to the reproductive organs that could produce defective children. The repair mechanisms, the assumption of a threshold dose, and the existence of apparently innocuous background radiation led to a minimizing of the cancer risks. Other types of hazards, such as perhaps impaired functioning of the body's immunological systems, seemed even smaller.

By the late 1960s and early 1970s evidence had begun to accumulate that suggested the risk of cancer induction had been underestimated. Among the survivors of the Hiroshima and Nagasaki bomb blasts, increasing numbers of malignant tumors began to appear. The radiation damage was producing cancer only after long latency periods. Similarly, patients exposed to X rays many years earlier for the cure of spinal disease were becoming victims of radiation-induced cancer. Uranium miners were suffering a high incidence of lung cancer from inhaling radon.

The newer evidence also indicated that for human populations it was inappropriate to assume a threshold below which radiation exposure was safe. Even if each individual has a threshold level, the level will vary from individual to individual and even for a single individual, depending on numerous factors, as, for example, age, genetic predispositions, and exposure to other health-impairing factors. It was then assumed that a threshold for the whole population would be determined by the lowest individual thresholds.

This new evidence led the National Academy of Sciences' Committee on the Biological Effects of Ionizing Radiation (BEIR) to conclude in 1972 that public authorities who intend "to minimize the loss of life that radiation exposure may entail, will not rely on notions of a threshold."[1] In other words, a noted body of scientists was calling the threshold assumption into question.

The newer data on human cancers from radiation exposure were consistent with (although they did not conclusively prove) a no-threshold, linear dose-effect relationship. In the linear hypothesis, the risk of cancer is directly or linearly proportional to the radiation dose, no matter how small the dose. With no threshold, any exposure carries some risk of cancer induction. The BEIR Committee recommended this hypothesis as the basis for risk estimates and standards.[2]

Although there was good evidence and logical analysis to support the no-threshold, linear hypothesis, many scientists and nuclear industrialists maintained that the hypothesis was "conservative" and overestimated the risk of small doses. These people said that the fact that the bomb victims and the irradiated patients had all received relatively large doses required that the risk of low doses be extrapolated down from the high dose–risk data. The absence of experimental data at low doses made it possible to downplay the risk from doses that workers in the nuclear industry and medical radiologists were routinely receiving on the job.

The linear no-threshold hypothesis may be regarded as conservative since it takes better account of the many gaps in our understanding of cancer caused by radiation. It is conservative in assuming that some members of the population have in effect no threshold for safe exposure. It does not follow, however, that risks derived from the hypothesis are overestimates. Uncertainties in the interpretation of the high-dose data make it possible to underestimate the low-dose risks. The BEIR Committee intended to give the best estimates available from the evidence, not conservative overestimates.[3]

Since the 1972 report, more evidence has accumulated

that may well require an upward revision of the BEIR estimates. Continued study of patients irradiated for spinal disease has led to an increase in the dose-risk estimate.[4] Likewise, Japanese receiving relatively low doses from the bombs are beginning to develop excess numbers of cancers compared to the general population.[5] U.S. soldiers exposed to atomic blasts and fallout in weapons tests in the late 1950s are suddenly developing a statistically significant number of leukemias and other malignancies.[6] Workers in the U.S. government's nuclear facilities at Hanford, Washington, seem to be showing increased damage from their occupational exposure.[7]

This evidence also tends to confirm the validity of the linear hypothesis. The data showing increased risks from high exposure, together with new data on effects of somewhat lower exposures, are consistent with the linear hypothesis. Consequently, both the hypothesis and the risk estimates derived from it in the 1972 BEIR report have been shown to be less "conservative" than many had previously believed.[8]

The delayed appearance of the cancers among both the high- and low-dose populations can probably be attributed to the long latency periods before malignancies develop. The 1972 report had, in fact, suggested that such latency periods could be keeping estimates low.[9] This phenomenon could result in periodic increases in the risk estimates for many years to come.

Although some of these studies are being challenged and not all the evidence on the exposed soldiers or the Hanford workers has been analyzed, scientists who have avoided "alarmist" stances in the past are expressing serious worries about the occupational and medical exposures. Leading radiation specialists have testified before the U. S. Congress that current regulations may allow occupational exposures that are two to ten times too high and that X-ray exposure for medical diagnosis should be reduced by 50 percent.[10]

Radiation Standards

Paralleling the scientific investigations of the biological effects of radiation, standards were established to regulate exposure from the newly developed nuclear technologies. Because of the financial and legal implications of governmental regulations, the early standards tend to be firmly locked in place. Changes in standards are strongly resisted, especially by vested interests.

The authority to establish regulations governing exposure to radiation within the U.S. government lies with three federal agencies. The Nuclear Regulatory Commission (NRC) carries on the functions of the former Atomic Energy Commission (AEC); it has responsibility for setting standards for occupational, nonmedical exposure. As licensing agency for individual nuclear facilities, the NRC also determines the allowable exposure to individuals of the general public at the site boundary as well as allowable releases of radioactive materials from the facility. The Environmental Protection Agency (EPA), however, is responsible for establishing limits on radiation exposures or levels, or quantities and concentrations of radioactive materials, in the general environment outside the site boundaries. It belongs to the NRC to regulate the various facilities so that the cumulative effect of the total nuclear industry falls within the limits established by the EPA. The Bureau of Radiological Health (BRH) within the Food and Drug Administration (FDA) has regulatory authority over radiation technology for medical uses.

Before 1976 the EPA did not issue general standards but merely continued the role of the Federal Radiation Council (whose function it took over in 1970) of issuing guidelines on radiation to other government agencies, including the NRC (AEC). The functional standards for the nuclear industry were those determined and enforced by the AEC over individual nuclear facilities, which standards had to be compatible with the EPA guidelines. Both of these agencies have relied, in general, on the recommendations of the National Council on Radiation Protection and Measurement (NCRP) and its international counterpart, the International Commission on Radiological Protection (ICRP). For this reason, the guiding philosophy and the scientific evaluation that lay behind the current standards actually evolved principally within these two private organizations.

The ICRP recommendations of 1966, which agreed with the earlier (1957) recommendation of the NCRP, stipulated that, except for medical purposes, the whole population should not be exposed, on the average, to more than 0.17 rem of ionizing radiation per person per year. Although the public commonly assumes that these limits represent safe levels of exposure—in the sense that such exposures cause no significant damage—this was not the point of view of the ICRP when it proposed the limits.

According to the *Recommendations* of the ICRP *Document 2* (1966): "This limitation necessarily involves a compromise between deleterious effects and social benefits. . . . The commission is aware of the fact that a proper balance between risks and benefits cannot yet be made, since it requires a more quantitative appraisal of the probable biological damage and the probable benefits than is presently possible. . . . However, recommendations in quantitative terms are needed in the design of power plants and other radiation installations and particularly in making plans for disposal of radioactive waste products. . . . It is felt that this level provides reasonable latitude for the expansion of atomic energy programs in the foreseeable future. It should be emphasized that the limit may not in fact represent the proper balance between possible harm and probable benefit. . . ."

This limit for exposure of the whole population was based on genetic considerations. The 0.17 rem per year as the population average exposure would result in a cumulative dose of 5 rems over the thirty years from birth to the "mean" age of reproduction. Such exposure, plus an estimated equal amount from medical X rays (totaling 10 rems per generation), continued indefinitely, was estimated to result in 5,000 new instances of inherited defects per million births; about one tenth of this number would be in the first generation after radiation begins.[11]

Radiation-exposed workers are allowed to receive thirty times as much radiation as the limit (average) for the whole population—up to 5 rems per year and as much as 3 rems in a thirteen-consecutive-week period. Thus, not all the 0.17 rem per year accepted as the maximum tolerable average dose for the general population is to be taken by the general public. The workers' exposure must be included in the total population average.

This relatively large dose allowed workers is justified by the assumption that their genetic damage will be shared or diluted by mating with the general population. As the ICRP explains: "Genetic effects manifest themselves in the descendants of exposed individuals. The injury, when it appears, may be of any degree of severity from inconspicuous to lethal. A slight injury will tend to occur in the descendants for many generations, whereas a severe injury will be eliminated rapidly through the early death of the individual carrying the defective gene. Thus, the sum total of the effect caused by the defective gene until it is eliminated may be considered to be roughly the same. The main consideration in the control of genetic damage (apart from aspects of individual misfortune) is the burden of society in future generations imposed by an increase in the proportions of individuals with deleterious mutations. From this point of view it is immaterial in the long run whether the defective genes are introduced into the genetic pool by a few individuals who have received large doses of radiation, or by many individuals in whom smaller doses have produced correspondingly few mutations. . . ."[12]

The AEC adopted these recommendations and required a 0.17 rem per person per year average population dose, with no individual of the general population receiving more than three times that amount per year. Occupational exposure limits were set at thirty times the average exposure of the whole population. In addition, in order to limit radiation doses to various internal organs, standards were set for maximum concentrations of various radiotoxic substances in air and water.

The higher limits for occupational exposure were established to satisfy the needs of the nuclear industry and were justified as allowing risk comparable to those taken in other occupations. An EPA radiation specialist estimated recently that the risk to nuclear workers might be comparable to those of agricultural workers who are subjected to high risk from agricultural chemicals.[13]

As is also clear from the method of calculating exposure and genetic risk to the total population, occupational exposure is considered a risk to the total population. In addition, the current scientific opinion holds that no plant or animal species is more sensitive to radiation than human beings. The limiting exposures for people are therefore considered as adequate protection for the whole living environment.

The recommendations and standards were based on the assumption that genetic damage was the greatest risk posed by radiation exposure, outweighing cancer and other risks. After 1966, however, scientific evidence began to indicate that these limits would in fact allow unacceptable levels of cancer risk.

On the basis of the new evidence, Dr. Arthur Tamplin and Dr. John Gofman, medical radiation experts at the AEC's Lawrence Radiation Laboratory at Livermore, California, strongly criticized the AEC radiation exposures standard, saying they were at least ten times too high. Their critique precipitated a nationwide controversy, congressional hearings, and finally a two-year study by the National Academy of Sciences. The NAS report by the BEIR Committee published in 1972 acknowledged that existing standards did allow an unnecessarily and unacceptably high risk of radiation-induced cancer.

The BEIR report concluded that "based on knowledge of mechanisms (admittedly incomplete) it must be stated that tumor induction as a result of radiation injury to one or a few cells of the body cannot be excluded. . . . Such calculations based on these data from irradiated humans lead to the prediction that additional exposure of the U.S. population of 5 rem per year could cause from roughly 3,000 to 15,000 cancer deaths annually. . . . The Committee considers the most likely estimate to be approximately 6,000 cancer deaths annually. . . . It appears that [society's] needs can be met with far lower average exposures and lower genetic and somatic risk than permitted by the current Radiation Protection Guide. To this extent, the current Guide is unnecessarily high." The committee's basic recommendation for radiation exposure from the nuclear industry was that it be kept "as low as practicable."[14]

The recommendation of "as low as practicable" radiation exposure from the nuclear industry has resulted in two changes in exposure standards. First, the Atomic Energy

Commission put quantitative value on the concept "as low as practicable." Design-specified releases must not allow more than 0.005 rem per year exposure to members of the general public at site boundaries. This new standard was a 100-fold reduction from that previously allowed.

More recently EPA has adopted an exposure standard of 0.025 rem maximum for the general public from a combination of all nuclear facilities except for exposures to releases from uranium tailing piles (ore processing wastes). Unfortunately, it is difficult to estimate the public exposure from the tailings or to control the tailing releases effectively and economically, although some action must eventually be taken. In addition, the EPA standard is no longer a guideline for other federal agencies but an umbrella standard that specific site standards in aggregate must meet.

To date, no changes have been made in occupational standards or in the maximum concentrations of radioactive materials in air and water. Many of these standards are under criticism and are open to modification.

Low Doses: Recent Developments

New evidence has been accumulating showing that even the 1972 BEIR Committee's estimates do not reflect the total risk from radiation exposure. The validity of this evidence is the subject of considerable scientific controversy, which has elicited renewed calls for a slowdown or even a moratorium in the deployment of the nuclear industry.

New evidence points to the possibility that low levels of radiation exposure can trigger diseases other than cancer. Thus the total risk of such exposure would exceed the estimate given by the BEIR Committee of 6,000 cancer deaths annually from a 5-rem exposure over thirty years. In general, the contested evidence indicates both that low doses of radiation received at low-dose rates interfere with the immune system's ability to protect the body from disease,[15] and that radiation speeds up the aging process, leading to an earlier onset of the diseases of old age.[16]

The evidence for the genetic and cancer risks from radiation has been drawn largely from relatively high exposures. Various factors peculiar to the exposed populations made it possible to overlook evidence indicating that radiation can cause other diseases. Consequently, the degenerative-disease risks controversy has arisen.

In a new approach to radiation research, the occurrence of degenerative disease in a large population has been compared statistically with the population's exposure to diagnostic X rays. The studies indicate that radiation exposure is related to early onset of diseases associated with age. In addition, experimental evidence with animals indicates that radiation received gradually in small doses does greater cumulative damage than would be predicted by the high-dose data used in most analyses. Since the scientific community is only beginning to see the importance of these analyses, the standards-setting organizations can insist that current regulations are adequate.

A similar controversy about the dangers of plutonium allows varied estimates of the health impact of the use of plutonium fuel in nuclear reactors. The so-called hot-particle controversy centers on the estimated cancer risks from the inhalation of plutonium particles into the lungs.[17] Evidence indicates that plutonium deposited in the bone is significantly more carcinogenic than is currently acknowledged.[18] Both these findings, if accepted by the scientific community and regulatory agencies, could necessitate that facilities handling plutonium be designed and operated to allow essentially zero release of plutonium even to the air inside the facility.

A brief description of the hot-particle battle indicates how scientists are able to miss significant empirical evidence, and how nonscientific factors can influence judgment in scientific research. Premature optimism and defense of established positions can restrict new insight. Also, the hot-particle controversy has intrinsic importance in the use of plutonium as a fuel and it reveals many of the problems of science, technology, and government regulation. If the hot-particle hypothesis is correct, it will be extremely difficult to design and operate plutonium facilities under regulations stringent enough to guarantee occupational and public safety. This potential difficulty has made regulators and their affiliated scientists loath to accept the troublesome theory.

The exact mechanisms by which radiation doses produce

cancer are not well known. The evidence does show, however, that alpha radiation such as that emitted by radium and plutonium is ten times more effective in producing cancer than are X rays. In addition, plutonium is five times more effective in causing bone cancer than is radium because the two distribute themselves differently in the bone. Thus, if the bone tissue is irradiated by X rays and by alpha radiation from deposited plutonium, the plutonium will produce fifty times as much cancerous growth as the X rays, even though the radiation energy absorbed per mass of bone tissue is the same.

Similarly, the hot-particle discussion centers around the fact that some chemical compounds of plutonium will tend to be distributed unevenly in the lungs, if they are inhaled. The question is whether intense radiation concentrated at a few small spots in the lungs is more likely to produce cancer than the same total radiation absorbed uniformly throughout the lungs. Clearly, for a given amount of plutonium inhaled, the radiation dose distribution will be different if in the form of very fine particles irradiating most of the lung tissue or in the form of a few hot particles that irradiate immediately surrounding tissue. The difficulty lies in determining whether the intense localized radiation will produce more cancerous growth than the lower uniform doses.

The NRC standards that set limits for the amounts of plutonium inhaled are based on the assumption that it makes little or no difference whether the inhaled quantity of plutonium is evenly distributed or trapped in a few spots in the lung. ICRP recommendations limit the maximum permissible lung dose (MPLD) for workers to 15 rems per year and for the general public to 0.5 rem per year. NRC regulations limit plutonium concentrations in the air to prevent lung exposure above this dose.

If, however, intense localized radiation from a hot particle is a more effective cancer source, then the permissible lung doses and air concentration will be far more hazardous than predicted by the more commonly accepted analysis. On the hypothesis that hot particles are more hazardous carcinogens, the Natural Resources Defense Council (NRDC) in 1974 petitioned the AEC (now the NRC) to reduce allowed plutonium concentrations in the air by a factor of 100,000 or more.

Such low lung burdens and air concentrations of hot particles would be below the limits of detectability. The only effective method of meeting these limits would be zero-release designs for the facilities. Effective monitoring and regulation of operations would be very difficult.

The scientists, on whose analysis the NRDC based its petition, submitted to the AEC the arguments and evidence supporting their reasoning. They also reviewed the arguments for maintaining the standards based on uniform irradiation of the lungs. As new evidence appeared, NRDC refined its estimates of the level of radioactivity in a particle that would constitute a sufficient cancer threat to be considered "hot."

In the spring of 1976 the NRC formally rejected the petition and disagreed with the supporting theory and evidence. Reviews of the issue by government laboratories and the NCRP preceded the rejection. Yet none of these reviews fully addressed the NRDC argument or evidence, and none attempted to counter the NRDC rebuttal of the accepted explanations of the experimental evidence. Scientifically, the issue was not satisfactorily settled; legally, the status quo was upheld. The existing standards, which are less conservative than the proposed standards in limiting health risks, were maintained despite their increasingly suspect scientific basis.

While the NRDC petition initially requested a 100,000-fold reduction in the standards, later and more refined evidence indicated that, at the very least, a reduction by 1,000 was necessary. Additional evidence on plutonium in bone indicated a reduction by 400 times would be needed. Yet the standards still remain unchanged.

At present, assurances from the nuclear industry and its regulators that the risks have been adequately assessed and protected against cannot be given full credence. An honest assessment of the current evidence would have to conclude that a policy of greater caution than is currently practiced is reasonable.

RADIATION EXPOSURE FROM NUCLEAR FACILITIES

Routine Emissions

Even under normal operating conditions, the various containment measures cannot prevent all radioactive emissions from nuclear facilities. Pinhole breaks and cracks in the fuel rod cladding allow radioactive gases to escape into the cooling water. These emissions are then released from the cooling water at the condenser. Such releases are planned in boiling-water reactors and are common, almost routine, for pressurized-water reactors, which frequently develop small leaks from the primary into the secondary cooling systems. Various filters have been designed to trap the longer-lived radioisotopes, and holdup systems allow short-lived radioisotopes to decay before release from the stacks. In addition, radioactive solids resulting from the neutron bombardment of the reactor structure, followed by corrosion and release into the cooling water, give rise to radioactive liquids and sludges that are purged from the cooling water.

The 1972 BEIR report presented estimates, based on computer models, of the dose that would be received by the total U.S. population from power reactors, assuming maximum allowed doses of 5 millirems (0.005 rem) per year at each site boundary. The average annual dose to the U.S. population was estimated to be 0.17 millirem per year from the 800 to 1,000 reactors then expected to be operating in the year 2000. Routine releases from fuel reprocessing plants were similarly estimated to give 0.2 millirem per year exposure.[19] This has formed the basis for claims by the nuclear industry that 1,000 operating plants plus auxiliary facilities would give an average population dose of less than 0.4 millirem per year.

When the NRC followed the BEIR Committee's recommendation to reduce the doses to "as low as practicable," it adopted the committee's assumed dose of 5 millirems per year at site boundaries as the numerical standard, or a 100-fold reduction from the previous standard. These exposure limits and predictions relate only to normal, designed releases. Necessary variances and accidental releases are not included in the calculations.

Clearly, these standards do not impose absolute limits on radioactive releases and exposures. To many critics these incomplete standards constitute no limit at all. Their reasons are reflected in the BEIR Committee's statement that its "predictions could be high because of improvement in technology or could be low if plant performance deteriorates with time; also no account is taken . . . of the possibility of local exposure due to accidents." As Three Mile Island has indicated, accidents do happen and in many cases inadequate monitoring can easily render the actual radiation doses unknown.

Many devices that prevent radioactive releases are complicated and can break down. When they do, utility managers face the choice of shutting down the reactors, with resultant loss of power and revenue, or of operating with abnormal releases from plant vents. Valve failures have frequently allowed releases of radioactive water. Despite regulations, utilities have allowed their plants to continue operating when emission controls were inoperative. With respect to responsible management, nuclear power plants are no better or worse than fossil fuel plants.

Guaranteed compliance with standards is difficult when an adequate radiation monitoring system is lacking. Currently, the primary responsibility for monitoring and reporting radiation releases lies with the nuclear utilities. Funding for the EPA's independent monitoring program has gradually been reduced almost to nothing. State health agencies monitor little more than radioactive contamination of milk and occasionally of other foodstuffs.

In general, however, there is little monitoring of releases independent of the nuclear industry itself. The existence of radioactive fallout from foreign weapons tests has allowed high levels of strontium 90 to be attributed to that source rather than to the nuclear plants, in the absence of independent analysis. Health studies of radiation effects have been vitiated because of the lack of adequate data on background radiation and plant emissions. Public confidence demands independent and properly funded monitoring.

Occupational Exposure

Besides exposure from the routine and abnormal releases from the reactors, there is another significant source of risk to the total population that has been generally overlooked. This risk belies the assurances given by nuclear industry proponents that "the average person in the United States will receive the following exposure: 102 millirem per year from medical X-rays and therapeutic radiation, but only 0.4 millirem per year from the operation of all 1,000 nuclear power plants and their supporting activities" (the number that was then predicted to be operating in the year 2000).[20] This prediction essentially repeats the estimates given in the BEIR report.

In reality, the U.S. population is experiencing an increased genetic risk from the excess exposure of workers in the nuclear industry. The BEIR group emphasized the seriousness of this risk: ". . . the Subcommittee is convinced that any increase in the mutation rate will be harmful to future generations." Despite this conviction, the group felt comfortable with the nuclear industry since "it appears to be technologically feasible to develop nuclear power, at least for the near future, with a genetic exposure that is a very small fraction of the natural background, and less than one per cent of present radiation guides." It thus anticipated that the genetically significant dose would be about one millirem per person per year.[21]

However, the genetically significant dose is far higher than either the industry or BEIR levels. As described earlier, the genetic risk is considered a risk to the whole population since workers are free to marry into the general population and the genetically damaged offspring is part of the total population. Because of this, there are several ways one can arrive at the equivalent of an average exposure of 0.4 millirem annually. One way is for everyone of potentially reproductive capability to receive the average dose. But the same overall genetic damage to the human species would result if one half the reproductive population received 0.8 millirem and the remainder received none. The average exposure remains 0.4 millirem and, over the generations, the defective genes will be just as widely distributed and will produce as many deformities and deaths as if the total population received an "average" dose. With about 100 million persons of reproductive age in the U.S. population, an average 0.4 millirem exposure will result in approximately 6 genetic defects per million births.

Nuclear workers, however, receive much higher exposures on the job. The NRC has summarized the data for all commercial nuclear plants over the period 1969–74.[22] Generally, worker exposure has increased with plant age because of both buildup of radioactive materials in the plants and the increasing need for maintenance. It is thus not unreasonable to assume that the hypothetical 1,000 plants will be giving the same exposures per megawatt year as occurred in the years studied.

Assuming that half the workers are of reproductive age, the total occupational dose can be calculated to produce about 65 genetic defects per million births. The occupational and general exposures combined, then, result in 71 genetic defects per million births, or 12 times the industrial prediction. While these genetic defects amount to only 5 percent of those from background radiation and 10 percent of the defects caused by medical exposure, they remain a significant human cost of nuclear power.

Nuclear Reactor Safety

Accidental exposure to radiation from nuclear power plants can range from the relatively minor to the catastrophic. Failures of filters and various mechanisms to delay releases of radioactive gases from plant vents have occurred numerous times, but the damage to the environment is difficult to assess. Contaminated fluids have leaked inside many plants and increased the risk to plant workers. Unexpectedly large maintenance operations have greatly increased exposure to welders and other technicians. Yet major public attention has focused on the possibility of catastrophic accidents leading to widespread and high radiation doses to the general population.

What had seemed to many merely a possibility came close to reality at the Three Mile Island plant near Harrisburg,

Pennsylvania, in late March 1979. Radiation releases forced a partial evacuation of the area and the nation watched experts from around the world struggle to bring the reactor under control.

While the peculiar series of events at Harrisburg had never been anticipated, the possibility of catastrophic accidents had long been a cause for public concern. While a small atomic explosion does not seem possible, other potential accidents can lead to widespread scattering of radioactive materials. Studies in the late 1950s concluded that the loss of cooling water could lead to a meltdown of the reactor core. The molten fuel would release dangerous fission products; sufficient pressure from the steam and other gases created by the heat would break the outer containment walls and spew the radioactive materials into the air. Depending on wind speed and direction, large populations could receive radiation doses resulting, over time, in many genetic and cancerous health problems.

While it has been argued that the analyses gave "worst case" estimates, they led to additional safety systems. Consequently the newer reactors have several systems to reflood the reactor core quickly if pipe breaks or other problems lead to the uncovering of the core. Pressure suppression systems have been designed to prevent the buildup of steam and explosive gases from heat-induced chemical reactions. Multiple mechanisms for shutting down the fission reaction and slowing heat production have been incorporated.

Yet critics claim the safety systems are not adequate and point to a number of reasons. Safety mechanisms have failed to produce desired results. Small-scale tests, even if successful, may not adequately predict behavior in large commercial reactors. Even the *Loss* of *Fluid Test* (LOFT) facility, which is the largest safety test system planned and completed, is only one sixtieth the size of commercial reactors. Computer models scaling up these test results to predict the behavior of full-size safety systems are difficult to validate. This holds true even after small-scale successful tests in the spring of 1979.

Assuming the designs are adequate, poor quality control in the construction of reactors, simultaneous failure of redundant systems, or human error in operating a reactor can make the safety systems ineffective. The possibility and likelihood of such failures are very hard to evaluate or eliminate. The Brown's Ferry, Alabama, reactor fire in 1975 made clear that the supposedly redundant systems guaranteeing reactor shutdown could be simultaneously destroyed by a single small fire. All three cables leading from the controls into the reactor vessel passed through a single tunnel and were engulfed in the one fire. Resultant testing by the NRC has shown that even sprinkler systems installed in older reactors of the same design cannot prevent this simultaneous failure. New shutdown systems will have to be installed. Yet safety analyses prior to the fire had ruled out any significant probability of such accidents. Human error also played a large part in worsening the near-disaster at Brown's Ferry. How many other oversights like this exist is a matter of conjecture.

In the Harrisburg accident, poor design, management mistakes, and operator error all appear to have contributed to the destruction of the reactor core and the release of radioactivity. Auxiliary buildings designed to receive coolant water during accidents were not equipped to prevent release to the outdoors of radioactive gases released from the water. Contrary to regulations, management allowed operation of the reactor with critical safety valves locked shut. Operators did not believe the unusual readings on control panels, and one failed to see warning lights hidden by his oversize stomach.

A major study to evaluate the possible accident types and their possibility of occurrence was initiated by the AEC and released in draft form in 1974.[23] The Reactor Safety Study (RSS), also called the Rasmussen study after the panel's chairman, was immediately proclaimed by industry as proof of reactor safety. However, it was challenged by many non-industry experts. NRC chairman Marcus Rowden stated in 1976 that the RSS showed that "the risks from potential nuclear accidents would be comparable to those from meteorites." Yet in 1978 a review panel appointed by the NRC, and including industry representatives and the former director of the AEC's safety division (who had been director at the time the RSS was in process), concluded that the safety study ailed to arrive at a credible evaluation of the probability of major nuclear accidents.

The review group found, for example, that the statistical analysis in the RSS "suffers from a spectrum of problems ranging from lack of data on which to base input distributions, to the invention and use of wrong statistical methods." The review continues: "We were unable to define whether the overall probability of a core meltdown given in WASH 1400 [the RSS] is high or low, but we are certain that the error bands are understated. *We cannot say by how much*. Reasons for this include an inadequate data base, a poor statistical treatment, an inconsistent propagation of uncertainties throughout the calculations, etc." Although admitting that the RSS provides to date the most complete single picture of such accident probabilities, the review group concluded that "WASH 1400 has been misused as a vehicle to judge the acceptability of reactor risks."[24]

Controversy over reactor safety will undoubtedly continue. Unfortunately, most analyses center on U.S. construction designs, where the NRC has regulatory and inspection capability. Reactors built in developing nations, even with U.S.-manufactured components, receive much less thorough design safety analyses, and often less attention is given to construction quality, proper siting, and worker safety. The nuclear industry is not immune from exporting products unsafe for American consumption.

WASTE MANAGEMENT

Nuclear fuel that has completed its useful life in a power reactor, or so-called spent fuel, contains a mixture of radioactive elements requiring careful management. This care is necessitated both by high levels of radioactivity and by the potential usefulness of a portion of the spent fuel as material for nuclear weapons. Decisions on the management of spent nuclear fuel involve, therefore, questions both of health and safety and of national security.

On an average, each 1,000-megawatt reactor produces 33 tons of spent fuel each year. Most of this is uranium that can be processed and upgraded into new reactor fuel. A small portion consists of a mixture of highly radioactive chemicals that, in general, must be disposed of as toxic wastes from the nuclear power industry. A third and smaller component is plutonium, a material that, like uranium, can fuel the fission reaction. This plutonium can be used in power reactors of various designs, but also as a critical mass for plutonium bombs. Moreover, plutonium requires extraordinary care in handling because of the toxic threat to health described earlier.

The spent fuel, when it is removed from the reactor core, has this radioactive mixture chemically locked into ceramic pellets and encased in long, pencil-like metal tubes. For use either as fuel or as weapons material, the plutonium must be separated from the uranium and the radioactive wastes; such separation is necessary also to reuse the uranium. As long as plutonium and uranium remain mixed in with the wastes, they cannot be handled without excessive exposure to radioactivity and are unusable for any purpose.

In an effort to encourage all nations to take a closer look at the threat to world security resulting from the possible diversion of commercially produced plutonium to weapons use, the United States has decided not to separate uranium and plutonium from the radioactive wastes. Diplomatic pressure is being exerted to convince other nations to follow suit. Various technologies and institutional arrangements are under examination in the hope of finding a commercial fuel cycle that will recover useful nuclear fuel but will guarantee it cannot be diverted to the production of nuclear weapons.

Before 1977, the United States wanted a nuclear fuel cycle in which spent fuel was chemically dissolved in order to separate the fuel mixture. The uranium and plutonium would each be separately recycled into fuels and the radioactive wastes prepared for permanent disposal.

Since the decision to postpone the use of this reprocessing technology, spent fuel has been accumulating in storage pools at reactor sites and at several special storage facilities. As the available space is almost filled, decisions will be needed on whether to expand on-site storage pools or to construct new away-from-reactor (AFR) facilities. Because this decision may require disposal of whole spent fuel rods, instead of only the separated wastes, the program for waste disposal may need modification.

In addition, the potential for exposure to radioactivity from the fuel cycle is changed considerably. While workers will not receive exposure at reprocessing plants or plutonium fuel manufacturing plants, exposure to uranium miners and to local populations from the crushed uranium ores grows because of increased demand for fresh uranium. Releases of plutonium from the plants or in transportation accidents is prevented, but away-from-reactor storage of spent fuel may double the number of rail and truck shipments of these dangerous materials. Storage of more spent fuel for longer times increases the possibility of accidental releases from the storage pools.

The development of policy remains uncertain regarding reprocessing, international safeguards, and permanent disposal, whether of spent fuel or of separated wastes. For that reason, the discussion of the toxicity of the wastes and of the technologies for managing them must cover both types of fuel cycles: the one including reprocessing and the other "once through" cycle.

The highly radioactive waste, whether separated out of spent fuel or not, has two major components—the fission products and the transuranics. The fission products are a wide variety of radioactive chemicals resulting from the splitting of uranium and plutonium in the fission reaction. The transuranics—for example, neptunium and americium—are produced from uranium by its absorption of neutrons. The distinction of these components is important because the half-lives of the transuranics are much longer in general than those of most of the fission products. In addition, the fission products emit beta and gamma rays, while the transuranics emit mostly alpha rays. The two components thus differ in their biological hazards, their heat output, and the duration of the hazards.

The toxicity of wastes can be estimated by computing the amount of water needed to dilute the wastes to levels specified in the Radiation Concentration Guides, or the maximum concentration of radioactive material allowed in water for unrestricted use. If the construction of nuclear power plants had continued at the rates estimated in the early 1970s, by the year 2000 the accumulated wastes would have taken 1.4 times 10^{19} gallons of water for dilution to "safe" concentrations. This is about 4 percent of the oceans' volume, and almost double all the global fresh water. Another measure of their toxicity is the potential for millions or billions of fatal cancer-causing doses that is contained in the wastes from one year of nuclear power production in the United States, if all the wastes were eaten.

While these estimates exceed the actual risk by ignoring the environmental barriers to full release of the wastes and their intake by humans, nonetheless they show the hazardous nature of radioactive wastes. Determining actual risks to humans is difficult because of not knowing the likelihood of waste release and the various pathways through the environment before wastes reach human beings.

Initially, the transuranics contribute less than one percent of the biological hazard. Most of the fission products, however, decay, quickly compared to the transuranics. After 800 years, the toxicity of the fission products has diminished to about fifty times that of natural uranium ore and stays at this level almost permanently. After these first 800 years, the transuranics become the chief biological hazard.

Because the transuranics decay through a long series of daughter elements and because many of these daughters are more dangerous than the transuranics themselves, the toxicity of the transuranics plus daughters gradually decreases over a period of 20,000 years, but then increases sevenfold again. The transuranics plus daughters remain one thousand times more toxic than uranium ore for most of 4 million years.

Similarly, the decay heat from the fission products makes handling of the wastes and their disposal difficult. Over the thousands of years of waste isolation, however, the presence of the transuranics and their daughters provides the major source of heat.

In a fuel cycle that reuses the uranium and plutonium, the management of the wastes involves a number of steps: temporary storage for cooling the spent fuel; chemical separation of the wastes from the reusable fuels; solidification of the wastes; and finally, the isolation from the environment through burial or other means. In the "once through" cycle, the fuel rods are stored intact until they can be packaged and disposed of permanently.

In both cycles, when the fuel rods are removed from a reactor they are stored at the reactor site in pools of water. They are kept there 150 days at least, until the heat and intense radiation from short-lived fission products have diminished enough to allow transportation off site. Most of the fission products and all of the transuranics are still locked into the ceramic fuel pellets that contained them in the reactor. As long as the metal cladding around the pellets remains intact, the waste products are safely stored.

Waste storage requires continuous security and maintenance of the facility. Two types of accident can be very dangerous. If the cooling water escapes the pool, especially when the fuel is very hot, the heat can melt the fuel and cladding and allow many of the fission products to escape. Also, if the fuel rods come too close together, a fission reaction can start, causing a rapid buildup of heat or a small explosion, again releasing the toxic wastes. Since such storage presents a continuous threat to national security in event of war or terrorist attack, and because of the maintenance required, such cooled surface storage cannot be a long-term management method.

In reprocessing, various chemical solutions are used to separate the uranium and plutonium from the fission products and the other transuranics. In this process, about 0.5 percent of the uranium and plutonium and all of the other transuranics remain mixed with the fission products in a liquid form. In this mixture the transuranics turn an 800-year waste problem into the several-million-year problem described earlier.

By completely extracting uranium and plutonium from the wastes the duration and magnitude of the problem would be reduced. Additional extraction is apparently technically feasible, but the value of the extra plutonium saved would not balance the cost of the process. Furthermore, the extraction process would generate increased quantities of radioactively contaminated chemicals needing proper disposal.

If transuranics were extracted from fission products, the waste problem would last for only 800 years. Of course, the extracted transuranics must be disposed of separately. Some suggest rocketing the transuranics to outer space. Rocket technology and encapsulation methods would have to be improved to protect against release of the radioactivity in a launch accident or an accidental reentry of the capsule.

Others suggest that transuranics be recycled with plutonium into reactor fuel. Under neutron bombardment they would eventually be transformed into elements that could fission, thus becoming wastes with shorter half-lives. This process, however, would require that the transuranics be recycled ten to twenty times, with attendant unavoidable losses at each step. In addition, the chemical separation of the transuranics may be difficult. In any case, the additional extraction processes are not now provided for at reprocessing plants. Presently, the question remains how to store and/or dispose of wastes that are highly toxic and enduring.

The next step in the process is the solidification of the liquid wastes, with considerable reduction in volume. The solidified high-level waste from the one-year operation of a 1,000-megawatt reactor will have a volume of 90 cubic feet and weigh about 5 tons. As now envisioned, the solidification results in a granular material, mixed with light powder, that must be enclosed in canisters to prevent dispersal by air movement or dissolution in fluids. These canisters of "calcined" wastes would be put in a cooled surface storage facility or in a permanent underground repository. Presently no commercial facility for this process exists. The only one built was a $64 million failure, an example of a transfer from pilot plant to commercial plant design that failed because of engineering oversight.

Ultimately it is hoped that the wastes can be solidified into a glass form, which would greatly reduce the possibility of dispersal into air or water. The Department of Energy is considering such a facility, but there are numerous unresolved problems. The process requires the development of very-high-temperature technology that is completely remote-controlled and -maintainable. Many of the fission products become gaseous at these high temperatures and can escape capture in the glass.

More important, the glass solid with the entrapped wastes may not be a very stable waste form. At the temperatures and pressures likely to exist in underground repositories, glass tends to crystallize and become a collection of crystal beads. The foreign wastes initially trapped in the glass are rejected by the crystals and settle at the crystal boundaries. Consequently, the wastes can be leached out by water. Thus the prime advantage of the glass waste form is lost. Recent tests under conditions similar to those in underground repositories have confirmed the likelihood of these reactions.

Because of these problems with glass, embedding the wastes in ceramics is now receiving more attention. Thorough testing under realistic conditions and commercial development of the necessary plants remain for the future.

The present status of this "reprocessing-solidification" approach to nuclear waste management consists of two commercial reprocessing plants, neither presently operational, and a demonstration plant that is calcining some military wastes. The NRC will not, however, let one reprocessing plant operate until an additional plant for converting plutonium from liquid to solid form is added on, in order to reduce the risks of transporting this fissionable material. To date, Allied-Gulf, the owner, has hesitated to commit its resources to building this addition. Another reprocessing plant in New York State operated for seven years but was shut down when worker exposure to radioactivity began to exceed standards. Several large tanks of liquid high-level wastes still await further treatment there.

Because of the national decision to reconsider the weapons proliferation problem that seems inherent in a plutonium fuel cycle, there is no active program to bring the commercial reprocessing system to completion. At present, spent fuel is stored in pools at reactor sites and at several large storage facilities.

The decision not to reprocess spent fuel raises a number of problems regarding its handling and disposal. While the current opinion is that the problems are not more (or less) difficult to resolve, a number of decisions must be made.

As has been mentioned, spent fuel rods are accumulating to the point of exceeding the capacity of the on-site storage pools at existing reactors. There is considerable dispute whether the on-site capacity can be enlarged sufficiently to handle accumulations that will occur before a waste disposal method is operational. Final disposal of entire spent fuel rods must differ in methodology from that for solidified wastes. The volume and tonnage is greater. The heat output is significantly different, but repository design or longer storage in pools can correct for this. The disposal method receiving the most attention is disposal in mined, underground repositories. The repository program is the prime focus of current government activity, but is by no means certain of success.[25]

Proposals for creating additional storage capacity for spent fuel are being debated at this time. The California Energy Resources Conservation and Development Commission has recommended that all new reactors be sized to store ten years' accumulation of fuel and designed to eventually hold forty years' worth—the expected lifetime of a nuclear power reactor. The Department of Energy is recommending construction of at least seven AFR (away-from-reactor) storage facilities, which would relieve the utilities of this burden at a fixed fee. Whether existing or currently designed reactors could be modified to allow such expansion is a disputed question.

Aside from economic costs, several difficulties with the AFR proposal need resolution. Larger concentrations of wastes at specific sites present greater national security risks. Handling and hauling spent fuel will increase occupational and transportation risks. The number of trips by highway and rail will more than double in certain peak years compared to at-reactor storage. Capability for manufacturing transportation casks will be severely strained and may produce casks of inferior quality.

No form of surface storage can be sufficiently secure from intrusion or free from deterioration for the needed storage duration. No institutional mechanisms to provide protection can reasonably be postulated to last for these periods. Disposal alternatives suggested for removal or isolation of the wastes are not perfect: some have failed; some are still under study; only one is being actively pursued. Rocket ejection or isolation in the ice sheets of Antarctica or Greenland provide incomplete waste disposal, are uncertain of technical success, or violate international treaties. No machinery and little technological expertise exist for disposal of wastes in deep-sea sediments or in super-deep wells. Disposal in continental rock formations in mined cavities is the only method that has progressed beyond the stage of conceptual studies.

Solid waste disposal in salt mines and formations has met with problems that to date have prevented the selection of sites meeting all disposal criteria. Although mining technology to handle and emplace the wastes is available, the ultimate criterion for the program is successful long-term isolation of the wastes, and this is not guaranteed. While success over the long duration needed can be evaluated only through computer projections, confidence in these projections requires accurate understanding of a large number of physical, chemical, biological, and climatic conditions. These conditions, even in the same type of rock formation, vary considerably from one site to another.

Emplacement of wastes and reaction of wastes with the rock material may disrupt the very features that make the site attractive. Bore holes and mine shafts open up pathways for water infiltration into the anticipated repository. The mechanical strength of the rock is weakened by mining. Earthquakes and seismic events can fracture formations and/or change rivers and underground water flow. Future generations may drill or mine the site in search of natural resources. The hot wastes themselves can expand and fracture rocks and perhaps let water in. Radiation from the wastes can change rock properties. Various chemical reactions of the hot wastes with surrounding rock can lead to seepage of the wastes from the repository.

Even salt-bed repositories no longer appear as free from difficulties as once thought. While salt will conduct heat away quickly, it also expands considerably, so that it can fracture the surrounding rocks that protect it from ground and subsurface water. Salt is very soluble and also corrosive to the metal canisters, so that access of water to the salt can speed up waste movement to the surface. Salt formations are not totally free of water, which will migrate toward the hot canisters and dissolve surrounding salt. Because of their weight, the hot canisters could begin to sink toward the lower boundary of the salt bed and perhaps break into water-laden rock formations below. Salt is frequently found with other valuable minerals and resources such as potash and natural gas, which makes a salt-bed site vulnerable to future human intrusion.

Although many problems are unresolved, such disposal remains the most feasible method at this time. Complete evaluation of the desirable characteristics and the development of criteria remain unfinished. The two sites tested between the mid-1950s and the present have not met even existing criteria. Consequently, President Carter set up an Interagency Review Group in 1978 to analyze the waste disposal program and recommend a future course. Among the primary recommendations was expanding research leading to underground sites in other rock formations besides salt beds. While the Department of Energy (DOE) prefers to locate the first repository in a salt formation, other federal agencies are turning their attention to other rock types. The review group projected that the earliest date for operation of a repository in salt would be 1988, while investigation of other rock types would postpone operation of a first repository to 1992. Such delay was seen as improving the success of the program but worsening the temporary storage problems for the spent fuel. Slippage of both programs by another three to five years was considered likely by the review panel.

Numerous political difficulties could delay or prevent the successful completion of either program. Citizens in many states are opposing the siting of repositories within their boundaries. Localities are restricting the transport of radioactive materials over their roads. State governments and Indian tribal councils are seeking closer consultation with the federal agencies on these programs.

In summary, a decade or more of difficult scientific effort and political activity is needed to provide even one waste repository. While the disposal program offers some promise, there is the possibility of failure. Even initial success could provide at best computer projections of the long-term isolation of the wastes.

While the disposal of high-level wastes has attracted much public attention, the crushed rock left after extracting uranium from the ore (mill tailings) was generally overlooked by the public and negligently ignored by the government. These tailings contain small amounts of uranium 234 and thorium 230, which decay over long time periods to radium 226 and its gaseous decay product, radon 222. Rainwater and streams easily dissolve radium from the waste piles, which all the while emit radon gas. Unless deep layers of clay or other materials are placed over the tailings, they can emit radon at up to 500 times the natural background rate.

Radon's decay products can cause lung cancer and have been responsible for the cancer deaths of many uranium miners in Europe and the United States. The hazard from the mill tailings may exceed those from the transuranics from the power plants. In fact, Victor Gilinsky, an NRC commissioner, has stated that unless the tailings are isolated from the atmosphere the radon releases will continue for more than 100,000 years to become "the dominant contribution to radiation exposure from the nuclear fuel cycle."[26]

The hazards of these wastes have been consistently underestimated by the regulatory agencies. Consequently, less than five miles from downtown Salt Lake City, in the middle of what is now a residential area of more than a half million people, 1.8 million tons of these sandy wastes stand open to the air. Thousands of people work and live near the pile and are exposed to radioactive dust, radon gas and its decay products, and external gamma radiation. Similar piles lie close to Grand Junction and Durango, Colorado. The largest and still-growing pile stands outside Grants, New Mexico, and contains 23 million tons. Besides 27 million tons of tailings at inactive sites, 113 million more tons have accumulated at active mine sites, and there may be as much as a billion tons in all by the year 2000.

The difficulty and size of the tailings cleanup can be seen from proposal estimates for the Salt Lake pile, which range from $550,000 to more than $30 million. Possible methods include a dirt covering with vegetation, all the way to rail transport of the pile along with two feet of radium-contaminated soil beneath to a desert site ninety miles away. Utah health officials prefer the latter method, since reduction of radon emissions in the city to near-background levels would require a covering of twenty-two to thirty feet of soil or eight feet of cement over the whole 128-acre site.

The need for a radical reevaluation of the handling of these wastes has been highlighted by numerous horror stories. In a Salt Lake City fire station built over the tailings twenty years ago, the radon exposure was found to be seven times that allowed to uranium miners. In 1959 the AEC authorized the sale of tailings for use as landfill material. In 1966 it was discovered that hundreds of buildings in Grand Junction and Durango were contaminated from tailings used as fill.

While Congress in 1972 authorized a multimillion-dollar cleanup of the Grand Junction buildings, more than half the 700 sites needing it remain contaminated in 1978. In that year, Congress enacted a bill to deal with the total tailings problem. The DOE has been given responsibility to eliminate the hazards of the twenty-some inactive tailings piles, at an estimated cost of $140 million. If the piles cannot be stabilized in place, removal and burial will cost far more. In addition, the NRC or authorized state agencies will have to insist on proper tailings management by uranium mill licensees.

Future licenses for mill operations may require backfilling the dry tailings into the mining pits created by ore extraction and deep burial under soil. For existing active piles, however, the NRC requires only regrading to control erosion and a covering of eight to twelve feet of clay and other soil. While this above-surface burial is estimated to reduce radon emissions to twice background levels, it is arguable that erosion and other events over the next thousands of years will negate these minimal corrective actions.

QUESTIONS FOR THE FUTURE

Past developments and the future role of nuclear power raise many questions that need satisfactory resolution. The risk to this and hundreds of future human generations from increasing amounts of radioactive materials requires sober

evaluation. The very real uncertainties over adequate technological solutions to the problems must force a national and
worldwide reexamination of the true benefits and the real
need for nuclear energy. Highly centralized electric power
generation must be questioned; it may prove to be an exces-
sively wasteful, uneconomical, and unnecessary method of
providing energy needs.

The resistance of the NRC to evidence on plutonium toxicity raises questions about the role of this and other governmental regulatory agencies. Mandated by Congress and paid
for by tax funds, the NRC is supposed to regulate the nuclear industry for the public's protection. Federal funds spent
for environmental and health research are likewise intended
to promote, not prevent, the development of evidence on
these important matters. Nuclear safety issues prompted the
division of the old AEC in order to separate the regulatory
from the developmental programs. Yet the NRC still vacil-
lates between promotion of public safety and that of nuclear
power. NRC holds that even high-priority safety research is
intended merely to confirm the safety of plant designs, not to
indicate any real inadequacy in the systems. Many NRC staff
people showed resentment of the criticism of the Reactor
Safety Study even by the panel appointed by their own
agency.

Part of the problem may be traced to a situation that exists
in many regulatory agencies but appears worse in the energy
agencies. This is the "revolving door" approach to meeting
staffing needs. Members of the regulated industry are re-
cruited for policy positions in the agencies, and staffers
trained by the agencies seek employment in the industry they
previously regulated. The conflicts of interest are intense.

When the Virginia Electric and Power Company discovered a seismic fault line under the site of a nuclear plant
being constructed, it did not formally report the discovery, as
required by the NRC. It was later convicted and fined for
the violation. When the Justice Department investigated the
situation for criminal violations, it decided that the NRC staff
had, in effect, cooperated in hiding the discovery. Justice refused to prosecute VEPCO because of the ambiguous role of
NRC. When asked to prosecute NRC staffers for their in-

volvement, they dropped the case because there was no evidence of bribery. Yet direct bribes are not necessary if jobs are waiting in a regulated industry.

The "revolving door" problem involves the training and maintaining of adequate expertise to perform the regulatory role and of adequately paying and motivating the government staffers. It is a serious and difficult problem that cries for congressional action.

An examination of the difficulties of establishing the relationships between radiation doses and subsequent health effects brings out a glaring need for continuous lifetime health records for exposed populations. The Japanese keep careful death records for the entire population, making it possible for the atomic bomb casualty study group to obtain its valuable results. The director of this group has stated that if the bomb had been dropped on a U.S. city no such study of the long-term effects could have been made because of the uneven and poor quality of the U.S. mortality record keeping.[27]

Only Connecticut keeps a cancer mortality record bank. No follow-up studies of the U.S. military exposed at the weapons tests were made until the sudden "epidemic" of leukemias and other cancers was brought to the attention of the Center for Disease Control in Atlanta by some of the affected military. Only because a few university researchers convinced the AEC of the utility of an occupational study was a reasonably careful record kept of the Hanford workers and other exposed employees of AEC contractors. Although regulated nuclear facilities must keep records of employee exposure, there is no requirement that these be kept as part of the employees' lifetime medical record. Death records do not include residential or employment history, and frequently not even a medically verified cause of death.

Protecting privacy and shielding workers from discrimination on the basis of health or previous exposure are problems. But the need for abundant and complete statistics on cancer and other diseases will require complete record keeping on exposure to radiation and other suspected carcinogens. Until epidemiologically valid records are kept, the risks of numerous technologies will continue to be vaguely estimated, at perhaps very high cost to workers and the public.

Besides technical problems with proper nuclear waste disposal, many policy questions also remain unanswered. Should the wastes be disposed of in a manner to allow retrieval if the site characteristics prove unsuitable? Since salt will corrode the waste canisters in about twenty years, a requirement of retrievability could rule out salt-bed disposal. Is disposal at one or two sites preferable to a multiplicity of sites with small amounts of waste in each? The latter option would reduce the potential for disaster at any one site, but at the same time allow for more mistakes in the choice of sites as well as increase the economic and political costs.

It is commonly believed that the amount of wastes that has been produced to date by commercial nuclear power are small compared to the wastes from nuclear weapons production. The urgency for commercial disposal sites thus seems relatively less. In fact, recent estimates indicate that commercial wastes already equal in toxicity (although not in volume) the military wastes. Consequently an already serious disposal problem is being compounded at an alarming rate.

The Interagency Review Group report of October 1978 on nuclear waste management represents a significant step forward in resolving this important but to-date unmanageable problem. The report for the first time allowed the government to appreciate the full breadth of technical and institutional problems encompassed in nuclear waste management. Among other things, the report acknowledged the failure of past plans to assess adequately the generic and site-specific questions concerning the interactions of the host rock and hydrology in all their complexity with the foreign matter (waste, canister, and so forth). It recognized the institutional aspects of the problem. Instead of outdated optimism over disposal in salt formations, the review group expressed confidence about evaluating several geologic media for *apparently feasible* isolation for periods of thousands of years by use of a "systems" approach.

While the "systems" approach and expansion to other media were welcome advances, they are not a new basis for optimism. Current limited knowledge indicates rather that some geologic media and sites may provide satisfactory disposal for long-term isolation of the wastes. Since the need is great, the United States must proceed with this approach as being likely to produce some reasonably satisfactory disposal capability at an earlier date than other approaches. As long as it remains uncertain what precise quantitative risks exist to human health and the environment from radioactive wastes, and as long as a reasonable hope of adequate disposal exists, it is difficult to argue that absolutely no additional nuclear plants should be built for this reason alone.

Yet to increase the admittedly sizable risk by a factor of 15, 25, or more, as implementation of current energy policy will assure, appears most irresponsible without comparably certain success in reducing risks through adequate disposal. The IRG report and subgroup give evidence that a lengthy and complicated program may eventually produce successful strategies and facilities for waste disposal. The same evidence indicates that generic scientific feasibility of waste disposal is no guarantee of site-specific, tested and proven, safe disposal. The past optimistic complacency has succeeded in producing a large backlog of military and commercial wastes that are managed by stop-gap measures. The proposed program may, or may not, produce in fifteen years what was promised twenty years ago. To continue the mistake of regarding promise as reality is foolishness.

As long as an essential component of nuclear technology is missing, nuclear power must be treated as burdened by a major disadvantage. In comparing the merits of various alternative energy strategies, the lack of a proven disposal method must weigh heavily against increases in the nuclear component over present capacity.

Solar energy use and many energy conservation techniques may be burdened by high front-end investments. But as long as nuclear power is burdened by its back-end weakness, energy strategies must attempt to overcome the problems in solar use and energy conservation efforts with at least as much vigor as the solution of nuclear problems requires. In fact, other advantages—for example, more employment opportunities and reduced capital demand—suggest that these alternative strategies be given higher priority.

Past mistakes have severely limited for the time being the potential contribution of nuclear power to a total energy system. Haste now may limit its contribution for all times. A high-priority effort to restrain growth in unnecessary electrification is essential for a successful long-term energy strategy that will meet the many needs of human life on earth.

REFERENCES

1. *The Effects on Populations of Exposure to Low Levels of Ionizing Radiations*, report of the Advisory Committee on the Biological Effects of Ionizing Radiations, Division of Medical Sciences (Washington, D.C.: National Academy of Sciences–National Research Council, Nov. 1972), p. 96. This BEIR report outlined the history of radiation toxicity experience and standards prior to 1972.

2. BEIR report, pp. 89 and 97.

3. Ibid., p. 90.

4. E. P. Radford, R. Doll, and P. G. Smith, "Mortality among patients with ankylosing spondylitis not given X-ray therapy," *New England Journal of Medicine* 297 (11) (Sept. 15, 1977), pp. 572–76.

5. J. Rotblat, "The Risks for Radiation Workers," *Bulletin of Atomic Scientists*, Vol. 33, No. 7 (Sept. 1978), pp. 41–46.

6. Testimony before U. S. House of Representatives, Committee on Interstate and Foreign Commerce, Subcommittee on Health and Environment, Feb. 1978.

7. T. Mancuso, A. Stewart, and G. Kneale, "Radiation Exposures of Hanford Workers Dying from Cancer and Other Causes," *Health Physics* 33 (Nov. 1977), p. 369.

8. Testimony before Subcommittee on Health and Environment, Feb. 1978.

9. BEIR report, pp. 86, 90, 99.

10. Testimony before Subcommittee on Health and Environment, Feb. 1978.

11. BEIR report, p. 43.

12. ICRP, *Document 2*, 1966.

13. W. Ellett, at Seminar on Effects of Low Level Radiation, U. S. House of Representatives, Committee on Interior and Insular Affairs, Subcommittee on Energy and Environment, Nov. 1976.

14. BEIR report, p. 2.

15. E. J. Sternglass, "The Role of Indirect Radiation Effects on Cell Membranes in the Immune Response," in *Radiation and the Immune Response*, Proceedings of the 1974 Hanford Radiation Symposium.

16. R. Bertell, *Health Effects of Low Level Radiation*, Presentation to the American Health Association, Nov. 1975.

17. A. Tamplin and T. Cochran, *Radiation Standards for Hot Particles* (Washington, D.C.: Natural Resources Defense Council, Feb. 1974).

18. Karl Z. Morgan, before the Environmental Protection Agency, Hearings on Radiation Protection Standards, 1976.

19. BEIR report, pp. 15 ff.

20. Congressman Mike McCormack, "Nuclear Power: the Nation's Salvation," *The New Engineer* (Oct. 1975).

21. BEIR report, p. 59.

22. U. S. Nuclear Regulatory Commission, *Occupational Radiation Exposures at Light Water Cooled Power Reactors 1969–1974*, Radiation Protection Section, Radiological Assessment Branch, Office of Nuclear Reactor Regulation, NUREG-75/032 (June 1975).

23. WASH 1400 (NUREG-75/014) Reactor Safety Study (Washington, D.C.: U. S. Nuclear·Regulatory Commission, Oct. 1975).

24. NUREG/cr-0400, Risk Assessment Review Group Report to the U. S. NRC (Washington, D.C.: United States Nuclear Regulatory Commission, Dec. 1978), pp. vi, x.

25. These materials are treated more fully in the following: *Report to the President by the Interagency Review Group on Nuclear Waste Management*, TID 28817 (draft) (Washington, D.C.: U. S. Department of Energy, Oct. 1978); *Geologic Disposal of High-Level Radioactive Wastes—Earth Science Perspectives* (Washington, D.C.: U. S. Geological Survey Circular 779, 1978); *State of Geological Knowledge Regarding Potential Transport of High-Level Waste from Deep Continental Repositories*, Report of an Adhoc Panel of Earth Scientists (Washington, D.C.: U. S. Environmental Protection Agency, 1978).

26. *Science* 202 (Oct. 13, 1978), p. 191.

27. S. Jablon, at Seminar on Effects of Low Level Radiation, Nov. 1976.

III

COAL: A STUDY IN FOSSIL FUEL ETHICS

> And Daddy won't you take me back to
>   Muhlenberg County,
> Down by the Green River
>   Where Paradise Lay.
> Well, I'm sorry my son
> But you're too late in asking
> Mister Peabody's coal train has
>   hauled it away.
>   John Prine "Paradise"

During the 1960s and early 1970s worldwide energy production grew an average of 5 to 6 percent annually. The growth in demand for electricity has been even more rapid— over 7 percent a year between 1958 and 1972. Increased use of petrochemicals in the production of plastics and other synthetics has led to the replacement of such solar-derived materials as wood, cotton, and natural rubber by fossil fuel materials. Modern energy-intensive agricultural methods demand hydrocarbon-based fertilizers and petroleum-powered farm implements. Thus the global growing demand for food has also become tied to fossil fuel supplies.

While the production and use of petroleum and natural gas entail a number of environmental problems (such as safety of transport and storage of liquefied natural gas, combustion products, and oil tanker problems), this chapter will concentrate on the complex issues relating to coal. In view of past trends and potential reserves of coal, speculators predict a marked increase in coal production and consumption over the next two decades.

COAL CONSUMPTION PROBLEMS

Coal, the king fuel of the pre–World War I period, was dethroned by cheap oil and natural gas. But the Arab embargo and subsequent oil price hikes has reversed that picture. Edwin R. Phelps, the president of Peabody Coal Company, America's largest coal producer, observes that the role of coal has changed from that of pariah to that of messiah. He may be right, since over 90 percent of U.S. recoverable fossil fuel, given current prices and technology, is coal.

Currently, coal accounts for 18.6 percent of U.S. energy consumption, two thirds of which is used to fire electric power generators, one quarter for other industry, and most of the rest exported. If widely held assumptions about the increase in demand for electricity prove true, then there will be an expanding reliance on coal until the year 2000. Nuclear fission, which was supposed to take up much of the electric generation load, is now subject to insurmountable economic, political, and environmental constraints, and solar energy, while becoming increasingly popular, does not have sufficient governmental support. There is also a strong bias in the U. S. Department of Energy and the Carter administration toward increased reliance on coal as an energy source. The future of coal, once spurned as an inferior fossil fuel, is now bright. However, economic promise does not translate into improved environment or human and animal welfare.

Ecological Problems

Fossil fuels, including coal, release a number of waste combustion products that can be harmful to the environment. These include sulfur oxides, nitrogen oxide gases, and some concentrations of other elements such as arsenic, lead, cadmium, mercury, selenium, and molybdenum. Smoke and dust from coal consumption blighted urban areas such as London and Pittsburgh for decades, and the ecological and health effects are quite obvious. Some of these pollutants have been removed or reduced by new technological innovations coupled with stricter environmental regulations.

Another coal combustion product is carbon dioxide, a normal component of the atmosphere, and not commonly regarded as a pollutant. But now the National Oceanic and Atmospheric Administration has reported a 5 percent rise in carbon dioxide levels between 1958 and 1976. Many scientists fear that if this trend continues the world could witness drastic climatic shifts through the so-called greenhouse effect.[1] This means that the atmosphere allows the sunlight to enter, but the carbon dioxide absorbs some of the reflected infrared radiation (heat) and radiates it back to Earth, which is similar to what occurs in a greenhouse. A recently convened National Academy of Sciences panel found that, if the use of fossil fuels continues to increase, atmospheric concentrations of carbon dioxide could double by the year 2050 and increase several times by 2150,[2] resulting in significant temperature increases in the lower atmosphere. However, some scientists still think the buildup of carbon dioxide is partly due to independently caused natural fluctuations in the temperature of ocean water. Other complicating factors such as the presence of human-made or natural dust could actually have a cooling effect upon the atmosphere.

What is known is that the ecological impact of burning enormous quantities of coal is not fully understood and that there is a possibility of causing major imbalances.

Human and Animal Problems

Increased consumption of coal is a serious health concern. Currently, as many as 21,000 people die prematurely east of the Mississippi each year because of pollutants expelled into the air by hydrocarbon-burning power plants.[3] The premature deaths are mainly due to heart and lung failure brought on by chronic respiratory diseases. There could be as many as 35,000 premature deaths by the year 2010 even if the new power plants installed scrubbers. The tall smokestacks installed in the past decade or so simply disperse emitted pollutants over a greater area.

Sulfur oxides are some of the most serious pollutants, especially when combined with moisture and mixed with dust and other particles. Besides affecting human beings, sulfur products can endanger farm animals and agricultural crops near power plant sites, and even do damage to marble monuments and relics in distant places.

Because the sulfur oxides are so serious, the Clean Air Act of 1970 requires the Environmental Protection Agency to issue regulations on the amount of sulfur oxides that can be emitted from coal combustion plants. The standards or limits the agency set are 1.2 pounds of sulfur per million British thermal units (a unit of heat measure). To meet these requirements, power plants seek low-sulfur coal either in Appalachia or in the West. However, western coal, while low in sulfur, is also lower in heat content, so it takes more to produce the equivalent amount of heat from eastern coal, thus emitting comparable quantities of sulfur products per unit of electricity generated as eastern coal. Higher freight charges and a recent ruling that *all* new coal-fired generators must have sulfur scrubbing devices diminish the otherwise superior position of western low-sulfur coal.

The use of lignite or "brown coal" in North Dakota during the 1960s resulted in a documented case of the toxic effects of a trace element in combusted coal. The contamination of a cattle and sheep pasture by molybdenum from a lignite ashing plant resulted in the deaths of several animals and severe sickness of the rest. The animals suffered from molybdenosis, which causes a decrease in the physiological availability of the trace element copper,[4] which is essential to mammalian life.

Other Problems

Besides ecological and health problems connected with coal consumption, there are economic ones. Industrial users of energy have traditionally paid less than individual consumers because of favored electric rate structures. Historically the price of electricity has been kept artificially low because the cost of environmental deterioration has not been borne by the utilities. There has never been widespread pressure to do this, and the understanding of the true cost of environmental deterioration has been limited. By bearing many of the environmental and health costs associated with the production of energy, and by underwriting subsidies to energy-related industries, the public has been subsidizing the low cost of energy.

Profligate electricity use by some does not necessarily guarantee prosperity for others. The Ford Foundation's Energy Policy Project suggests that the scenario of high energy growth and questionable prosperity need not continue.[5] In fact, a reduced energy growth accompanied by more efficient use will not only expand the number of available jobs, but will protect public health and the environment as well. The nation could use half the projected energy slated for the year 2000 and still increase total employment.[6]

Historically, industry has sought to substitute energy for labor. The total number of workers could increase only if the demand for products rose. Planned obsolescence notwithstanding, the demand for products is tied inexorably to the supply of inputs needed to produce them. Because of the limitations inherent in what is called the "Round Earth Theory," the rise in demand cannot be sustained forever. Thus increased electrification has meant job losses. In fact, for every quadrillion Btu's of fuel (about 1⅓ percent of the U.S. annual consumption of energy) changed into electricity, 75,000 jobs are lost over the whole economy.[7]

Increased use of coal for electricity means nonrenewable resource waste, especially during generation and transmission of electricity and also through electric appliance inefficiencies. In fact, three fourths of the fuel content is lost before final use. Energy is also lost by being mismatched, as when a high-quality energy fuel is used to boil water to produce power plant steam for electricity destined for home heating. Some estimates are that electricity use by the year 2000 will result in a fuel waste equal to the nation's total energy consumption in 1971.

COAL PRODUCTION PROBLEMS

Different methods of coal production affect ecosystems, human health and welfare, and the economy in different ways. Since many influences (such as topography, population, and transportation systems) are associated with these methods of production, it is difficult to weigh benefits in one area against costs or problems in others. Yet production decisions must be made with imperfect knowledge, and in the context of a set of values whose implications for quality of life are often little understood.

For those outside the coalfields, coal production methods may be somewhat unfamiliar. A little less than half of the coal in the United States is mined from *underground* mines, which may be of a shaft, drift, or slope type. The major portion is now mined from *surface* mines, which may be of a strip or auger type. Underground mines are sometimes referred to as "deep" mines, as opposed to strip mines, but the nomenclature is not perfectly accurate, because drift mines are often only slightly below the surface and strip mining does not account for all (though over 90 percent) of surface mining operations.

Prior to World War II only one tenth of the nation's coal was surface-mined, but the advent of heavy earth-moving machinery increased the amount to almost 60 percent by 1978. Strip mining is far less labor-intensive and also requires less capital investment than underground mining. It is quite profitable, especially in parts of the coalfields where *reclamation* of the land (restoration either to some previous condition or to a more productive state) is neglected.

Surface mining is performed on layers of coal near the surface of the land. It involves simply removing the outer earthen layer, or *overburden*, and scooping the exposed coal into vehicles. In flat and rolling terrain such as in Illinois and in the Great Plains states, a subtype of surface mining called *area* mining is performed by the use of large draglines or power shovels that remove the earthen layer or overburden and expose the coal, which is then removed. When this is done, a parallel cut is made next to the first, and the first is back-filled by use of the material that is the overburden of the second cut, and on and on, much like a plow making furrows in a field. In fact, area surface-mining operations leave giant parallel mounds of dirt or ridges of earth that stretch for miles, the indelible tracks of methodical draglines.

In mountainous terrain such as Appalachia, another form of surface mining is used, called *contour* mining because the layers of coal project out of the hillside on a contour. To obtain this coal, the bulldozer or other instrument removes the surface layer of earth down to where it becomes unprofitable. This removal of earth creates a *highwall*, or a vertical section of mountain where the surface contains too much overburden to remove. The earthen layer is called *spoil* and has generally been pushed over the lower slope, where it is prone in highly elevated areas to wash or slide down into the valleys and stream beds below.

Ecological Problems

All large-scale underground and surface mining operations have environmental impact on air, water, and land. The air near surface-mining operations is often filled with dust generated by the movement of heavy equipment and blasting, posing a health hazard for all living creatures near the mine site. Underground mining creates similar problems, but these are restricted for the most part to the miners themselves and will be discussed later.

Watersheds in coalfields are vulnerable to seepage of water containing some of the acidic materials previously trapped in the coal layers. In surface-mining areas there is in addition a problem with soil erosion and the heavy siltation of streams and rivers. Mining acids and soil erosion are said to have contributed to the pollution of over 12,000 miles of streams.[8] As water runs over unconsolidated mounds of earth generated by mining activities, it erodes these materials and carries off sediment, which is not always captured by artificial settling ponds or lakes near the site; instead, the materials choke the local streams and rivers with silt and sedimentation, and thus destroy fish life and fill the riverbeds.

Surface mining directly affects at least 153,000 acres of American land each year,[9] with the actual disturbed area sometimes being three to five times as great. This is due to clearing for machinery and coal haul roads and for mining spoil and wastes. Nothing since the glaciers has had such an impact on the land of surface-mining areas. As one Appalachian says when referring to the disturbance of a cemetery for the coal beneath it, "They bury the living and dig up the dead."

In Appalachia, where considerable land disturbance from surface-mining operations occur in regions of heavy rainfall (sixty inches per year), clogging of streams and waterways has created severe ecological problems, including a series of disastrous floods in 1977 and others up to the present. The relationship between land disturbance and flooding was proved by a study of Harlan County, Kentucky.[10] While all types of land use/disturbance (including road and building construction, farming, and forestry) played some part in producing sediment and exacerbating flood levels, strip mining was found to be by far the most dominant and intensive type of land disturbance. Since 1970 over 14 percent of the county has been disturbed by surface-mining operations. One former resident of Harlan County returned after two years' absence and was shocked to find she could not recognize her native hollow. Everything—the homesite, the hills, and the rivers—was drastically altered.

The filling of the stream beds from the eroding soil reduces the carrying capacity of these watersheds by as much as 75 percent in some sections of Appalachia. Since the valleys are quite narrow, the water has nowhere to go in times of heavy rainfall but across the flood plain and often into dwellings on those plains. Furthermore, the disturbed land does not have the vegetative covering required to retain or retard the flow of water. In 1969 approximately 4,800 miles of Appalachian streams had been adversely affected by sedimentation,[11] but this has perhaps since doubled because of vastly increased surface-mining operations in the last decade.

All land areas yield some sediment in areas of heavy rainfall, but the relative contributions depend greatly on the way the land is covered or disturbed. Thus a homesite has a heavy "sediment yield" for a few months during construction, but once the ground is seeded and covered this drops dramatically. The exposed dirt from surface mining operations, the "spoil," has as much as one thousand times the sediment yield, and coal haul roads—dirt roads used for trucking out the coal near or on the surface mine site—about two thousand times the yield, of unmined watersheds.

The type of eroded materials is dependent upon both the land composition and the manner in which the land disturbance is performed. If in more conscientious surface-mining operations the top soil is removed and segregated, and then used to cover the more acidic layers that occur nearer the coal seam, erosion will contain that type of soil. If, as occurs in many careless surface-mining operations, the layers nearer the coal are allowed to erode and be exposed to air and water, then acidic materials are formed that can carry minerals in large amounts into the waterways. Layers near coal contain pyritic or sulfur compounds, which on contact with air and moisture produce sulfuric acid. A U. S. Geological Survey study found that the rate of chemical degradation of spoil banks in Cane Branch, Kentucky, was 126 times higher than that of nearby unmined lands.[12] This problem occurs in both area and contour mining operations and represents one of the gravest environmental hazards associated with surface mining.

In the western part of the United States a myopic faith in coal development technology exists, accompanied by a false trust that no environmental deterioration will occur. Coal beds lying close to the surface, which are prime candidates for surface mining, are able to hold water in place or serve as aquifers in these arid or semiarid regions. In parts of the Great Plains they are a major water source for livestock and irrigated cropland.

Fossil fuel processing industries such as power plants, coal gasification units, and refineries require vast quantities of water and compete for the limited water supply of the arid West. Another such fuel-industry water user is the so-called coal slurry pipeline program—a form of transportation that pulverizes coal, mixes it with water, and sends it through pipelines much like any liquid. One coal slurry pipeline proposal talks of tapping the Madison formation, a huge underground water reserve or aquifer that underlies the Dakotas, Montana, and parts of Wyoming and Nebraska, to supply water at 10,000 gallons per minute for a pipeline system to extend from Wyoming to Arkansas.[13] Such a project would, however, radically modify the fragile ecosystem of the entire region.

Energy development industries also compete with other groups, including wildlife management programs, municipal water systems, and agriculture, for surface waters. Perhaps the largest problem area will be in the development of coal gasification plants in the 1980s. The ones now being planned have an enormous appetite for water—using up to 20,000 gallons per minute per plant and creating air and land as well as water pollution problems. In parts of Appalachia, plans for new dam construction are coupled with those for future coal gasification plants.

While water conservation issues are becoming quite important in areas with increased surface mining, land conservation is not to be forgotten. Much of America's prime grazing and farming land is located over coal deposits. The process of soil formation occurs over millions of years; this can be undone in a matter of weeks by mining operations. In their haste to dig coal, operators invert the layers—that is, the topsoil ends up at the bottom and the less fertile and more acidic spoil will become the new surface. As biologist Charles Riley notes:

> Seldom will the ecologist in his research of ecosystem dynamics of natural landscapes encounter the diversity and the extremes of geochemistry present in the surface medium or in the drainage that may follow the disturbance and exposure of the strata of the various coal measures.[14]

While segregation of the various soil layers is possible, it is costly and little heeded by miner or operator. It is hoped that the enforcers of the Federal Surface Mining Control and Reclamation Act of 1977 will address this problem.

Restoration, in the sense of re-creating the former conditions, is not possible, for the original condition of the land took millions of years to evolve.[15] Certainly deep-soiled, moist-climate, and level regions are more easily restored than are shallow-soiled, arid, or elevated ones. Duplicating prior conditions demands, as a minimum, proper segregation of the topsoil and attempts to reconstruct a suitable topography for water drainage. Much care must be given to proper soil cover, compactness of soils, and stability of materials, all of which influence rainfall retention, infiltration, leaching, and erosion. Original ecosystems are almost always more complex than restored ones. At any rate, the particular land-use plan that reclamation efforts are based on is usually dictated by the values of a moment in human history, and it may or may not be in accord with the long-term development or succession of a habitat toward its climax state.

The complexity of evolutionary processes, as well as the length of time inherent in the formation of any ecosystem, makes it extremely difficult for any reclamation procedure to mimic nature. The land-use plan settled upon often seeks an ecosystem that has a profoundly different and less complex nature than the one that characterized the original. Dictates of "economics" and inescapable time constraints often make society content with such a strategy. However, strategies deemed advantageous in the short term may not produce an ecosystem or human society that conforms to the requirements of succeeding generations. An illustration of this dilemma exists in the confrontation between coal and agriculture in Illinois.[16]

Illinois farmers have certainly contributed to global food production. About 25,500,000 acres of Illinois land are in crop rotation. However, land in Illinois is lost at a rate of 80,000 to 100,000 acres per year—because of forces such as urban sprawl, highway building, and strip mining. This loss of cropland represents a threat to continued increases in food production. Even more problematic is the lack of concern of citizens and government for the fate of this land or the forces that change it. The prospect of some sort of benign technological savior diverts attention from the forces responsible for taking some of the world's best agricultural land out of production.

The Illinois Geological Survey estimates that 161.6 billion tons of coal lie under the state. About 13 percent of these reserves lie close enough to the surface to be strip-mined. Since strip mining began in Illinois in 1866, over 181,000 acres of land have been disturbed. The Illinois State strip-mining law includes several strong provisions to help protect the land. Row crop land must be rehabilitated to row crop standards, but there is no provision that areas of prime agricultural land will be returned to the same level of productivity that existed before mining. Thus land that once supported soybeans is rehabilitated to grow silage or wheat. While these uses are important, they do not require the same quality of land as the production of soybeans.

Communities in the ecosystem, including the human community, develop over time. To threaten the stability and the continued evolution of these communities without a thorough understanding of all aspects of the development process, and of how far it is safe to proceed, is to risk the end of this process, and of life. Isolated degradation of water, air, and land probably have no lasting consequences for either the human or the more inclusive natural communities; however, wholesale degradation of air, water, and land—which can occur as a by-product of coal production—warrant careful consideration and reflection.

Problems for the People

Both underground and surface mining have serious impacts on the quality of human life, as well as on the environment. Often these effects are less publicized than the environmental ones, and they often go unnoticed outside of the coalfields. In other cases they are intermixed with the ecological impacts.

The most graphic examples of such problems occur each time there is an underground mine disaster, usually due to explosions, mine fires, inrush of surface water, or fall of a roof. The most serious mine disaster was an explosion at Monongah, West Virginia, on December 6, 1907, which killed 361 miners. But that accident was not isolated; accidents have been happening throughout the history of mining. Since the U.S. government has kept statistics, over 100,000 coal miners have been killed in the mines, and the injured number over five times that figure. Coal has always been a dirty, dangerous occupation, but only through the insistence of the United Mine Workers and others has safety in underground mines improved in the last few decades.

Underground miners are often forced to breathe in dust generated in the extraction of coal. This, over a period of time, results in "black lung" disease, which constricts breathing. Part of the cause of this occupational hazard has been the introduction of high-speed drills into underground mining operations. To a lesser degree, surface miners are also subjected to increased dust levels due both to blasting operations and to movement of equipment. This airborne dust can cause *pneumoconiosis*, a generic form of black lung disease. The problem is exacerbated in surface mining areas by the fact that local residents must also be subjected to increased dust levels and must breathe fine rock and siliceous particles.

Surface mining, especially in rocky regions of Appalachia, uses considerable amounts of blasting material. When these operations occur near towns and dwellings, people are affected in a number of ways: drained wells, cracked and crushed homes, temporary and permanent hearing loss, and personal injuries such as lacerations and broken bones. Less identifiable effects include the psychological damage caused by blasting. The anxiety created in persons living near blasting sites is very real. The noise from blasting has an unnerving effect on many Appalachian residents. Bertha Mulkey of Stanville, Kentucky, who lives near an active mine, likened the situation to a war. She explained that she never knew when a charge would be set off. When one is, she becomes deathly afraid that she will be crushed as she was in 1977 when a boulder ripped through her home.

Blasting or vibrational pollution has been known to cause extensive mental and physical duress to residents in such places as Norton, Virginia, and Jefferson County, Alabama, who live near major surface-mining operations. Part of the problem has been the lack of care on the part of the blasters; part is the unpredictable character of the blasting material, which is often a mixture of fuel oil and ammonia fertilizer (ANFO). The extent of blasting in the eastern coalfields is comparable in terms of tonnage to the amount of explosives used in the Vietnam War. During that war the Defense Department delivered an average of 30 tons of explosives per square mile in Vietnam; from 1965 to 1975 strip-mine operators detonated 35 tons of blasting materials per square mile in the Appalachian coalfields.[17]

With the use of such quantities of materials it is no surprise that the property damage suffered by residents in central Appalachia alone is estimated to be over $200 million per year.[18] In the past the fear of loss of home insurance and other harassment has kept citizens from openly seeking retribution for damages; but now, armed with the Federal Surface Mining Control and Reclamation Act of 1977 and its attendant regulations, they are starting to speak out. They demand a "good neighbor" blasting policy, which means that blasters are to communicate with residents before blasting occurs, informing them what to expect and whom to contact if problems develop, being considerate of citizen concerns, and contacting citizens after blasting to remedy any damage done.

Another area where human beings suffer from surface-mining operations is the trucking of coal. Because contour mining disturbs widely scattered areas, construction of railroads to mining sites is deemed uneconomical. Thus about 58 percent of Appalachian coal is transported by truck in its journey from mine to consumer. This coal movement affects over 15,000 miles of Appalachian roads. More than 75 percent of these highways are presently or in the process of becoming badly deteriorated. It takes only ten heavy coal trucks per day to destroy some of the secondary roads of the region. In eastern Kentucky a loaded coal truck does 86 cents damage to the roadways for each mile it travels—damage for which the taxpayers are ultimately responsible.[19] It will cost citizens of that state alone $2.7 billion to upgrade eastern Kentucky roads to coal haul standards.

Citizens in the surface-mining regions suffer from trucking in a number of ways: continual exposure to roadway dust, causing severe respiratory problems; potholes and broken pavement, making driving more difficult; spilled coal denting autos and breaking windshields (a very frequent occurrence); noise and vibration jeopardizing the psychological well-being of residents; less accessibility to consumer goods and services due to road damage; instilling a disdain for law and order by laxity in enforcing weight limits; and added extra auto expenses for tires, brakes, mufflers, and towing services.

Other problems, already mentioned, include increased potential of flooding due to surface mine disturbances. The flood of April 1977 is estimated to have done $175 million worth of property damage in eastern Kentucky alone[20] and perhaps twice that much when considering the regions flooded in West Virginia and Virginia. Lives were lost and businesses were wiped out. No one has calculated the psychological damage and fear that accompany each subsequent heavy rainfall in that region, and the unstabilizing effects on families and especially young children.

Underground mining has affected residents in one way: through *subsidence*, or collapse of the surface layer over abandoned mine shafts. Out of the 8 million acres of land that have been undermined in the United States, some 2 million have experienced some subsidence.[21] It is possible to arrest this phenomenon somewhat by backfilling the mine with refuse from coal mining and cleaning operations, although this process is expensive. Such a practice would help solve the problem of disposal of underground mine-related solid wastes. An estimated 122,000 acres of land were used for surface disposal of underground mine wastes between 1930 and 1971, the equivalent of 14 percent of the area disturbed by surface mining during the same period.[22]

A more general problem in coalfields is the lack of local control over coal resources. Mining operations are most often owned by nonresidents who are not accountable for the welfare of the residents or the environment where the mine is located. Large landholding companies are sensitive to the speculative value of their holdings, not to the needs of victims of mine blasting, flooding, or subsidence. From an advantageous position of distance they can make people and the environment pay dearly.

Nowhere is this scenario more evident than in the case of the so-called broad form deed. This type of land title allows the person to gain access to mineral rights regardless of the wishes of the people who own rights to the surface land above the minerals. The potential unjustness of this legal instrument was not so apparent at the turn of the century, when broad form deeds became popular. Then almost all coal was extracted from underground mines, and little thought was given to the possible ramifications of surface mining on dwellers who had title to land in their families for a century or more.

The legality of the broad form deed has been overturned in most states, though it continues to be upheld in Kentucky despite many legal attacks on it. That such an instrument could be perpetrated is a powerful testimony to the hegemony of the mining institutions; it is, however, a more telling indicator of the helplessness of the people and the environment of the region. Residents generally lack the power to deal with coal companies.

Land use and ownership problems abound in coal-producing regions, but are not particular to these areas. In many parts of Appalachia the most favorable land for construction of homes is owned or controlled by mining companies. Residents are forced to choose inferior sites, often on flood plains.

Land prices are beyond the reach of the average citizen. In parts of West Virginia over two thirds of the land is owned by outside companies and railroads. To compound this problem, the company-owned land has only minimal tax assessment, thus placing still greater burdens on often land-starved residents.

Surface mining is also an aesthetic blight on the countryside. Thousands of miles of unreclaimed highwalls mar the landscape. These wastelands of ruined beauty depress the resident, discourage tourism and business, and challenge those who want to attempt to reclaim the land.

Economic Considerations

Mining costs vary tremendously according to the technology involved, the geology encountered, and the constraints imposed by the environmental and human health and safety guidelines. In most areas, surface-mined coal is somewhat cheaper to produce than underground-mined coal. Estimates of the cost differential range from $3.00 to $5.00 per ton,[23] which is a considerable difference when judging on a base selling price of $20 to $25 a ton. These savings are now in question, however, because new surface-mining regulations may be costly. The Federal Office of Surface Mining estimates in 1978 rates that regulations will add no more than an average of $2.16 a ton to the price of Appalachian coal. White House economists in the President's Council on Wage and Price Stability estimated on November 27, 1978, that the cost of transporting spoil into a valley and packing the material as proposed in the regulations would increase the cost of coal $2.00 to $3.00 alone.[24]

The major price difference in underground- and surface-mined coal stems from the degree of reclamation demanded. The extent to which any disturbed landscape can be rehabilitated depends on many factors—physical, ecological, geological, social, economic, and technical—and on the values that people cede to these various factors. If decision-makers do not have full knowledge about production impacts, the coal is not accurately priced. For instance, mined land can only be rehabilitated, not completely restored in the sense that the conditions at the mine site prior to mining will be duplicated

—which means that the cost of coal does not reflect full restoration. And it is impossible to predict or anticipate the value to society of the land in its original condition. The momentary euphoria of "cheap" surface-mined coal has to be tempered by the realization that the cost of this coal has been determined by short-term values embodied in narrowly perceived land-use schemes. These values may not necessarily coincide with the value of leaving the land and its ecology undisturbed.

Another fly in the ointment concerns the distribution of the cost advantages of surface-mined coal. The equity of surface-mine-related savings depends on the structure of mineral ownership. In Appalachia and in western coalfields much of coal-bearing land is in the hands of a relatively privileged few; thus this elite group is further benefited by cost advantages. Other recipients of these savings are consumers of coal, principally electric utilities. Direct beneficiaries of the good fortune of the utilities are those electricity consumers that benefit most from electric rate structures—the large industrial users. It is somewhat ironic that surface-mined coal, which accounts for a legacy of social and environmental destruction, is mined to the advantage of large industries, themselves often the cause of adverse disturbances in the human and natural environment. Other "externalities" that are seldom accounted for by industry include road damage by coal trucks, blasting damage, and failure to rehabilitate orphan (abandoned) surface mines.

The Bureau of Mines estimates that the United States has a *reserve base*[25] of 297 billion tons of deep-minable coal, and 141 billion that could be surface-minded.[26] The U. S. Geological Survey identifies total U.S. coal deposits of 1.7 trillion tons at depths of less than 3,000 feet[27] but much of that is not economically and technically minable. Thus, while 60 percent of current coal production is from surface mines, 70 percent of the U.S. reserves are accessible only via underground mines.

Underground mining can be made more safe by use of proper equipment, procedures, and work rules. Safety technology is improving and thus accident rates are being reduced. Conventional underground American mining technology allows coal pillars to remain in the mine to support the roof of the shaft, thus affording only a 57 percent recovery rate for coal mined.[28] On the other hand, European *longwall* mining methods employing hydraulic jacks recover 95 percent of the coal and are safer because they protect miners from roof falls, the current major source of fatalities in underground mining.

For both ecological and human reasons it would appear that we should favor underground over surface mining. While there is a greater safety disadvantage of underground over surface mining, this could be narrowed if, in the United States, we followed many European practices. In the British nationalized mines the fatality rate in 1974 was 1 person per 7 million person-hours; in Germany, 1 in 3 million, and in the United States 1 in 2⅓ million person-hours (or only one-third as good a record as in Great Britain). Surface-mining fatalities in this country are over twice the rate of deep-mine ones in Great Britain and only slightly lower than underground ones in this country.[29]

In making the choice between underground and surface mining, one factor is the widespread use of newer technologies, especially those that reduce the danger of explosions by withdrawing all combustible gases from underground mines. This process could make underground mines safer than surface ones. The U. S. Bureau of Mines agrees that through the full use of technology we could bring the accident rate to a vanishing point. The failure in the past to introduce this technology is due in part to the relative cost advantages of surface mining. With increased demands for enforcing surface-mine regulations, these advantages should disappear.

From an employment standpoint, underground mines furnish more work than does surface mining. For instance, surface-mined coal from the Great Plains requires one fifth as much labor per energy unit as do Appalachian underground mines.[30] If existing underground mines were operated on a three-shift-per-day, five-days-per-week, fifty-weeks-per-year basis, with an allowance for absenteeism, labor disputes, and necessary "down time," underground mine production would increase by 110 million tons,[31] or about one third of U.S. annual surface-mined coal production. This method of increasing underground coal production could also create 28,000 additional jobs. So it is possible to increase underground coal production substantially with relatively little additional capital expenditure.

Many factors, tangible and otherwise, contribute to the actual cost of coal production. The cost of coal should account for ecological and human considerations as well as the more conventional "costs of production." From every standpoint—of resources, environment, employment, and even safety—it appears that the choice must be made for underground over surface mining.

TOWARD AN ETHICAL COAL POLICY

In evaluating the consequences of coal production and consumption, policy-makers must not only become aware of the environmental, human, and institutional "facts," but must also reflect upon the motivations, principles, and values responsible for these facts. Attempts at remedying environmental and human destitution require such a holistic reflection, for it is these values and principles that underlie our patterns of production and consumption.

Coal policy-makers have a difficult task ahead of them. They have to recognize technical and physical realities along with social and political considerations; they must also be aware of the ethical values that should guide the development of such a public policy. The national coal policy in the past has been haphazard at best, guided by a mistaken perception of environmental and human welfare. Since so much is at stake—miners' health, community economic well-being, proper land use—any lack of proper reflection will have immense social ramifications on large populations and areas of this land.

Ethical Guidelines
Ecological Wisdom

Human beings have a dual responsibility of stewardship and transformation of the earth.[32] (See Chapters V and VIII for further development of this theme.) We do not have a right to subjugate human or nonhuman environments for short-term gains. A deterioration of a region due to massive strip mining or removal of the benefits of coal from a region while leaving people destitute are forms of subjugation.

Transforming nature and appreciating nature are complementary. But this transformation must be wisely undertaken or else it becomes reckless domination and a danger to all ecosystems. Human interactions with the environment have far-reaching repercussions, many of which are cumulative and apparently irreversible. Ecology speaks of interdependency and integrity of biotic systems. Thus a coal policy that is forgetful of the whole is quite risky to the environment. Can all damage be repaired? While some speak of the resiliency of nature, still the first-hand experience of Appalachians in coal-producing areas is that some damage is beyond repair. How do you repair a black-lung victim or a highwall-laced mountain? Prudence dictates that when irreversible or irreparable damage is highly likely, as occurs with coal mining, we must go slow or even avoid performing the act. Some types of coal mining can be done safely and with little environmental impact, but are there not exceptions?

A full assessment is required before development of energy systems, including coal, that have widespread consequences. "Acceptable" degrees of social and environmental deterioration have to be developed from an ethical perspective, for, as ethicist J. Hartt says, ". . . man has no effective way of living beyond or outside the kingdom of life. So whatever diminishes that kingdom diminishes him, both as a form of life and as a form of spirit."

Social and Ecological Justice

Exploitation of human beings and of nature are really two sides of the same coin, for we are inseparably bound to our earth. Poverty and pollution, the products of exploitation, hurt us all, whether we live in a coalfield, near a power plant, or far removed from both. As we seek a comprehensive coal policy it is wise to ask serious questions about potential or actual energy exploitation. How does energy consumption fulfill us as human beings? Who pays the cost and who receives the benefits from current energy production and consumption? How do we calculate the cost of human health or of the destruction of natural beauty of a region? Is it right to develop coal in a manner that causes some of the poor to bear the costs (victims of blasting, trucking dust, and air pollution) while the privileged few benefit? Is it just that lucrative governmental subsidies are involved in coal production and consumption while victims are ignored? Does coal use respond to needs based on true human fulfillment and welfare? Are not structural changes required for a just coal policy?

Citizen Participation

Electricity is generated at a relatively small number of large facilities and then distributed over considerable distances to consumers. Although much can be said for how electricity has benefited our material growth, it has come to us with a cost. Besides the environmental and health costs already discussed, there is the resource cost due to electric conversion and transmission inefficiencies. These highly capitalized systems are often beyond the control of local consumers and in the hands of less accountable distant institutions. This situation jeopardizes individual choice and determination. The bureaucracy inherent in concentration and institutionalization enhances alienation among citizens and between people and the environment.

Participation in decision-making should be widespread, not limited to a privileged few. Since energy consumption, especially electricity use, has social and environmental impact, the control must rest to some degree where it is produced and used—in the local communities that are directly affected.

Responsible Coal Consumption

Coal consumption is in response to needs, legitimate and otherwise, felt by people. These needs rarely heed the fact that coal, like all fossil fuels, is a finite resource. Unlike solar energy, it is not renewable in the finite time of human civilization. Since certain organic materials and synthetic products can be made only from fossil fuels, it is imperative that we conserve coal regardless of whether the supply will last several hundred years by current production standards. Furthermore, there are limits to the environmental assimilation of product wastes.

Policy Implications

An ecologically sound coal policy requires making proper and often difficult choices among several competing goals according to ethical guidelines, while retaining the vision of a better world.

Redirection of Energy Subsidies

Historically, governments have subsidized economically "advantageous" forms of energy development. These subsidies are a direct reflection of accepted priorities and values. Underassessment of mineral holdings, special tax breaks, depletion allowances, failure to enforce transportation requirements, funded technical research and promotion, special water privileges, and leniency in imposing fines all speak to this governmental sponsored approach. These efforts must now be redirected to aid black-lung victims, repair highways, reclaim orphan lands, and promote deep-mine safety. Such efforts would undoubtedly result in such beneficial side effects as reduced surface devastation and flooding and reduction of accidents in deep mines.

Decentralization of Energy Production Systems

Concentrated and centralized energy-producing systems are considered more efficient by many citizens. This may, however, be disputed when considering transmission losses and network vulnerability, among other things. Moreover, centralized systems are responsible for weakening democratic and locally controlled decision-making. The growing horizontal integration (control over coal, oil, uranium sources) by large energy producers may create even more distance between production and consumer. In place of this, solar and biomass advocates stress the need to use solar water heaters, small hydroelectric generators, local windmills, and wood for heating and cooking.

Decentralized energy systems are deemed preferable for a number of reasons: they facilitate democratic control and decision-making on a local level; they do not require as much capital investment; they do not require transmission systems that include energy losses; they are less harmful to the environment; they may more easily tailor energy needs to lifestyle requirements and permit consumers to become more conscious of wastes.

Federal, state, and local governments could provide a significant push in the direction of decentralized energy systems. Governments could conduct demonstration programs and, through procurement programs, could provide a means to realize commercial production. Comprehensive energy planning could require that new structures accommodate solar equipment. Electric utilities should be made to buy back excess electricity produced by wind generators. Economic incentives, both related to taxes and subsidies, could assist in promoting the development of energy alternatives.

Communities and individuals provide the most significant support for increased local energy self-reliance. Citizens should be responsible for assembling a profile of local energy resources and the development of a community energy plan concerned with how energy is used, and how well, and where improvements should be made. It is crucial for communities to meet regularly to discuss problems and share ideas and ideals. Without strong support at the local level, decentralization cannot come about. Decentralization is possible, for all areas of the United States have ample sun, wind, and other local energy resources that can be developed in ecologically sound ways. Perhaps the primary policy goal in this area is that subsidies advantageous to the proliferation of nuclear and other centralized power schemes be redirected to aid local energy self-reliance.

Equitable Distribution of Coal and Electric Services

The concern for equity should make us examine coal policy according to whether its effects are justly distributed to various segments of society. Coal is allocated according to its price. All too often the pricing mechanism cannot adequately account for all environmental and human factors. An artificially low price for coal shifts the true burden of coal use onto these marginal elements. Also, because of widely used rate structures, the benefits from coal use are skewed in favor of the privileged, while environmental costs fall heavily on the poor and the workplace. Coal costs must account for human and environmental degradation. Utility rate structures must be revised to become more progressive. Finally, higher energy costs to the poor should be subsidized through taxation and energy stamps.

Discouragement of Extravagance

It is more difficult to influence individual lifestyles than to change institutions that play a role in determining how we live. Energy defines the way we live. If we produce our own energy, our lifestyle will reflect this fact. If we are susceptible to advertising and large-scale electrification, then our lifestyle reflects this. Thus, if induced to waste, we assume an extravagant lifestyle. Since energy waste is intolerable, policy-makers should consider limiting unnecessary electrification and offer practical substitutes such as solar water heaters and geothermally heated greenhouses. Advertising that promotes increasing electrification of homes, especially when consumer-financed, should be eliminated. Unless institutional changes such as these occur, it will be difficult for people to match energy consumption with their basic energy needs. Unnecessary electricity usage should be actively discouraged and energy conservation should be viewed as an alternate source of energy.

Development of Coal as an Interim Fuel

Coal should be regarded as an interim fuel that will carry the burden in the transition between the age of fossil fuels and the coming age of renewable or environmental energy sources (solar, tidal, wind, geothermal, and so on).[33] Coal is nonrenewable and environmentally costly. When needed to meet legitimate energy demands, coal should be deep-mined, but only under vigorous health, safety, and environmental controls. Social disruptions should be minimized. Strip mining, which is environmentally disruptive, should be phased out as soon as possible.

In line with this policy, several coal development suggestions follow:

* Massive coal-fueled energy parks, high-voltage transmission networks, and large-scale on-site power

generation are all incompatible with ecological justice and should not be pursued.

* Transition between conventional and alternative energy systems should be accomplished in such a way that communities are not destroyed. Provisions should be made for employment opportunities that aid in the development of the alternative energy sources and systems. Subsidies should be redirected in support of these efforts and toward assisting the acquisition of local and/or regional control of coal resources.

* Reclamation of remaining strip-mine operations must attempt to restore mined areas to full pre-mining ecological diversity and productive capacity. Mining must be planned and conducted to minimize injury to persons and damage to property; any damage that does occur must be fully compensated, even though it has occurred in the past.

* Reclamation of mined land must be based on a plan for post-mining use. This plan, in turn, should reflect awareness of: the proven capacity of the land to support a desired end use; an expressed need and commitment by local people to be responsible for following a desired plan; and the social, economic, and environmental characteristics of the region where the mining occurs. The application for a mining permit should contain a precisely articulated post-mining land-use plan in addition to the reclamation plan.[34]

* The Federal Power Commission collects information on the source and quality of fuel purchases for the power plants of most utilities. Reported on FPC form 423, it lists tonnages, state of origin, sulfur content by weight, and energy content. This valuable information assists citizens in monitoring the impacts of coal usage. The service should be continued and the information made more accessible.[35]

* Permits for mining operations should be issued on a watershed basis and distributed to minimize the amount of disturbance at any one time. Where watersheds cross state lines, some procedure should be provided by affected states for the federal government to coordinate

mining activity. Techniques for evaluating the amount of mining that can occur without adversely affecting water quality and stream carrying capacity must be developed.[36]

* It is necessary to obtain accurate and reliable data on the amount of trace elements present in coal, their distribution, and their volatility during the combustion of coal.[37]

Coal production that does occur needs to be in response to basic human needs and never at the expense of basic values. The health and safety of workers and of the environment take precedence over economic and technical productivity criteria in mining processes.

> If we could first know where we are and whither we are tending, we could better judge what to do and how to do it.
>
> A. Lincoln

Ethical decision-making is a process with limitations. Many of our decisions are subtle and obscured from intentional reflection. Our current lifestyles, for example, represent the cumulative effect of many seemingly insignificant decisions. Yet the sustenance of our lifestyles certainly has ethical implications. The consumption of electricity links us directly with the entire spectrum of consequences arising from the extraction and use of coal.

Reflection that does take place is based on the knowledge that is available. Decisions are made in terms of the expectations of consequences established by this limited knowledge.[38] Ethical reflections on the development of coal policy must be based on a thorough grasp of all the physical "facts." These facts must also be subjected to critical scrutiny and reevaluation, with an eye to constantly improving our understanding of all the implications of coal development.

The statement that we can "have ample energy without sacrificing our standard of living or the environment" can be evaluated only in light of physical consequences associated with coal-based energy. An evaluation that accounts for these facts and the above ethical guidelines indicates that we cannot have an ample supply of coal-based energy without substantial sacrifice of human and environmental quality of life.

REFERENCES

1. W. Lepkowski, "Carbon Dioxide: A Problem of Producing Usable Data," *Chemical and Engineering News* (Oct. 17, 1977), p. 26.
2. Washington *Post*, July 27, 1977.
3. Washington *Post*, July 4, 1977.
4. Mining Task Force, "Where We Agree": draft report (Washington, D.C.: National Coal Policy Project, 1977), Sect. 2.2, p. 17.
5. Ford Foundation Energy Policy Project, *A Time to Choose* (Cambridge: Ballinger, 1974), pp. 12 ff.
6. R. Grossman and G. Danker, *Jobs and Energy* (Washington, D.C.: Environmentalists for Full Employment, Spring 1977), p. 4.
7. Ibid., p. 5.
8. D. Pimental et al., "Land Degradation: Effects on Food and Energy Resources," *Science* 194:4621 (1976), p. 150.
9. Ibid., p. 149.
10. "Harlan County Flood Report," ASPI Research Series (Corbin, Ky.: Appalachia-Science in the Public Interest, 1978), pp. 44–47.
11. Mining Task Force, op. cit., Sect. 3.4, p. 6.
12. R. C. Austin, *Spoil: A Moral Study of Strip Mining for Coal* (New York: Board of Global Ministries, The United Methodist Church, 1976), p. 39.
13. H. Smith, "The Wringing of the West," Washington *Post*, Feb. 16, 1975.
14. C. V. Riley, "Ecosystem Development on Coal Surface Mined Land, 1918–1975," in *Recovery and Restoration of Damaged Ecosystems*, J. Cairns, Jr., ed. (Charlottesville: University of Virginia Press, 1976), p. 3.
15. *Rehabilitation Potential of Western Coal Lands* (Washington, D.C.: National Academy of Science, 1974).
16. D. Ostendorf and J. Gibson, *Illinois Land* (Carterville: Illinois South Project, 1976), pp. 8–19.
17. *Strip Mine Blasting* (Corbin, Ky.: Appalachia-Science in the Public Interest, 1977), pp. 91–93.
18. Ibid., p. 1.
19. *Citizens' Coal Haul Handbook* (Corbin, Ky.: Appalachia-Science in the Public Interest, 1978), p. 38.
20. *The Floods of April* (Frankfort, Ky.: Department of Natural Resources and Environmental Protection, Commonwealth of Kentucky, Nov. 1977), p. 2.
21. Mining Task Force, op. cit., Sect. 3.4, p. 27.
22. Ibid., p. 29.
23. R. E. Mintz, "Strip Mining: A Policy Evaluation," *Ecology Law Quarterly* 5:46 (1976), p. 473.
24. H. Fineman, "Economists, U.S. Agency Leaders Call Pro-

posed Strip-mine Rules Too Costly," Louisville *Courier-Journal*, Nov. 28, 1978, p. 1.

25. The reserve base figure does not subtract for losses due to coal recovery.
26. *Demonstrated Coal Reserve Base of the U.S. on January 1, 1976* (Washington, D.C.: U. S. Department of Interior, Bureau of Mines, Aug. 1977), p. 2.
27. Ibid., p. 1.
28. J. L. McCormick, *Facts About Coal in the United States* (Washington, D.C.: Environmental Policy Center, 1975), p. 28.
29. "Coal Mine Injuries and Worktime—April 1977," *MESA Safety Reviews* (Denver: U. S. Department of Interior, June 1977).
30. R. Neill et al., "The Transition of Coal," *Technology Review* 78:1 (1975), p. 10.
31. McCormick, op. cit., p. 30.
32. This section is indebted to ideas suggested in: Norman Faramelli, "Acts of Transformation," *Journal of Current Social Issues* 14:4 (1977); The Committee on Ecology and Christian Lifestyle, "The Energy Crisis: A Study Paper for the United Church of Christ," *Journal of Current Social Issues* 14:4 (1977); I. G. Barbour, ed., *Western Man and Environmental Ethics* (Reading, Mass.: Addison-Wesley Publishing Co., 1973); and A. Okagaki, *Solar Energy: One Way to Citizen Control* (Washington, D.C.: Center for Science in the Public Interest, 1976).
33. National Council of Churches Energy Study Panel, Energy Ethics Consultation, Stony Point, N.Y., Oct. 12–14, 1977.
34. Mining Task Force, op. cit., Sect. 2.3, pp. 2–3.
35. Ibid., Sect. 2.2, pp. 11–12.
36. Ibid., Sect. 2.4, p. 10.
37. Ibid., Sect. 2.2, p. 18.
38. J. Cobb, "Ecology, Ethics and Theology," in *Toward a Steady-State Economy*, H. E. Daly, ed. (San Francisco: W. H. Freeman and Co., 1973), p. 319.

IV

CONTROLLING THE CHEMICALS WE USE

> The morality that pollution is criminal
>   only after legal conviction
> is the morality that causes pollution.
>
>   Aileen Smith
>   *Minamata*

> Once the public becomes accustomed to enjoying the re-
> wards of a technological advance, returning to the state
> of affairs prior to this advance becomes difficult, often
> almost impossible.[1]

Chemicals have left the laboratory and entered everyday
life. They range from synthetic fibers and plastics to cosmetics and cleansers. A major industry has been born which
takes petroleum products and other natural materials and,
through elaborate engineering procedures, synthesizes the
70,000 or more chemicals in commercial use.

In the manufacture and use of these chemicals, a number
of ethical issues arise regarding health exposure of workers
and consumers, availability of information on health effects,
and individual and group decisions on use of materials. However, these are all overshadowed by the trade-off that policy-
makers and citizens must confront—the cost of controlling an
economically valuable chemical versus the threat to the lives
of people who handle it. Du Pont says it will cost the industry an estimated $3.25 million, because of the need for cer-
tain engineering changes, to save a single life in textile plants
using acrylonitrile, a common chemical that causes colon and
lung cancer.[2] This is but one of many such examples where
reduction of exposure levels to chemicals comes in terms of
dollars and cents.

The placing of money value on chemicals is relatively recent. Few chemicals were commercially important in the
nineteenth century. While the transposition from laboratory

to industry and commercial products came with great benefits, such as new cheaper and longer-lasting products and employment, it also came at the price of chemically induced dangers. Hardly a week passes without some exposé of a chemical causing harm to some group of workers, consumers, or those living in the neighborhood of chemical processing plants. Citizens are now reading about a host of dangers due to chemicals:

* The National Cancer Institute estimates that 60 to 90 percent of cancer is environmentally induced,[3] that 20 percent of the population now dies from cancer, and that one fourth of the people will develop some form of cancer in their life.

* Each year, 200,000 infants are born with physical or mental damage, one fifth of which damage may be due to environmental factors.

* Between 200,000 and 500,000 illnesses are caused by occupational disease, much of which is induced by harmful chemicals. One million Americans have worked with asbestos, and fully 300,000 have been projected to die from cancer—a far higher rate than in the normal population.

* The pesticide DBCP causes reduction in sperm levels among workers producing it, and dangerous levels of other pesticide residues are found in the milk of nursing mothers.

* Fluorocarbons used in refrigerants and aerosol sprays may destroy the ozone layer in the upper atmosphere and expose us to dangerous levels of ultraviolet radiation.

* Fluorides destroy forest seedings, dioxin kills horses, PCB's contaminate fish, chloramines kill oysters, zinc damages wheat crops, and on and on.

These stories have been highly publicized and need not be retold here. While an exposé of a new chemical threat-of-the-week might be fair journalism, it is not ethics as such. However, the publicity informs the public that we have a major problem of control of materials that are economically valuable, and such awareness is a first step toward prudent use of these hazardous materials.

Control includes knowing the scope of the chemical pollution problem, discussing benefits and risks, delving into the rights and responsibilities of involved parties (workers, consumers, producers, government, scientists), and coming to some decision-making mechanism. Controlling chemicals may be looked at from the end use and include an evaluation of whether or not a potentially dangerous chemical is really "necessary"; steps to resist the commercial pressures to use harmful chemicals; and citizen actions that prod regulators into doing their duties.

Juxtaposed to controls of a technical nature at the factory are controls by the human beings who transport, use, and dispose of chemicals. What are the values that entice us to use chemicals such as fertilizers, pesticides, and detergents in larger amounts than needed? What alternatives exist to highly harmful chemicals? How are we to know what chemicals are harmful and to what degree?

The public is still basically unaware of the need to curb chemical use. A foul-smelling chemical may be relatively harmless, a pleasant one deadly. Most people who are not experienced in handling chemicals do not know how to store, pour, or dispose of a particular chemical. They often lack practical judgment of the safety, efficiency, or environmental impact of chemicals. They share a common ignorance with experts of what are the synergistic effects of many household, automotive, and yard chemical products.

The blame for this ignorance does not rest solely with consumers. The absence of revelation of content, warning labels, and proper chemical testing stems from a recalcitrant government and irresponsible producers, which hides vital information behind the walls of trade secrecy and proprietary rights. The Toxic Substances Control Act (TSCA) of 1976 was the first federal attempt to regulate hazardous chemicals. In this matter of legislation the United States is ahead of most of the industrial world, but so it should be, since such a volume and so many different kinds of chemicals are used in this country. The European Economic Community is considering a proposal for the coordinated review of new chemical substances.

TSCA is a broad-based act dealing with the whole life cycle of chemicals—through manufacturing, distribution, use, and disposal. It gives authority to the Environmental Protection Agency (EPA) to review notices of industry's intent to market new chemicals and to collect data on chemical production, use, exposure, by-products, and impurities. Likewise, the act requires pretesting of suspected chemicals.

Workers, consumers, and citizens in general are subjected to many modern hazards: electrical, mechanical, and thermal as well as chemical. Enough of almost any chemical will have a deleterious effect on living organisms. Here we speak of the toxicity, or poisonous nature, of chemical substances in either minute amounts or within the range of normal usage. Our modern lifestyles complicate matters by encouraging heavy use of numerous chemicals—thereby increasing the range of potential harm. Chemical hazards are present to us in four different ways:

In manufacturing—A 1978 hazard survey by the National Institute of Occupational Safety and Health (NIOSH) shows that 9 out of every 10 U.S. workers are unprotected from exposure to at least 1 of the 163 most common industrial chemical and physical hazards, among which are asbestos, benzene, and isopropanol. While about two thirds of companies provide employees with protective devices, these are geared to only special types of hazards. However, only 3 percent of plants offer services to reduce chemical exposure, but the plants with industrial hygiene services cover almost 25 percent of the work force.

In distribution—While the greatest chemical dangers are in the workplace, one cannot minimize the seriousness of the almost weekly railroad or highway spills and accidents involving chemicals. Not only are travelers placed in danger but so are residents near accident sites. Oceans and rivers have also been polluted by spillage of petroleum and chemicals during water transportation.

In consumer use—Chemicals can be quite hazardous when used by inexperienced people, especially consumers of household and garden products. Injuries and deaths are recorded from using farm and yard pesticides. Many consumers do not know how to read complex labels or instructions or how to handle dangerous chemicals properly.

In wastes—Many chemical, biological, radioactive, and explosive wastes are generated through extraction, conversion, and use of chemicals, especially by industrial and governmental facilities. Agricultural runoff also includes pesticides and fertilizers that can contaminate the waterways and general environment. Among problems related to the hazardous-waste phenomenon are: industrial waste and sludge that cannot be dumped in oceans or streams; lack of procedures to properly dispose of such common consumer products as waste motor oil and herbicides; and old community dumps such as ones in Niagara Falls, New York, and Toone, Tennessee, which have seepage of highly toxic chemicals. At Niagara Falls more than eighty chemicals taken from the ground have been identified as causing cancer, miscarriages, and birth defects.

A serious problem that cuts across all four of these areas is a failure to enforce a number of specific federal laws now on the books dealing with proper handling of these chemicals in manufacture, distribution, use, and wastes. For instance, the Environmental Protection Agency in 1978 listed some 638 chemical dump sites that could be considered hazardous, but a canvass of regional offices of that agency revealed over 32,000 nationwide sites that may be threats to human life. Some 90 percent of the estimated 40 million tons of hazardous wastes produced each year will be disposed of in ways that violate the intent of Congress; and yet EPA officials say the matter is largely a state and local government problem or something requiring citizen vigilance. Environmentalists fear that excellent chemical pollution regulations are becoming prime targets of anti-inflation battles.

CHARACTERISTICS OF HAZARDOUS CHEMICALS

Chemicals may possess some characteristics that are harmful to individual health, cause genetic damage to the human race, or are detrimental to the environment. Some of these characteristics are:

* They are *alien* to the environment; they have not existed for a sufficient length of time for natural processes to furnish protection for existing species from their harmful effects. Members of this group include certain uncombined elements and many synthetic compounds such as plastics and silicone resins. The problems become more complex here since the variety and magnitude of the plastics industry has increased so enormously in recent years.

* They are *persistent* and remain over a long period. Such chemicals as the insecticide DDT and polychlorinated biphenyls (PCB's), which have been used for carbon paper and for electric transformer fluids, are known as global pollutants. They accumulate in the environment because there is no biological mechanism to break them down and cleanse the environment of them. Later harmful effects cannot be easily remedied because of their pervasiveness. Examples of classes of persistent chemicals that are not presently known to be injurious are polyethylene glycols and silicone fluids found in industrial solvents and lubricants, and in numerous other uses.

Persistent chemicals may exhibit the phenomenon called *bioaccumulation*, which means that the chemical may concentrate in living tissue in amounts greater than in the surrounding environment. Presently little is known about the chemical's effect on the host tissue, its movement through the environment, and the conditions causing bioaccumulation. DDT and PCB are known to bioaccumulate in animal tissue and dairy products.

* They are *toxic* to living organisms, whether these be the lower forms or plants, animals, and human beings. They may be acutely or chronically toxic; they may have a variety of perverse effects such as shortening life or reducing resistance to stress. Some of the better-known chemicals of this category include cadmium, lead, mercury, selenium, arsenic, and beryllium.

Compounds released into the environment can undergo a variety of chemical conversions, with or without the mediation of a biological system. When the compound decomposes to free elements or oxides, they are not usually harmful. But that is not always the case, especially with a number of pesticides (for example, heptachlor epoxide is a harmful product of heptachlor, and dieldrin is derived from aldrin). Also, ordinary smog is a by-product of fuel combustion.

Many chemicals unite with certain metals and elements to form what are called *complexes,* which can alter the properties of the uncomplexed metal with respect to movement through the soil and water or across membranes. In some cases harmful properties of a substance are more easily able to manifest themselves. Some nonessential (to living organisms) elements, such as mercury and cadmium, are prone to complexification, and their complexes are more mobile and thus more able to contaminate the environment; other essential elements such as iron, manganese, chromium, and copper can become harmful in the excessive amounts available through complexes that enter the living organism.

* They are *mobile* and diffuse, or are carried widely throughout the environment by such natural forces as wind and ocean currents. Examples of such diffused materials include the sulfur oxides, mercury, and lead. Little is known about the mechanism of global dispersal of these materials.

Some chemical substances may appear innocuous at their point of production or release, but may be transported to another part of the ecosystem where they may be harmful. An example is the effect of fluorochlorocarbons (Freons) on the ozone layer in the stratosphere. Materials released in a rural environment may be harmless until mixed with oxidants from an urban area. Or materials stable in fresh water may react with pollutants in the ocean to form toxic materials. Merely saying that chemicals occur naturally does not mean that they are immune from becoming environmental threats. Naturally occurring petroleum becomes a menace when a tanker breaks apart; chemicals like carbon tetrachloride and other halomethanes, originally thought only human-made, are now purported to be produced by meteorological, geological, or other natural phenomena—they are still dangerous when concentrated in the workplace.

Once we have seen areas where chemicals might prove harmful and in what manner, we must begin to fashion some form of analysis that could limit use of a particular chemical (risk-benefit analysis) and develop alternatives that mitigate chemical pollution problems.

RISK-BENEFIT ANALYSES

Chemical Risks

Chemical risks occur with greater frequency as larger quantities of synthetic materials enter the marketplace and larger volumes are produced in industry. These are the disadvantages or liabilities of our chemical age, and they can affect us either directly or through our contact with a polluted environment. One cannot really escape these risks. Modern homes lack proper ventilation to handle the many cleaning agents, hobby materials, and solvents used there. Foods are often contaminated, either deliberately with additives or inadvertently by pesticides and outdoor pollutants. Highways, the automobile, playgrounds, schools, and numerous other places all contain chemical risks of varying degrees.

One may wish to distinguish risks according to a number of categories: necessary risks, negligible risks, acceptable risks, reasonable risks, and so forth. For us to understand more fully the degree and kind of risk involved in a particular chemical practice or use, the following questions are important.

1. Do the chemicals cause harm in manufacturing? A number of workers have contracted asbestosis due to exposure to asbestos in the manufacturing stage. These workers deserve to know when they are exposed to even small quantities of this material, and what precautions should be taken to guard against inhaling the minute fibers.

2. Does the process involve emission of hazardous by-products? A chemical plant on Minamata Bay, Japan, used a mercury catalyst, which was allowed to contaminate the nearby fishing grounds of many poor people living in the vicinity. These unsuspecting fishermen would eat two to three meals of fish per day and thus were severely affected by the mercury contamination. Some died, and others were crippled for life. For several years after the cause of contamination was known, the plant continued to discharge wastes directly into the bay.

3. Are intentional toxic effects part of the product's commercial value? Powerful herbicides and pesticides used to kill weeds and pests are produced by the millions of pounds. Some are nerve gases, which are gradually released over long periods of time. Others can hurt and kill unsuspecting persons who contact or inhale them in a variety of ways. It is important that the dangers and toxicity of this class of compounds be understood and made known.

4. Do the chemicals remain in the environment for long periods of time? Persistence often is a selling point for chemicals, especially those which resist biochemical degradation. Such chemicals as polychlorinated hydrocarbons enter air and water and gradually disperse throughout the ecosystem. Chemicals like DDT and PCB (polycholorinated biphenyls) are commercially beneficial, but, although they have been in use only a few decades, they are found in tissues of animals and fish throughout the world.

5. Do the chemicals degrade into harmful materials that remain for short periods of time before degrading into other end-products? Here the problem is the opposite of the preceding. Biodegradable intermediate products are often hard to detect, yet they may be quite toxic to humans and animals. Propanil, a major pesticide, degrades into a short-lived intermediate that is highly cancer-causing but proceeds to break down under normal circumstances into harmless final products.

6. Are the chemical additives used in large quantities? In a heavily consumption-oriented economy like ours, a new product can be developed and introduced into the market in immense amounts in a short period before adequate testing is completed. A few years ago the detergent industry came under criticism for including both phosphate and caustic ingredients in their products. They announced the use of nitrilotriacetic acid (NTA) in place of these, but an anticipated 2-billion-pound production of NTA per year alarmed toxicologists, since little experimental information was available about the chemical. When one common food color, Red II, came under attack, the industry converted to Violet I and increased use of Violet I from 3,000 to 66,000 pounds in a single year. In early 1973 the Food and Drug Administration received evidence from Japanese scientists that Violet I material was cancer-causing, and thus it was banned.

7. Are the chemicals subject to misuse? Printed regulations and instructions on methods of application, however strict, are insufficient when pesticides and other potent chemicals are used by unsophisticated workers. In early 1972 illiterate Iraqi farmers allowed their families to eat mercury-contaminated seed wheat, and hundreds of deaths and injuries ensued. Parathion [an insecticide] sprayed on tobacco in North Carolina in 1971 killed two farm children. Dozens of deaths have occurred from children sniffing or misusing aerosols containing a dangerous Freon propellant. Labels and warnings are hardly enough to keep children from being poisoned by these chemicals now found in many households.

Mere public knowledge of harmful materials will not prevent accidents, but better dissemination of information to the public would make it possible to balance the marginal benefits of such products against the immense risks involved. Removing some items from the market entirely, making safety caps on drug bottles mandatory, requiring licensed applicators in some cases, and banning many aerosols from home use would be the fruits of such information. We are prone to forget that the number of dangerous items within the reach of children is rapidly increasing. Aspirin, a supposedly harmless drug, has the dubious distinction of being the number-one drug killer among children.

8. Do fuel and other chemical additives add to the pollution burden? We hear a lot about such air pollutants as nitrogen oxides and carbon monoxide. The gasoline and oil sources of many of these better-known pollutants also contain additives whose identities are held to be trade secrets by manufacturers. Little or no testing of the effects of these billions of pounds of additives has been done. Their investigation has been buried under the sheer volume of research on better-known toxic substances. Tetraethyl lead and other antiknock additives, certain deposit modifiers, and the lead-removal agents (called "scavengers") in gasoline are highly toxic. Some enter the environment directly, while others slip in through careless disposal of waste motor oil and accidental spillage.[4]

Chemical Benefits

No one can deny that many of the chemical uses that have become prominent in our age are beneficial to human beings. Advantages accrue to society as a whole and to individuals through such chemicals as soaps, cleaners, and polishes. If chemicals were unbeneficial, the discussion would shorten itself to "thou shalt not use." A synthetic garment or rope or tent may be longer-lasting; a plastic garbage container may be less noisy when emptied; many synthetic chemicals may be cheaper than their natural counterparts (e.g., rubber). While some of these synthetics are derived from precious petroleum feedstock that should be conserved, still others actually extend the life of natural resources (e.g., detergents in motor oils). Besides the consumer and environmental benefits, the more often discussed ones are economic, such as employment, regional development, and balance of trade.

Advertising and the mass media have done a fairly good job in publicizing chemicals, but they have done little to help us in assessing benefits. The following questions may help us to analyze chemical benefits:

* What needs of society are met from use of the chemical? Are these real needs? If the threat of toxicity is significant, merely aesthetic values may not be sufficient for allowing use.
* If the chemical should be proscribed, are adequate alternatives (safe, inexpensive, easily usable) available?
* What is the extent of public use in volume? In dollars?
* Would restrictions on the use of a chemical cause unemployment or other local, regional, or national economic dislocation? International ramifications?
* If the chemical is too hazardous for continued use, how can economic and social impacts be minimized by proscription?
* How would proscription affect the export market to nations without restriction? Balance of trade?[5]

Questions about the overall technical merits of the beneficial chemical are not included. The presumption is that it is good if safe enough to be marketable, but a host of poor-grade consumer products made from chemicals refutes that notion. Regulation leads to inevitable economic and technical adjustments, but when corporate profits alone determine which products are available in the market, a balanced analysis of consumer goods is impossible.

In order to see economic benefits to the public and not just to special interests, we might ask further questions such as: Is the economic benefit shared by many or by a few? Does the benefit improve the quality of life to a greater degree than the suspected risk may harm it (as may occur with a number of medicines or the use of saccharin)? Is the benefit and/or risk short- or long-lived? Does the benefit or risk have spin-off effects such as the increase of future benefits or risks? Are the risks overlooked or neglected for the sake of obvious benefits? Is the risk a severe health problem or a minor one for a major portion of the population, or for a select, susceptible fraction of that population?

Necessary, Acceptable, and Reasonable Risks

Production and use of chemicals involve some degree of risk. Environmentally speaking, producing chemicals presents threats or "risks" to the ecosystem itself. Use of chemicals by a variety of consumers includes other levels of risks. A toxic-substance public policy must involve some form of risk-benefit analysis so that citizens might have a complete assessment of whether certain chemicals should or should not be produced or used, and to what degree. Some components for a proper risk-benefit analysis include:

* a shared goal in protecting and improving the environment and the quality of human life;
* a participation by all knowledgeable and interested parties including scientists, laborers, consumers, and businesspeople;
* an openness to include all data;
* a common desire to set general benefit/risk priorities;
* and a sufficient time period for assembling the perceived benefits and costs to both the environment and the affected human population.

While these components appear quite straightforward, the resolution of the analysis is more difficult. While benefits are often amenable to quantification (dollar sales and employment), risks are not. Furthermore, quantifiers have subconscious value judgments that they are not willing to acknowledge. Benefits are relatively more concrete and immediate than are risks. The persons most qualified to speak about benefits are not the ones who may be able to discuss risks. Issues are generally emotionally charged, and the measuring tools are not fully developed. Even with shared goals there exist differing levels of priorities, economic and health interests, and degrees of willingness to bear certain risks.

The National Academy of Sciences says that those who must resolve these analyses are "faced with the necessity of weighing incommensurables. Decisions of this kind must primarily reflect the underlying social values."[6] Unfortunately this recognition of the difficulties is not shared by all scientists and technical experts. The promoters of a "science court" believe that the entire procedure of analysis is merely a technical one, and their goal is to eliminate biased persons, emotions, and all subjective judgment. Ultimately the clear technical fact would be able to generate a definitive resolution.

Fortunately this court procedure has never received general acceptance. Values are involved in accepting risks or defining benefits. Decisions will ultimately be made not by experts but by others influenced by amorphous emotional and political factors.[7] Furthermore, what some technical people tolerate as acceptable, to ensure the maintenance of a particular lifestyle, others will reject as not commensurate with the risk involved. What is necessary for some is folly for others.

Identification of economic benefits is a strongly supported function of the private sector. These benefits, however, are often defined in business-centered and profit-motivated terms and regarded more highly than health or environmental considerations. Health-conscious people perceive costs in terms of medical and hospital bills, but, ironically, an economics-centered person may regard the same bills as benefits to our economy and GNP. Again, a health-conscious citizen may be aware of the toll of human suffering, while profit-conscious people regard the sufferers as "unproductive" and burdens.

Today environmentally conscious citizens call into question such institutionalized values as success, aggressiveness, competitiveness, achievement, individualism, and bigness. Behind the tension in this struggle is a conflict over which values are beneficial to society as a whole.

Together with this lack of consensus on what constitutes a particular benefit to society goes an equally serious difference over the necessity or acceptability of a particular risk. When one takes an airplane ride a certain risk is involved, albeit a lower risk on a mile-by-mile basis than an auto ride. We might rationalize taking this risk—even when unnecessary—but should we force the risk on a friend or relative who is terrified by air travel? For a vacation? For needed medical attention? If we grant certain personal freedom in choosing such risks, then we ask, should we define the necessity or acceptability of certain hazardous chemicals in terms of our own perceived benefits? Perhaps in answering this we become aware of personal biases and preferences. To what degree must those of others be honored?

In speaking of risks one must remember that what is acceptable or necessary for individuals may not be so for the population on the whole. One individual may consider air pollutants acceptable because of residing in a remote location removed from traffic; this individual may also regard the pollutants as necessary for the continuation of personal lifestyle and mobility. On the other hand, this person might be reasonable enough to admit that the risk is far from being negligible—a term that may be less value-laden.

Of the three terms (*acceptable, necessary,* and *negligible*) related to risks, the most elusive is *acceptable*. William W. Lowrance, who wrote *Of Acceptable Risk*, says *acceptable* may be just passive or even stoical continuance of historical momentum; it may persist because no alternatives are seen; it may result from ignorance or misperception of risk.[8]

In the setting of radiation protection criteria and standards, *acceptable* can mean different things: "(1) a conscious decision perhaps based upon some balancing of good and bad or progress and risk; (2) a decision implying a comparison, possibly subjective, with hazards from other causes, these latter being 'acceptable' in turn in one of the senses given here, or perhaps just historically and possibly unconsciously; (3) the passive but substantive fact that nothing has been done to eliminate or curtail the thing being deemed 'acceptable.'"[9]

A portion of the population could be made to accept a risk it would refuse if aware of health and safety dangers. It is hardly ethical to attempt to make a hazard acceptable as such, and thus some prefer not to speak of *acceptable* in relation to toxic substance control, but only of *necessary* risks that should be allowed. Of course, here again is ambiguity since the word is used differently by the profit- and health-conscious person. It does, however, seem to lend itself to a more precise definition.

We may speak of basic necessities (food, clothing, shelter, fuel) and broader-term necessities regarded for living in a civilized manner (roads, recreational facilities, government, courts, schools). *Necessity* may be extended to include things and operations required for functioning properly in one's state of life. Surgery may be a necessity for a father of a young family, but not so for his elderly parent who has no dependents. Because of modern habits, the word *necessity* is often extended to elevator service, air conditioning, and central heating. So the degree of risk must be analyzed in the context of basic or broader-term necessities, and the parameters clearly determined.

In an ethical treatment it appears best to speak of reasonable and unreasonable risks, rather than acceptable and unacceptable ones. Several criteria for judging a risk reasonable include: a long-standing custom of use giving presumption of safety (such as the Food and Drug Administration's "generally recognized as safe" [GRAS] list), prevailing standards of safety within a profession (such as among architects building to conform to "prevailing local standards"), best available technology (such as the best available means for noise abatement), and necessity or benefit.[10] Of course, all of these are subject to discussion, since in some cases industry pressure has helped set standards that may have overlooked health risks.

Concerning the reasonableness of risks to consumers, the following proposed guideline is enlightening:

> Risks of bodily harm to users are not unreasonable when consumers understand that risks exist, can appraise their probability and severity, know how to cope with them, and voluntarily accept them to get benefits that could not be obtained in less risky ways. When there is a risk of this character, consumers have reasonable opportunity to protect themselves; and public authorities should hesitate to substitute their value judgments about the desirability of the risk for those of the consumers who choose to incur it.

> But preventive risk is not reasonable
> —when consumers do not know it exists; or

—when, though aware of it, consumers are unable to estimate its frequency and severity; or

—when consumers do not know how to cope with it, and hence are likely to incur harm unnecessarily; or

—when risk is unnecessary in . . . that it could be reduced or eliminated at a cost in money or in the performance of the product that consumers would willingly incur if they knew the facts and were given the choice.[11]

Even for those who champion acceptable risks reasonableness plays a part: Given a reasonable calculation of the genetic hazard posed by an environmental mutagen, it then becomes necessary to consider how acceptable such a risk will be to the population at large. The guiding principle in all cases should be that no risk whatsoever is acceptable when the mutagen compound presents no clear benefits, or when an alternative non-mutagenic compound is available.[12]

Burden of Proof

Determining the degree of chemical risk involves various components of society: producers, government, workers, scientists, and citizens. A reasonable proof of chemical safety rests with the producer who creates the potential environmental disturbance by making the chemical. The government has the burden of establishing workable regulations for guarding health and environment. When producers are remiss in alerting the public to a chemical hazard, the burden rests on industrial workers and scientists. Public-interest groups also accept the burden of producing evidence that others are not doing their duties.

Society's biases are such that it often wishes to overlook possible risks, but pressures within a democratic society tend toward exposing them. A seemingly harmless chemical may be quite hazardous when used differently or in higher dosage. By mid-1979 the first EPA inventory of suspect chemicals whose safety requires investigation approaches five thousand. Still thousands of new uses are devised annually for these many chemicals, which challenges EPA to bring some form of control and order to the rather chaotic modern chemical situation.

Injured persons bear the greatest burden of proof. They are burdened by the toxic effects of mercury, asbestos, lead, and other pollutants and are living—or else dead—proof that chemicals can harm us. They are proof that no chemical risk is really negligible when human populations are threatened. They testify to the human cost of chemical risk-taking.

While such burdens may not be lifted from victims who are seriously harmed, steps can and should be taken to see that such incidents do not recur. Some guiding principles include:

* Restrict the use of chemicals known to cause cancer, genetic changes, or birth defects to essential practices. The National Academy of Sciences says that normally only very low risks, except in lifesaving drugs, will be allowed when dealing with dangerous substances.

* Handle dangerous or potentially dangerous chemicals under proper supervision. In the case of pesticides, only instructed applicators should be allowed to dispense the chemicals.

* Concentrate on finding safe alternatives through governmental encouragement.

* Restrict use, prohibit certain manufacturing methods, and remove chemicals from the market when found harmful. The federal government has this power under TSCA.

Even when all such measures are fully operative, absolute safety cannot be guaranteed—but relative safety, and thus reduction of risks to nearly negligible levels, can be. Proof of safety is more economically but less socially burdensome to the producer than proof of harm, because such safety involves foreseeing all possible ways the substance can be misused. Proof of harm may require only the examination of a medical doctor or coroner.

The burden should rest on the producer before marketing the product. While pre-market testing is costly and leads to no absolute proof of safety, it does possess a number of benefits:

* It prevents some highly toxic materials from reaching the marketplace. It can generally discover acutely toxic substances, though overlooking the chronically toxic ones.

* It requires producers to anticipate possible misuses of the chemical once on the market, and thus to be able to make some forms of compensation.

* Its cost leads to more basic and applied research; families and classes of chemicals do behave similarly, and good toxicologists can predict with some certainty whether one compound might be more dangerous than those of another class.

* It opens up the possibility of degrees of testing. Chemicals which are more suspicious, or which are produced in greater quantities, or which are in close proximity to people should have more refined testing.

* Lastly, it enhances the service economy by employing more toxicologists.

While chemical testing is costly and cuts profits, it should be regarded as a built-in cost to be repaid by consumers much as are market surveying and advertising campaigns. Waiting for dead bodies to be the test results of a certain chemical is to turn the public into the chemical industry's guinea pigs. So often the delayed effects of environmental and human harm appear long after the chemical has reached peak profitability. Producers do not perform "innocent" acts until proven guilty; a new chemical is a threat to us and we have the sad experiences of vinyl chloride and kepone to show us this. The best procedure is to put the burden upon the producer in the form of pretesting.

TECHNOLOGY ASSESSMENT

All chemical production, distribution, disposal, and even use involve some form(s) of technology. A risk-benefit analysis of an existing or new chemical is not sufficient in itself, for it may fail to consider how the chemical technology is utilized or is being expanded, or all the alternatives that could replace the substance in question. In order that reasonable controls and decisions can be made, some type of general assessment is required including all factors—economic, societal, and technical. Furthermore, the affected parties must be able to have a voice in helping to frame the ultimate decision about the controlling of chemicals.

General Procedures

Technology assessment (TA) is a systematic approach to gathering and analyzing information required for making a decision. It is not meant merely to evaluate the functioning or performance of a certain technology, though these may be part of the total assessment. Rather, TA focuses on the anticipated or existing impact of a technology on society. Insofar as that impact includes the health, safety, and general welfare of human populations and the whole ecosystem, it includes an ethical component. What is said here may just as easily apply to the problems of the previous chapters (agricultural or animal husbandry practices, fuel alternatives, or nuclear disposal techniques) as to chemical controls.

A chemical TA includes technical analyses of manufacturing and engineering techniques, transportation containers and materials, loading and storage practices, characteristics of various chemical components (such as toxicity and persistence), economics of chemical alternatives, employment and job dislocation, profitability, and so forth. These analyses require expertise from the respective fields of engineering, science, and economics. Divergence of opinion exists even over technical matters and these differences should be publicly discussed. Obviously a consensus on technical matters is desired. The technical analyses should set out the options as clearly as possible.

The second compartment of an ideal chemical TA is not technical but rather involves the social, political, cultural, and ethical aspects of the particular problems. Questions of value judgment may arise here, such as: Is this technology appropriate to the kind of society we want? (More will be said about appropriate technology in the next chapter.) Will this technology weaken our societal structures and values?

Are all affected parties being considered? Who wants and who needs this technology? Ideally, the broadest form of consultation is sought in this TA, because so many people are affected. Within the practical limits of TA, the decisions should be democratic and not those of technocrats.

While TA processes differ, some common components are usually present—descriptive, assessment of impact, policy analysis, and dissemination of results phases.[13]

The descriptive phase attempts to place the problem in perspective. It involves a state-of-the-art review; it tries to characterize the technology and the existing "environment," which is both biophysical and social; it defines the problems listing sponsor objectives and available study resources; it projects alternative futures, technology choices, and socio-economic and institutional/legal climates.

The assessment of impact phase compares effects of different technologies and includes a sensitivity analysis. Criteria for selection of importance of various impacts must be established here, so that the effects of different technologies on citizens in general—consumers, workers, and others—might be better understood.

The policy analysis phase includes further identification of issues arising from the development and characterization of social environments. Also, the development of alternative policies, technology mixes and timing, and means of controlling development are discussed here. An assessment of policy implementation is made including constraints and barriers to implementation. The dissemination of results phase is highly dependent on who the target group is and who makes the final decision.

An example of a very elementary TA was that involving the congressional decision in 1972 not to fund development of the supersonic transport (SST). Questions of technological feasibility, estimates of development costs, market surveys of airlines and passengers, evaluation of comparative fuel efficiency, noise level estimates, possible impact on the ozone layer of the stratosphere, predictions of job gain or loss, and impact on national balance of payments were considered. Experts were called in. Disputes over scientific conclusion were aired, as, for example, over whether danger to the ozone layer was significant or not.

A discussion of values proceeded from there. Are we willing to surrender our number one status in aircraft technology? What values do we place on quick, quiet, cheap, economic flights? Would our people tolerate frequent sonic booms? Were the benefits of the SST enough to justify the risk to thousands of possible additional cases of skin cancer each year? Should we develop an SST when people go without proper social services, so an executive might save a few hours? These value questions would probably have been only peripherally considered if the SST had not required governmental subsidy. But an TA decision was made, even before the time that an Office of Technology Assessment was set up by Congress.

More complete and systematic TA's are now being conducted, but many do not presume to make the final technical decision. Often they are part of a general resource, energy, or development policy-making process. For instance, there is a current TA of Appalachian energy development being conducted by the EPA and the Appalachian Regional Commission (1979). It is seeking to assess how energy development will occur over the next quarter century within a particular physical, economic, and social setting. It is looking at problems related to development of coal resources and the technologies involved in extraction, conversion, transportation, and utilization. Nuclear-generated electric power and oil and gas are also being investigated.

A problem area where a technology assessment is most urgent is that of transportation of chemicals by railroad. Numerous serious accidents have occurred, especially on certain lines, because of faulty equipment, deteriorated railbeds, or deliberate damage. Chemicals such as chlorine and sulfuric acid have harmed local residents and forced the evacuation of whole towns. In the cases of explosives and inflammable materials, a number of residents have lost their lives and property. A TA could determine whether other routes could be utilized, whether chemicals need not be shipped at such distance, to what degree equipment and services must be improved, and how to better alert local residents and disaster teams as to the dangers involved. Still other alternative policy options might be presented through a complete TA.

For a valid technology assessment, several general laws or rules have been formulated by Henry Skolimowski:

* No system can adequately assess itself. It must be assessed by agents outside itself.
* The more quantitative a model for a technology assessment, the more it eliminates value judgments, and therefore the less effective it will be from a social point of view.
* Every valid technology assessment must be an assessment terminating in a human value and judgment, otherwise it is a fraud.
* The real expertise for conducting a technology assessment is not just technical, but also biological and social.[14]

An added axiom is: Not everything that becomes technologically *possible* is necessarily *good* for the entire people or *worth developing*.

Ultimate Decision-makers

Someone or some group must make the ultimate decision on an assessment. Some technologies affect a local area; some have impacts regionally and some nationally or even internationally. To the best means possible, the decision should be tailored to the impact area. Thus decentralized decision-making is better where the question to be answered is of local consequence.

Ultimate decisions on a technology assessment could be made by direct referendum (locally, statewide, or even national perhaps), by a professional mechanism such as a jury of peers, by governmental administrative or legislative routes, or maybe by the courts. The courts seem the least equipped to handle such an added load and such a technical subject. Democratic processes would break down if we were to have a referendum on each issue, but on some rather important decisions the procedure does not seem farfetched, such as whether to launch a nationwide solar development program.

Coupled with area considerations is the seriousness of a particular problem. Both are factors that should influence the choice of decision-maker(s). Other such factors might include a guarantee of being balanced and well-informed and freedom from undue influence by special-interest groups. The overriding aim is that the decision should be made with as much openness and public participation as possible. Granting that all decision-makers exhibit competency for the task at hand, the following scheme might be recommended:

* Major decisions—involving entire populations (local, state, national) and dealing with serious health and safety issues that threaten these populations, such as nuclear power development (direct referendum or legislative action);
* Intermediate decisions—involving a select portion of the population on serious health and safety issues such as establishing occupational safety guidelines in chemical factories (federal administrative or jury system);
* Small-scope decisions—potentially harmful but not definitely proven health effects on a select portion of the population, such as those decisions on the use and transportation of numerous chemicals (proper local, state, or national regulatory agency).

Discontinuation of current potentially dangerous practices is always difficult, especially where those practices are profitable to a special-interest group. Though legal action ought not to force a specific decision, it should require the decision-maker(s) to act when evidence exists that a hazard is imminent. When proof of safety is required, the burden rests with the producers, not the users. Whatever the decision-making mechanism, time for such demonstration of proof must be allotted, and the means available to assemble all data needed for making a proper one.

Other Approaches to Assessment

Technology assessment as now practiced is an incomplete art; several approaches of varying degrees of validity are now used:

* Single-contract method—Seeking assessing data from a single think tank, research institute, or academic department. This method is currently used by Congress's Office of Technology Assessment. Advantages: quick, concise recommendations; Disadvantages: technologically and narrowly based with little tradition for social inputs.

* Dual-contract method—Seeking identical assessing data from several competing institutions. Advantages: cross-referencing and double check for completeness; Disadvantages: types of research institutes are so similar that the same often unrecognized biases exist.

* In-house method—Developing a staff of experts to handle the entire assessment. Advantages: shorter time and fewer logistic problems; Disadvantages: no method of thorough criticism.

* In-house modified method—The same as the in-house method but with external advisory panels of experts. This is the general method for critical report writing at the federal level.

* Advocacy method—Similar to the technique used to assess the guilt or innocence of a party in a criminal suit by a jury of peers. This method is backed by public-interest groups and includes assembling in the public forum data on both sides of the issue; subsidizing intervention of any interested parties that lack resources; if necessary, appointment of a citizen advocate; time given for the results to be digested and re-examined or submitted to the final judge(s).

To incite the respective governmental body to begin action on an assessment is most important. Thus there are some questions for review of existing technology needing an assessment, and some for taking precautions before adopting a new technology:

Existing Practice

* Is there scientific proof (injuries, a body count, animal chronic effects, and so on) that harm is done or could be done by this practice?

* Is there growing abuse of a product beyond legitimate intended use (sniffing solvents or taking chemicals as drugs)?

* Is there sufficient reason to suspect long-term harmful effects (chemicals in drinking water)?

* Is some scientific datum lacking that is critical to a decision?

Added Questions for Anticipated Practice

* Do we have sufficient economic and scientific data: quantity, use volume, nature (physical and toxicological)?

* Are there close analogies with existing chemicals already in use?

* Has there been sufficient testing of this substance?

Whatever approach is used to collect and weigh evidence, several qualities ought to characterize the final assessment:

Promptness—A decision should be rendered speedily once all data are collected.

Prudence—All sides must be weighed properly (by quality of evidence and not just quantity) and risks and benefits ranked and assessed.

Thoroughness—Advice and evidence must be gathered from all parties concerned, especially those not normally heard from because of their poverty or lack of political skills. A range of alternatives to the proposed technology should be presented. The weighing of various factors should be subject to public comment.

Detachment—There must be no *a priori* commitment to one side or another by the decision-makers. Care should be taken to screen out factors of political expediency or strictly personal ideology. Appearances or credentials must not be given special favors. Evidence from all sides must be presented fully and intelligently.

Recognition of Fallibility—All sides should be aware of the pitfalls of decision-making in complex issues and of the likelihood of a degree of error in any decision.

Broadness of Base—Considerations must include not merely economic feasibility but also environmental, legal, social, ethical, and health factors.

Updating the Decision

No technology assessment is ever finished. The many factors that go into the decision are in flux: testing methods; control techniques; social and economic needs and goals; relative priorities of the decision-makers; alternative technologies. A periodic updating and review of major technology assessments should be built into the process.

Technology, while ever changing and improving, has been with us a long time; technology assessment is a relatively new procedure. In a restricted sense, TA has existed as an ongoing critical evaluation of the economic worth and technical feasibility of a particular procedure. But the incorporation of the social dimension is quite new, and our abilities to incorporate this aspect will surely grow in the coming years.

Perhaps the one aspect of TA which will develop is that of citizen participation in decision-making. Programs of citizen monitoring of water and air deterioration, land misuse, poor forestry practices, weather changes, road violations, and a host of other programs will make citizens more sophisticated in understanding the social dimension of technology. Better ways of finding and developing citizen opinion will be found. Citizens will look upon technology more realistically and find it limited by the natural, financial, and human resources available. It will be for them more a tool than an overlord.

This promise of a developed TA will be welcome news for those struggling against chemical pollution. Assessing a chemical technology includes the set of alternatives by which a particular substance can be either processed in a more environmentally sound manner or replaced.

RIGHTS AND RESPONSIBILITIES

The public has a right to be protected from the unreasonable risk of working or using untested chemicals. Chemical producers have the responsibility to do or have these tests performed, and the government should see that they are properly executed. These duties follow from the individual's right to bodily integrity and "life" under the Constitution, which, broadly speaking, includes the right to clean and healthy environment, safe working conditions, and safe consumer products. These citizen rights or entitlements to certain modes of conduct are not new but newly threatened existing ones. The threatened conduct or "freedom" must be clearly seen, so that proper decision-making can be performed with regard to toxic substances.

The Consumer

We are all consumers. Some of our chemical consuming practices are quite harmless, and some threaten our bodily integrity and life. In such matters the dignity of the human person demands that consent be obtained before anything is done to his or her body—and the individual can void that right by giving consent. An ethicist, Deborah Johnson, has developed some important arguments for consumer rights in this matter by working from recent developments in bioethics and medical ethics.[15] She emphasizes that consent is the important concept here and that valid consent must be freely given, the person competent at the time, and the person informed as to risks and what is being done to people. *Competence* implies being adult and possessing proper mental health; *information* includes knowing the substance (chemical), the duration and degree of the threat, and how to handle or dispose of it; *free choice* means not having some sort of circumstance that induces risking beyond what would otherwise be desired (absence of readily accessible alternatives to harmful chemical products; fear of unemployment allowing a plant to remain open even when unsafe, and so on).

Unfortunately, not all chemical consumers can make proper consent. A young boy is seen in a supermarket sniffing toxic pesticides to see which to purchase; consumers admit that they never read labels and simply trust that their household products are safe; advertising pressure and product placement in stores limit free choice. Part of the problem is impressing on consumers the dangers of many chemicals; part is arousing an awareness of such consumer rights as access to health and safety information, freedom from harassment, and organizing freely for consumer protection.

Subsidiary consumer rights include requirements for adequate labeling and warning, access to performance standards and complaints, and communication with experts on all sides of a given issue.

When injury is done without a person's knowledge, the first responsibility rests with the offending party, and then with other individual citizens or groups having knowledge of the harm. This responsibility falls on those with a knowledge of the injury, a capacity to make it known, an awareness of the need for such information, and an availability to be the last resort for action, made necessary by the unresponsiveness of those with primary responsibility.[16]

Consumers have the responsibility: to preserve their own health and safety and those of their neighbor; to protect the environment by proper use of resources and by disposing of waste materials properly; to educate themselves and others about the risks involved in hazardous chemicals; and to use existing judiciary systems to further the reduction of chemical insult on human beings and the environment.[17]

In a democratic society faced with large and powerful special interests, citizens have a right to organize to be better able to carry out their responsibilities. In this context, public-interest or citizen groups serve as surrogates for individuals and offer an effective voice in the political arena. Citizen groups do represent certain interests rather than others, such as a community-accepted moral value of health, or collective goods that might be neglected or abused by multiple private actions. As groups, they have certain rights and responsibilities.

Regarding health and safety information, public-interest groups have the rights: to organize and share in the privileges and exemptions of other incorporated bodies; to have access to information; to communicate and have access to printed and electronic media so that the message can be delivered to the public; to freedom from harassment (they should not suffer intimidation from the Internal Revenue Service, corporate groups, or governmental policing bodies); to confidentiality of sources according to the canons of good journalism; and to redress (petitioning of regulatory agencies and standing in court).[18]

Regarding health and safety information, public-interest groups have the responsibility: to remain open to public scrutiny to preserve an atmosphere of purity of public-interest spirit; to educate the public and prepare it for more responsible citizenship; to use all available means to acquire information that will prove the truth of the issue; to be accessible to the needs of the public; to provide follow-through and not jump from issue to issue, thus producing an air of shallowness or lack of long-term commitment to the cause; and to report reasonably and not be drawn into the temptation to sensationalism that is present in many public-interest issues.[19]

The Worker

Often workers have their own lives shortened or their health threatened by chemicals in the workplace. A common and shameful practice reported to exist in the chemical industry has been to transfer older workers to the manufacture of highly toxic chemicals that the industry knows will shorten lives. Their increased death rates will be "hidden" by their advanced years. This is an ethical issue that needs considerable exposure and discussion, especially by professional medical groups and labor unions.

Workers as citizens exposed to special chemical threats have rights: to a safe and healthy workplace; to knowledge of the risk involved in processing a certain chemical; to the seeking of outside medical help for their own protection; to freedom from job loss due to occupational health concerns; to a safe neighborhood environment; and to reasonable job security.

Workers as such also have certain responsibilities: to consider the general public's health and safety; to put aside company and employment interests for a greater environ-

mental or public-health good; to resist pressure to engage in
company polluting practices, especially when they know regulations are lax or inspectors are absent; and to produce safe
consumer products.

These worker duties are often burdensome, especially
when job insecurity and the need for higher wages are a
threat. A number of labor unions like the Oil, Chemical and
Atomic Workers (OCAW) keep occupational health and the
public interest very much before the rank and file.

The Producer

Chemical manufacturers have a tradition of keeping much
information under a trade secrecy cloak. Secrecy has been
their hallmark. The National Science Foundation's Panel to
Select Organic Compounds Hazardous to the Environment
found in 1975 only 28 percent of survey questions sent to industry were usable as answers in compiling data.[20] While the
public does not have easy access to data, some of the more
pertinent materials are actually accessible to competitors
within industry itself through analytical resources, intelligence systems, and experts who know what others are doing.
Few outside the industry have the sophisticated instru-
mentation and expertise to do this detective work.

Prompted by the need for revelation of chemical data, the
Toxic Substances Control Act partly remedied the situation
through the persistence of public interest spokespersons. The
act calls for disclosure of such data to the Environmental
Protection Agency, but both nontoxicological data and those
designated "trade secrecy" material are inaccessible to the
general public—and, for all practical purposes, to other governmental agencies. The TSCA tried to bypass the sticky
question of conflict of rights: the right of citizens to know
the chemicals they use and are exposed to; the right of the
industry to so-called proprietary and confidential information.

The right to compete among producers within the framework of a market system is generally regarded by industry as
a fundamental right of each individual—and this, for industry, includes individual companies. Others might concede it
to be a derived right—granted by the public as a way of preserving more fundamental rights guaranteed by the Consti-

tution, such as life and liberty. Industry generally regards trade secrecy as instrumental to the competitive demands of the marketplace and to the fundamental rights of the groups and individuals that the marketplace is meant to serve.

Another line of reasoning is that the right of trade secrecy may be part of a broader right to private property guaranteed by the Constitution. The corporation, being a legal and not a natural person, does not possess this as an inherent right as do individual citizens.[21]

Chemical producers, amid many governmental regulations, are still free in many ways such as in the sharing of relevant information—at least, what they think is important. The act is somewhat vague about what constitutes a trade secret, and yet the corporation may define some information as secret—from not just competitors but also consumers and workers. The industry might opt for an openness that makes use of licenses or patents and still be as healthy as the food or drug industries, which have been forced to disclose ingredients for years.

One argument concerning public disclosure is that producers are to give the public information about *known* toxic materials, but merely notify governmental agencies about *suspected* ones.[22] But why should not consumers know even suspected effects? The credibility of the chemical industry might be enhanced by such revelation. Besides, the argument that the marketplace is free in such choices is really a corporate one. Information—even of possible dangers—ceases to be private when it involves human and environmental health and protection. It must be public, for otherwise our democratic institutions might fall into the hands of a technocratic elite with often unrecognized biases who are able to make the final decisions.

Corporate responsibility extends beyond information dissemination. It includes setting up an atmosphere wherein consumers and workers can make free decisions with regard to use and production of chemicals. A threat to close a factory does not allow a financially threatened community to make free choices about the chemicals produced. The development of a product line that will inevitably lead to consumer overuse or misuse is corporate irresponsibility, especially when subtle advertising conditions consumers to take up such harmful practices.

The Scientist

The public's right to know stands in sharp contrast to scientists' duty to reveal what they know about chemicals. The reason for this duty is found in the very nature of the scientific profession (to profess publicly) and scientific knowledge (to be made public). Scientific societies and journals were founded for the sake of communication. Repression of scientific information—a common practice in the early years of science—exists today in the corporate research laboratory where valuable scientific information is regarded as private and proprietary. The scientist is caught in this conflict of a professional commitment to reveal scientific knowledge and a loyalty to the company, which wants the information kept within its walls.

The matter is far more than merely academic. If particular scientific knowledge leads to a judgment on environmental and health effects of a chemical, then to withhold it is both scientifically and socially reprehensible. Protection of the consumer, worker, and local inhabitant must extend to protection of the concerned citizen-scientist who is moved to reveal pertinent health and environmental information he or she is privy to.

In order to be prudent in such revelations, such scientists should take the following preliminary steps: carefully assess their own level of confidence in the information; consider the degree and type of risk involved, which might cause environmental damage, harm to animals, and/or injury to human beings; recognize that in considering a course of action the timing factor can be most significant; and consider all rights and responsibilities to their families, professions, employers, and other relevant parties.[23] Some, however, regard this as far too cautious and say that scientists must do their utmost to correct a potentially dangerous situation. "The level of effort applied must be commensurate with the degree of seriousness, and consideration of career, family, and so on, must be secondary if death or serious harm to humans is likely."[24]

Some further guides to revelation of important corporate information (whistle blowing) for the scientist and engineer include the following:

* Reflect on the seriousness of the issue. Does the knowledge really need to be revealed for the public interest? Has it already been made public somewhere else? Does public awareness outweigh legitimate corporate rights? How valid are the data?
* Reflect on the reason for revelation. Is there a sense of grandeur in publicity? Is it an excuse to leave a job? What are all the ramifications of revelation?
* Reflect on the method of revelation. Have intimate friends been consulted who can offer wise counsel? Has a professional ethics committee been approached? Are all remedies within the company exhausted? Is the party concerned willing to go to a regulatory agency before the mass media? Is he or she protected in the event of misinterpretation of data or intentions? Has the best time for the revelation been considered?
* Reflect on what can be offered as an alternative. Is it practical? Is it a costly remedy and can it be done in the present situation?

Scientists also have rights in relation to employment: to periodic performance reviews available in writing; to freedom from arbitrary discharge through provision of both advance notice and severance pay; to judgment by at least two higher levels of management in cases of dispute and also by peers; to application for patents and publication of technical papers; to affiliation with appropriate professional societies; and to protection of individual fringe benefits.[25]

The Government

The government must protect its citizens' health and safety. It must point out the risks involved in a new chemical technology and conduct an assessment of a scientific "advance" before it reaches commercial utilization. It must provide an atmosphere where the proper decision-making may occur. Democracy's glory is that time is required to make technological decisions; its shame is that procedures curtailing existing hazardous substances are so cumbersome.

Among the governmental duties are: to ensure that chemical production and use do not pose unreasonable risk to health and environment; to regulate distribution and use that pose such unreasonable risks; to proscribe uses that are proven to be imminently hazardous; to monitor chemical plant emissions; to so regulate as not to unduly impede technological innovations; to protect workers from harmful chemicals; to encourage research into the toxicology of existing and used chemicals; to notify other nations of known chemical dangers; to keep potentially dangerous chemicals out of the hands of the young and incompetent; and to inform citizens of the toxicity of manufactured chemicals.

Regarding the last duty, difficulties arise when industry prefers to keep information secret. In such cases several governmental guidelines are helpful: information is eligible for protection from disclosure when such revelation would foreclose governmental access to necessary future information, or do serious economic harm to the informant; it should not be protected if public harm from ignorance exceeds the value of the detriment to governmental or private interests from disclosure.[26]

The government must see that the conditions for the free consent mentioned earlier are provided. The needs for curbing excessive or misleading advertising and for checking on consumer product labeling are part of the government's responsibility, as is the monitoring of safety testing and distribution practices.

FURTHER ETHICAL QUESTIONS

Besides playing active roles in risk-benefit analyses, technology assessments, and the establishment of rights and responsibilities of involved parties, skilled ethicists may play important roles in the following problem and policy areas related to chemicals:

Worker and victim compensation—If a worker has worked at several places, who bears the liability for his or her disability? Is compensation sufficient to warrant workers' exposure to toxic substances? To whom does a worker appeal for redress when incurring a chronic disease? To whom does the general citizenry appeal? What level of protection from toxic substances should be afforded the general public? Should we assign responsibility in multiple-agent cases? How is someone to be compensated for irreversible, as opposed to reversible, harm?

Environmental compensation—What patterns of responsibility are formed in relation to damage done to the commons? Does nature provide an enduring standard for environmental integrity and well-being? Are there priority rules for adjudicating between competing values?

Consumer use—Is it ethical to distribute or retain in the home or workplace chemicals that may be easily misused? Does some governmental agency or corporate entity know what is best for the consumer? How much does consumer behavior depend on consumer information and private decision-making and how much on governmental regulation? How does the corporate role in advertising and production enter into consumer choice? Are there some chemicals that should simply not be available to the average consumer (e.g., in foods, cosmetics, and household products)? Should those who encourage overuse of chemicals be held culpable?

Limits to chemical technology—Should there not be an environmental impact statement for every new chemical telling harmful properties, potential for misuse, and resource expenditure? Should some chemicals simply not be produced, distributed, or used by industry or individual consumers? Are there times when we must say no to experimentation with hazardous materials?

Trade secrecy and information flow—When may trade secrecy be retained and when must information be revealed for the common good in matters regarding hazardous materials? Is there really such a thing as a trade secret in regard to the properties of a hazardous material? In other words, is it not necessary always to reveal characteristics that could be harmful to others? Are not all chemical toxicity data public information? Is not a manufactured or processed chemical always a potential environmental threat, unless proven harmless in a particular use? Is it not the government's task to ensure that the burden of proof rest with the parties that benefit from a certain chemical production?

Citizen participation—Who has the right to be heard when it comes to assessing the worth of a particular chemical technology? Who determines the use of a chemical—producer, government, user, general public? What weight is placed on the testimony of those who are heard? Are the technologically elite to be listened to more carefully?

International and global dimensions—Should we work for international controls over certain hazardous chemicals? What should be done about "escape industries" seeking to operate in countries with less stringent safety regulations? What about the export of toxic substances banned in another country? What course of action ought a corporation to follow when countries have differing standards for production, distribution, use, and disposal of toxic materials? Do transnational corporations bear a special responsibility in promoting international standards of exposure for workers and the public to toxic substances? Are there ethical principles upon which to base these laws and regulations? Are not polluting chemicals so mobile that they are almost automatically of global concern, and thus not to be left to the discretion of certain user or producer nations? What obligations exist between highly developed technological countries and less developed countries regarding chemical pollution? Ought the global commons to be protected from chemical pollutants?

REFERENCES

1. *Principles for Evaluating Chemicals in the Environment* (Washington, D.C.: National Academy of Sciences, 1975), p. 36.
2. Behr, "Controlling Chemical Hazards," *Environment* 20 (July/Aug. 1978), p. 26.
3. M. Eisenbud, "Environmental Causes of Cancer," *Environment* 20 (Oct. 1978), p. 15. When epidemiologists write that 60 to 90 percent of all deaths from cancer can be attributed to environmental factors, they use the term *environment* broadly to include food, sunlight, alcohol, smoking, chemicals, and radiations to which individuals are exposed in the course of their occupations.
4. A. Fritsch, *The Contrasumers: A Citizen's Guide to Resource Conservation* (New York: Praeger Publishers, 1974), pp. 87–89.
5. *Principles for Evaluating Chemicals,* pp. 39–40.
6. Ibid., p. 23.
7. H. Green, "Cost-Risk-Benefit Assessment and the Law: Introduction and Perspective," *The George Washington Law Review* 45 (Aug. 1977), p. 901.
8. W. W. Lowrance, *Of Acceptable Risk: Science and the Determination of Safety* (Los Altos, Calif.: Wm. Kaufman, 1976), p. 78.
9. The U. S. Congress, Joint Committee on Atomic Energy, "Radiation Protection Criteria and Standards: Their Basis and Use," Summary-Analysis of Hearing, May 24–25 and June 1–3, 1960.
10. Lowrance, op. cit., p. 78.
11. National Commission on Product Safety, *Final Report* (Washington, D.C., 1970), p. 11.
12. "Environmental Mutagenic Hazards," Report of the Environmental Mutagen Society, Committee 17, *Science* 187 (1975), pp. 503–14.
13. B. L. Blaney, "Appalachian Energy Development: The Need for the Assessment and the Workshop" (Cincinnati: U. S. Environmental Protection Agency, 1979), pp. 6–7; also J. E. Armstrong and W. W. Harman, "Strategies for Conducting Technology Assessment," NSF Contract No. NSF-ERS-75-22788 (Dec. 1977).
14. H. Skolimowski, "Symposium on Technology Assessment," Philosophy of Science Association, Notre Dame University (Nov. 1974), as reported in *An Interdisciplinary Newsletter on Science, Technology, Public Policy and Society* (West Lafayette, Ind.: Purdue Univ., Sept. 1975), p. 10.
15. D. Johnson, "The Consumer and Public Decisions," Toxic Substance Conference, Washington, D.C. (Feb. 19–20), 1979.

16. "Rights and Responsibilities of Citizens," *Toxic Substances and Trade Secrecy*, Technical Information Project, Washington, D.C. (1977), p. 89. (These and the following references are condensations of the rights and responsibilities as drawn up at the Conference at Coolfont, W. Va.)
17. Ibid., p. 90.
18. Ibid., p. 91.
19. Ibid., p. 92.
20. *Final Report of the National Science Foundation Workshop Panel to Select Organic Compounds Hazardous to the Environment* (Washington, D.C.: National Science Foundation, Sept. 1975), p. 8.
21. "Rights and Responsibilities of Chemical Producers," *Toxic Substances and Trade Secrecy*, pp. 93–94.
22. Ibid., pp. 94–95.
23. "Rights and Responsibilities of Scientists and Engineers," *Toxic Substances and Trade Secrecy*, p. 97.
24. Ibid., P. Lombardo Subsequent Comments, p. 99.
25. A. J. Fritsch, "Societal Responsibilities of Chemists," *Legal Rights of Chemists and Engineers*, Advances in Chemistry Series 161, Meyer and Niederhauser, eds. (Washington, D.C.: American Chemical Society, 1977), pp. 82–90; see also A. C. Nixon, in ibid., pp. 54–66.
26. "Rights and Responsibilities of Governmental Agencies," *Toxic Substances and Trade Secrecy*, p. 103.

For Further Reading

A. B. Early. *Trade Secrets in Federal Environmental Law*. Master's thesis. George Washington University, Sept. 1973.
M. Juergensmeyer. "The Ethics of Secrecy." *Ethics and Policy*. Berkeley, Calif.: Center for Ethics and Policy Study, April 1976, p. 1.
Papers of a Seminar on Early Warning Systems for Toxic Substances. Washington, D.C.: Office of Toxic Substances, Environmental Protection Agency, July 1975.

V

GROWING DURING A
CONSERVATION ERA

> Earth provides enough to satisfy
> every man's need,
> but not every man's greed.
>
> Mohandas K. Gandhi

We endanger plants and animals, threaten future generations with nuclear materials, squander precious fossil fuel reserves, and poison ourselves with certain chemicals. We hear versions of "We have no other choice. How else can we grow and provide opportunities for all our citizens? How else can we fulfill our destiny? How else can we be faithful to the rich heritage of creativity, imagination, and ever-expanding frontiers? Growth has made us great. It is part of our Western genius."

Indeed, how else? That is the question of this chapter. If we are devoid of practical alternatives, then why is it unethical to continue our current growth practices? The cancer of modern material growth would continue and we would inevitably die. "Growth" at nearly any cost, the operative philosophy of our current system, our workplace, our universities, and even our churches, would continue unchecked.

However, ethics does not exist to confirm the status quo. Ethics deals with what is reasonable. Ethics raises fundamental questions about human actions that otherwise may be taken for granted. Ethics may raise further questions about whether or not this or that action is needed or necessary. Are the current risks to this earth worthwhile, or can alternatives be found that protect the environment? Can we not preserve the psychic urge to grow, and do so in a manner that will not threaten our earth and its inhabitants?

The problem of material growth can be examined under a number of aspects: its historical and cultural roots; difficulties arising in growth-oriented societies; a series of limited strategies for answering the material growth problem; and lastly, a preferred, ecologically sound strategy. What this means in our individual and collective lives will be discussed in the following chapter.

HISTORICAL AND CULTURAL BACKGROUND

An Overview of the United States

When European settlers came to these shores, they found a continent already inhabited. The native Americans, whom they mistakenly called Indians, lived at peace with the environment. Members of the various tribes and nations were born, lived, hunted, and died in the prairies, forests, and deserts of this vast landmass of North America, and yet the land they were wed to remained for the greater part unspoiled. These natives were in harmony with nature; they knew the woods, herbs, and animals; they had a reverence for all their fellow creatures, because the plants and animals that provided them with fibers, food, dyes, medicines, tools, and building materials were their friends and coinhabitants. The native Americans hunted for meat and skins, but realized they could not wantonly slaughter or endanger the species of their friends.

Native Americans were not purely hunters. In many regions, including the Great Lakes area and eastward into what is now New England, they cultivated the land, fertilizing it and harvesting a variety of crops not known to the Eastern Hemisphere: corn or maize, squash, pumpkin, tomatoes, and tobacco, to mention but a few. However, they did not exhaust the soil. Their footprints were tiptoes on sacred land. Nature continued to flourish.

Into this setting of relative ecological balance came the shiploads of white people from Europe: English, Scots, Irish, German, Dutch, French, Swedish, Spanish, Portuguese. On and on they came. These people stormed ashore with gun and ax and plow and private enterprise and notions of growth. Charters, land boundaries, property rights, and corporate profits—concepts unknown to the native American—became part of the American lifestyle. Surveying and recording land grants, purchases, and charters became important operations from the time of the earliest settlements.

Attitudes about the land and property were somewhat varied even among the colonists, for they espoused different religions and had different reasons for coming. From Maryland and Virginia through the Carolinas, tobacco lands merged with cotton, rice, and indigo plantations. The economy differed from that farther north or in the French and Spanish settlements. To produce these agricultural raw materials, cheap labor was needed, but the native American resisted, owing in part to a fierce sense of independence and the ability to withdraw from the coastal settlements. And so the slave trade was born and the galleys of human misery found their way, mainly to southern ports.

In the New England and neighboring coastal regions, small farms with mixed grains and vegetables and livestock prevailed. The people were not established planters but often those fleeing religious persecution. Northern settlers did, however, use slaves sometimes and more often indentured servants, but the latter generally gained their freedom after a number of years of work. The farms mostly stayed small, allowing the tillers a certain affinity with the soil. In the South, however, where the plantations and the labor force were large, a greater psychological distance from the soil resulted. Owners soon became indifferent to the place where they farmed as land became exhausted from intensive, unscientific farming. The soil eroded and the fields became bare. These plantation owners soon pulled up stakes and moved farther west into the seemingly endless interior territories. By the time of the Revolutionary War, sizable amounts of farmland along the Atlantic Seaboard were already abandoned, and the more venturesome pioneers were already crossing the Appalachians.

The end of the eighteenth century saw the movement westward in full swing. Independence had been won, and the new nation's national policy was one of expansion. It would not cease until the old Northwest Territory, the Louisiana Purchase, Texas, and California had felt the heavy foot of white America. Patterns of this migration were generally directed due west from coastal settlements, so that the ethnic and language characteristics of the Middle Atlantic States stretched first into Ohio, then into Indiana and Illinois. The single-crop, slave-holding farmers of Virginia and the Carolinas moved into Kentucky, Tennessee, and Alabama. Native Americans retreated before the onslaught, leaving history with such sorry pages as the trek of the Cherokee across the Mississippi. By 1820 woodsmoke had hung for a decade over these newly settled regions, as the early pioneers decimated the forest regions east of the Mississippi River.

By 1840 large numbers of settlers were crossing the Mississippi, entering into Texas—a newly independent nation—and moving across Missouri and Iowa to become the sodbusters of Kansas and Nebraska. Prairie flora disappeared under the steel plow. Settlers moved northwestward into Michigan, Wisconsin, and Minnesota, and the first covered wagons were being fitted for the long journey to the Oregon Territory. To Americans, growth meant leaving a previous settlement for virgin territory. And the resistance of native Americans only made the adventure more enticing.

Over the period of a century and a half from the founding of the Republic, concepts of growth broadened to reflect America's transformation from a rural to an industrial society. Inventions in both America and Europe in the early nineteenth century of the reaper, steam engine, cotton gin, and steel plow gave settlement a more industrial flavor. The first birth pangs of industry in the post-revolutionary years saw the advent of the steamboat and railroad. Waterfalls offered cheap power for cotton and textile mills in such towns as Springfield, Massachusetts, and Paterson and New Brunswick, New Jersey. The mills were hungry, and so were the dispossessed of Europe; thus waves of immigrants came from Europe. Husbands, wives, and even children were pressed into dawn-to-dusk work in these factories, leaving social scars on this land.

Railroads and canals stretched westward to handle the flood of people and goods. With the Civil War, the most bloody of American conflicts, heavy industry expanded. After the conflict, railroad tracks and telegraph wires networked the whole country. Perhaps no expansion had a greater ecological price than that of the railroads, as native Americans were subdued and driven into out-of-the-way reservations on the Great Plains and in the western desert regions. Their main native food source, the buffalo, was nearly exterminated from the Dakotas to Texas.

As the industrial age progressed, mechanization, irrigation, and commercial fertilizers transformed growth concepts from mere land acquisition to increased yields per acre per farmer. But such growth was not without a price. Bankruptcies, bank failures, soil erosion, and later dust bowls became familiar events in the history of American expansion.

Fuels also underwent change. Wood, which was bulky, becoming more expensive, and of varied quality, was being replaced in the late nineteenth century by coal for industry and transportation. Coal would soon have to share its glory with petroleum and then natural gas. These fossil fuels became the raw-materials base for a new chemical industry after German sources were cut off during the First World War. Coal mines and oil wells proliferated and became the keystones of a new growth philosophy. The invention of the airplane and mass production of the automobile added to fuel needs as these items in turn became the instruments of an ever more mobile America. Speed and mechanical efficiency became primary values; communications grew easier; travel passed from a burden or adventure to a leisure pastime.

During America's first two hundred years the concept of growth itself was transformed. At first, growth meant simply territorial growth, but as the Pacific shores were reached and homestead tracts were exhausted in the interior, growth became economic—the acquisition of goods by individuals and corporations, and an expanding national economy. Rural America was now industrial. Growth was defined by tons of plastics, steel, and rubber, by numbers of autos produced, by miles of new highway, and by numbers of power plants constructed. The American appetite looked outward from our shores, first to Alaska and Hawaii, then to the lands taken from Spain, then to distant undeveloped regions of Africa and Latin America.

From the start of the nation, no one questioned whether growth was good and necessary. A vast fertile and unlimited land presented no foreseeable limits to growth. But that growth has almost always been associated with quantitative measures: first with territorial expansion and growth of population, later with miles of railroad and tons of steel, and now with technological sophistication and salary levels. This is tangible, measurable growth, easy to point to and easy to celebrate. However, some less recognized qualitative growth trends paralleled quantitative growth: extension of voting privileges to blacks and women; public education opportunities for all children; better health and welfare systems; growing ease of communication through telephone, radio, and television. Through this qualitative growth we are beginning to realize that frontiers are conquered and domestic resources are limited.

From the early nineteenth century a few thoughtful Americans saw excessive expansion and its side effects as often undesirable. Such naturalist-romantic writers as Thoreau, Emerson, and John Muir presented a love for nature untouched or preserved from the frenetic activity of fellow citizens. The shock of the near-extinction of the buffalo and destruction of natural habitats led people like Theodore Roosevelt to advocate wildlife conservation and national park and forest lands. In the 1930s soil conservationists sought to halt the spreading dust bowls. Of a less naturalistic tone, the movement toward conservation of human resources—improved health, education, child care, labor conditions, and sanitation; the stress on human rights; and the interest in organic and health foods—and toward protection of the consumer added to the crosscurrents of opposition to an unreflecting growth "ethic." Rachel Carson's *Silent Spring* focused attention on what increased use of commercial pesticides has done to our environment. All of these countermovements and critics added to a mosaic of opposition that would gather enough momentum in the 1970s to arouse widespread questioning of America's growth. A deeper look at the roots of Western civilization might help us obtain a more balanced view of this growth in an age of scarcity.

Cultural Roots of Growth

Many cultural anthropologists locate the antecedents of the predominant growth philosophy of our culture in the Old Testament of the Bible. Primitive societies have, with few exceptions, viewed time as endlessly repeating cycles. For them, human history was a yearly reenactment of patterns set by the gods—annual fertility cycles, bird migrations, changes of seasons, lengthening and shortening of days, and so on. The cycle of human life, from birth to death, repeated itself over and over. A culture could hardly progress; it simply was as it had always been. Social change was scarcely recognized; nor was human responsibility for caring for the earth as such. Human cycles followed natural cycles, and harmony was to be passive before nature's forces. Nothing was new under the sun.

But Israel and its culture were unique. It was a nation going somewhere. Yahweh's people were part of a covenant and destination. For them time was linear—directional. They *became* a special or chosen people who give direction to their world by free choices. Christianity also grew up with these concepts, calling upon people to bring about a "Kingdom of God" on earth, meaning a society marked by faith, justice, and love. It was an imperfect world that could be, if not perfected, steadily improved. The good news of this development was to go out to all people throughout the world. The ideal of improvement is in origin and aim fundamentally religious.

While this Judeo-Christian tradition has, with some justice, been accused of being too otherworldly, it does attempt to teach people a responsibility for developing this earth. It does not escape or flee from earthly needs, but in its liturgy, reflection on doctrine (incarnation, redemption, resurrection), and emphasis on good works, it attests to the dignity and continued worth of human beings *and* the human habitat—the earth. Thus, ironically, the same tradition which has been accused of being too otherworldly is also accused of being too worldly, because of the present and future aspects of its belief.

Western civilization, which is founded within the Judeo-

Christian tradition, has undergone periods of stagnation and hibernation. When spring came, it would be almost imperceptible, and few noticed the light becoming stronger. It took centuries for people to sense change on more than an individual level. But the printing press, new expressions of art, more sophisticated weaponry, and tales from distant lands all had their effect. People were beginning to stir and recognize growth within their own ranks. With the Renaissance, and more so with the period of the scientific revolution, the idea of human beings as systematic agents of progress took deeper root. The philosophers of the Enlightenment believed nature's laws were finally uncovered. They thought it possible to reconstruct rationally a natural and fully human social order according to conceivably perfect universal laws. It was an exciting concept that gave birth, to give just one example, to the U. S. Constitution as a sort of social analog to Newton's laws of motion.

But the Enlightenment's scientists and political architects had to share the age with others more bent on controlling than on understanding nature. These found allies in a rising middle class imbued with the capitalistic ethos of competitiveness, rugged individualism, and economic efficiency. There was also the other offspring of the Enlightenment: the process of industrialization, and its stepchild, big industry. Early industrialization was characterized by laissez-faire capitalism, or classical liberalism.[1] Here the principal manufacturing nations fashioned a labor-intensive technology with accompanied severe exploitation of the working people, and kept governmental regulation or provision of social services to a minimum. A network of European colonies to supply abundant, inexpensive raw materials was developed over three centuries. This industrialization matured into a corporate-dominated, social-welfare type of capitalism with advanced technology, different capital/labor balance, workers' movements, and increased governmental regulations. The less-developed countries became both sources for cheap raw materials and new markets for finished products.

In the current stage, industrialization has spread from its original center in the North Atlantic nations to the Second and even some Third World countries. The multinational corporations of the second stage of industrialization are now faced with a competitive nationalism that seeks to bend First World transnational capitalism to the purposes of the host country. The ruthless competition that was the hallmark of laissez-faire capitalism has been revived on a worldwide scale. What corporations were to the domestic market, large transnational companies are to the global market.

Growth in quantitative terms is certainly not an exclusively American phenomenon. Many industrial nations are driven by the notion of advances in GNP, material production, and maximization of profit. It is commonly assumed that wants and resources are boundless and thus production should continue growing ad infinitum, with technology making up for any unforeseen resource discrepancies.

Industrial growth has helped spawn a social and cultural setting of ambivalent quality. On the positive side, scientific and technological advances have enabled sizable numbers of people in advanced countries to lead affluent lives. On the other hand, material affluence has come at the price of significant depletion of nonrenewable resources and a deterioration of the quality of environment and life. Industrialization and transnational capitalism has led to exploitation of our earth. The young American republic provided a laboratory for testing Enlightenment concepts. For some people the experiment was successful; for others—especially those outside the system—it meant harder times. American progress became synonymous with quantitative growth. An inflated GNP became the sign of our society's health, along with rising per capita income and energy consumption. Few asked, however, whether quantitative growth corresponded to quality of life.

MATERIAL GROWTH PAINS

Our lifestyle individually and collectively is characterized by conspicuous consumption, extravagant waste, widespread pollution and extensive destruction of natural resources. Economic growth is almost axiomatic in our nation with the false assumption that more consumption is necessary to fuel the nation's economic engine and continuous growth. In a society where success is usually equated with wealth, and access to "the good life" is dependent upon wealth, gross inequalities develop. It is the poor and middle class citizens of our nation who increasingly bear the burdens of unplanned economic growth. It is they who feel the widening gap between excessive consumption by the few and poverty of the many.

"The Moral Demands of the Energy Crisis"
National Council of Churches, December 14, 1973

Limited Resources

There's no denying it. Our vision of the world's future is in flux, and, with it, our vision of the growth needed to bring us to a desired future. Two decades ago an entertaining exercise consisted of conjuring up the technological paradise of A.D. 2050—vast concrete and steel skyscrapers, automated high-speed transportation, moving sidewalks, personal helicopters, holiday weekends on the moon, robots doing household work, twenty-hour work weeks and plentiful leisure. These imaginings were quite in tune with trends of the previous century, such as the doubling of electrical energy consumption every twelve years. But such growth cannot continue indefinitely, for reasons that are also the ones which make these visions outdated.

This is certainly true of population growth. Finite availability of food, natural resources, and living space suggest that the earth cannot sustain a continually increasing population. World population has recently been doubling every thirty-five years. Even if zero-population-growth policies were accepted, the human family would continue increasing for several generations because of lowered death rates. And mere high birth rates and decreased death rates are not the only points to focus on. There is no uniform international population policy, even though Western nations have generally encouraged decreased birth rates. In fact, in Germany and several European countries death rates are now higher than the birth levels. On the other hand, many Third World nations feel that population control coupled with a continued status quo of the international economic order poses a dire threat to already oppressed peoples. These nations insist that for population control to be acceptable it must be joined by a radical reorganization of economic and political power.

Shortages of readily available fossil fuels are evident (see Chapter III). Shortages of minerals such as lead, manganese, and tin will also become a serious problem by the year 2000. We may not be actually running out of these minerals as such, but rather running out of high-grade ore deposits that can be mined conveniently. Unlike fossil fuel resources, mineral resources will generally remain plentiful, but at higher costs since energy prices, to which mineral extraction costs are directly related, will continue ballooning. Thus the combination of rising worldwide demand with dwindling cheap resources will require a fundamental rethinking of mineral use.

Finally, the earth's biosphere has a limited capacity to assimilate the waste products of all processes. While the normal working of the system may exceed natural limits in isolated instances, for the most part the biosystem can handle its wastes. Human beings, though, have the ability to disregard the limits of this natural self-renewal process and to pollute the system with excess and nonbiodegradable waste products. Pressures from increased human consumption of material goods increase the probability that these natural limits will be exceeded.

Global and Domestic Injustice

The dimensions of today's environmental crisis make it truly a world problem, not confined just to industrialized nations with their air and water pollutants. This is both because air and water pollutants are mobile and because a major element of the environmental crisis is the global problem of resource depletion. The poor, who have contributed least to creating the crisis, suffer its consequences most severely. The rich make the world's problems and the poor pay for them.

Western patterns of overconsumption have global effects, for there is a competition for the limited raw materials—and the poorer nations come out on the shorter end. This extends to manufactured goods as well. Rising fertilizer prices reflect rising oil prices, and some poorer countries can no longer afford even the limited fertilizer that they have used in previous years. Some 15 percent of American commercial fertilizer demand is for lawns and golf courses. This practice exacerbates the cost problems for fertilizer- and food-short Third World countries. In the area of food consumption, the more affluent Western appetite for grain-fed beef and other meat leads to greater competition for limited grain on the world market, and so the poor can afford less for the essentials of life. The examples go on and on.

In the beginning of this century when international economics was less understood, many thought that developed lands aided the underdeveloped when advancing their own cause. The Western world would get its raw materials and produce consumer products, and the Third World would get business and new employment opportunities. However, there were serious flaws. Third World prime agricultural land is diverted from essential food crops to cotton, tobacco, coffee, and rubber for export to the developed nations. Hotels are more for tourists than for inhabitants. Showcase steel mills and high technology were ill suited to the economies of the Third World. Overall, the lack of good planning has forced an exodus of much-needed capital from poorer to richer lands.

Unchecked material growth may likewise cause serious injustice to the domestic population. Industry in the West has sought to substitute energy for jobs,[2] so that the only way the total number of employees could increase would be by increased demand or expansion. The major energy-producing and consuming sectors of the U.S. industrial economy consume one third of the nation's energy and directly provide only about one tenth of the jobs. To counteract job losses entailed by adoption of energy-intensive laborsaving devices, the economy has had to expand. This growth has come at the expense of environmental deterioration and human health costs, increased energy consumption, job loss through automation, and the sustaining of a vicious circle. This automation has drained the capital market of funds that might otherwise have been directed to expanding the service sector.

"Ecojustice" has been denied in the cycle just mentioned.

Energy-intensive industries say they are unable to release funds toward meeting environmental protection standards, and threaten to close or curtail production in the face of increased enforcement. Environmentalists are convinced that job-loss threats and regulatory foot-dragging are red herrings and diversions from the more fundamental structural problems associated with an energy- and capital-intensive economy. Again, the critical curbing of excessive energy use would go a long way toward improving air and water quality.

Increased consumer goods do not guarantee higher quality of life, but instead may even lead to deterioration through increased wastes and resource depletion. No other culture ever moved about as much as ours or, ironically, spent so much time getting about. While mobility has salutary effects, it diverts much physical and psychic energy and money to travel expenses. While mobility can acquaint us with other places, E. F. Schumacher points out how excessive mobility makes people footloose, tends to separate them from essential commitments to communities and places, and leads to a progressive and harmful urbanization of the human population.[3] We can overlook the richness or poverty of the local neighborhood because we are never there when needed. Human relations require time to build, and local communities require citizen participation. Thus we may both move about and be in place, and yet give each its proper time.

Just as we can limit our travel, so can we be satisfied with limiting the varieties of consumer products. Supermarkets and refrigerated freight give us out-of-season "necessities" such as winter tomatoes shipped three thousand miles from farm to market; when they arrive they are fleshy, hard, and bland and hardly resemble their summer cousins. Supermarkets contain 10,000 items today versus 4,000 thirty years ago. More real consumer choices? Not always, when 25 corn breakfast cereals simply differ in color, shape, and amount of sugar. Human-intensive practices, however, often find and promote authentic variety through spices and herbs, creative textile and furniture design, and a variety of games and home entertainment.

Overuse of resources is both cause and effect of insecurity.

Goods acquired for use must be stored and made secure, and this defense of private or national store soon becomes a primary preoccupation. People are diverted from basic values. This problem accelerates the drive to obtain the money needed to maintain these goods. It thus weakens willpower, loosens social relationships, reduces time spent with and for others, and turns people into objects of productivity. It makes the striver egocentric and inclines to shunt aside the "worthless" members of society—the ill, the elderly, the retarded, the poor. Overconsumers become overworked, devoid of spiritual practice, tense, and insensitive. Sharing gives way to selfishness and greed; silence and relaxation, to hyperactivity and mobility.

An Overdeveloped Society

Booming consumption of material goods has supported growth in a variety of technologies and professional support personnel bent on creating the new frontiers. Such skilled professionals as aeronautical and nuclear engineers have been trained for certain sophisticated technologies (such as space travel or breeder reactors) that may not be realized. American urban centers such as Seattle, Wichita, and Boston have large numbers of overqualified but unneeded technicians and professional people educated and trained for jobs that did not materialize.

Our society is overdeveloped not only in terms of excessive production and consumption, but also through misdirecting valuable human resources. Little creativity is shown today in reorienting people to areas of services where both technical and human skills and experience can be properly utilized. An unemployed or underemployed person is a wasted valuable resource. Unemployment is degrading to the person in such a situation; it shows a wasted educational opportunity; it breeds discontent and resentment and offers no positive alternatives. The technocratic production economy cares little for the human side of life and is blinded to the tragedies of the overqualified.

One can die from either thirst or drowning, from want or excess. Maintaining sophisticated gadgets means higher pollution costs, waste disposal problems, repair bills, and greater worries about damage and theft. Affluence leads to a high incidence of obesity, drug addiction, alcoholism, highway fatalities, and poisonings.

Superabundance does not lead to utopias—witness the social ills of the affluent nations. It allures many people struggling for the necessities of life, it enthralls the wealthy, it beckons the middle class; but it does not guarantee a better quality of life.

EVOLVING STRATEGIES

The very notions of "equilibrium" in economics and ecology are antithetical. In macroeconomics "equilibrium" refers not to physical magnitudes at all, but to a balance of desires between savers and investors—equilibrium means full employment at a stable price level. This implies, under current institutions, a positive flow of new investment to offset positive savings. Net investment implies increasing stocks and a growing throughput—i.e., a biophysical *dis*equilibrium. Physical boundaries guaranteeing reasonable ecological equilibrium must be imposed on the market in quantitative terms.

Herman E. Daly
Toward a Steady-State Economy

In response to the problems of excessive material growth a variety of strategies have been proposed. The variety reflects the seriousness of the problem, the global extent of its impact, and the diversity of philosophies at work on the question. Many of these offer some promise of solving one or other aspect of the total problem; no single solution offered can remedy the pervasive ill-effects of what E. J. Mishan calls "the cornucopia of burgeoning indices."

Population Limitation

Population limitation is often the first solution proposed, for it is widely recognized that the earth has a limited ability to serve an ever-expanding human population. Some areas of the world where the income is not properly distributed face continuation of high birth rates and overpopulation problems, regardless of how fast their economies grow. On the other hand, in China, Taiwan, Sri Lanka, and Malaysia, where income distribution has become more equalized, birth rates have dropped dramatically over the past two decades.[4] Aggressive birth control programs without better distribution of wealth are not panaceas for growth-related problems.

Affluent nations often favor voluntary methods of family planning, both because of their own stabilizing populations and their libertarian cultural heritage. However, these methods are seen by a radicalizing Third World as requiring few sacrifices for the affluent, and as self-righteous finger-pointing (see Appendix III).

Recent hopeful signs of population stabilization have appeared, with world population rates dropping from an annual increase of 2.0 percent in 1966 to 1.9 percent in 1976.[5] However, those overly concerned at absolute growth of human populations must realize that population is one of a spectrum of interrelated issues arising from the economic and political realities accompanying material growth. While the affluent often feel threatened by the rising Third World demands, the most viable solution must include disassembling the structures that deny the world's poor control over their own destiny. This needs to be coupled with some form of economic stability so that the poor do not feel obliged to bear numerous offspring as insurance against an uncertain old age. Population limitation and social ecological balance go hand in hand.

Consumption Limitations

A modification to mandating population limitations for expanding Third World nations is to couple population curbs with a limitation on consumption of goods in the more wealthy nations. This approach avoids Western chauvinism and latent racism. However, minority groups within affluent countries are threatened by across-the-board consumption limitations, which would lock them into permanent economic inferiority. This could be avoided, however, through rationing programs that penalize unnecessary consumption (such as gasoline rationing severely limiting use by recreational vehicles and motor boats, private air travel, and heavy automobiles). Special financial allocations may be made during periods of readjustment for the poorer portion of the population.

Redistribution of Wealth

The poor cannot improve their lot with restrained material growth coupled with a political status quo. Either they will have to remain resigned to a permanent inferior economic position in society, or else they will have to fight for a redistribution of the finite wealth. Once aware of their power, the poor will no longer be satisfied with crumbs. They will want to sit at the banquet table as equals. Knowing that their cause is just, they will seek their goal of equality by either violent or peaceful routes. For the sake of all, one strategy proposes redistribution schemes such as graduated taxation or governmental subsidies, loans, or grants to the poor. No lasting redistribution of wealth is possible without substantial sharing of control over wealth-generating institutions.

Reordering Production

Another strategy that attempts to meet the weaknesses of some previous ones is to curb excessive production through strict regulations and expand world production of essential materials to meet people's legitimate basic demands. Population limitation would be deemphasized and consumption of goods in Third World countries recognized as necessary. Without new social and economic restraints, however, consumption would only continue to rise. The practicality of such a strategy taken alone is questionable. World resources could be depleted if curbs remain unenacted, with the poor remaining poor and the rich continuing their excessive consumption. Water shortages, land misuse, deforestation, and fossil fuel depletion would only accelerate.

Purchase Time

A fifth strategy does not question existing consumption levels so much as stress a movement to environmentally sound energy sources and methods such as active and passive solar, wind, and biomass. But a massive conversion to such forms and practices may include some untackled environmental, political, and economic problems. Institutional barriers are formidable. The business establishment may show little interest; the government is slow to provide sufficient fiscal support, although some say that with governmental support these so-called exotic energy sources would be commercially viable in a few years.[6]

Confusion exists about whether or not these alternative technologies can sufficiently complement the existing mix of energy-producing sources, and whether or not they are compatible with the "growth ethic" itself. Will they be accepted by a public mesmerized by traditional fuels? Will they require an expensive incentive program? Will sufficient capital be released to develop these alternative technologies? And if so, will the reordering of investment priorities make it possible to expand the service sector, and thus available jobs? Finally, is the move to alternative energy sources merely to purchase time so that the current high rates of consumption may be maintained?

One rationale behind the "purchase time" strategy is that the alternative technologies will become part of the mix of existing technologies. They will allow current energy-use rates to continue, but slow down resource depletion until some new technological "savior" such as fusion appears. Another rationale is that these alternative technologies are meaningful only if accompanied by basic changes in the social and economic structures.

To propose any of these strategies alone risks an infatuation with their promise that ignores technical and institutional shortcomings and realities. Human population continues to grow; consumption of energy-intensive goods climbs; wealth remains in the hands of a few; reserves dwindle; and capital needed for alternative technologies is in short supply. Time purchased without fundamental changes in consumption patterns is of relatively short duration. This philosophy simply postpones the day of reckoning a few years.

From the advantages and shortcomings of the above five strategies it seems that an ideal "growth" policy must both account for real human needs and be conscious of environmental demands. Such a policy must:

* be able to work now, given the human condition and the urgent need for action;

* help promote human labor as a fulfilling occupation;

* be joined by an equitable distribution of its costs and benefits;

* respect both the human and physical environment through reduced resource depletion and pollution;

* be mindful of the psychic, social, and spiritual as well as the physical needs of citizens

PREFERRED STRATEGY: A MOVE TOWARD QUALITATIVE GROWTH

We must change, not only our habits, but some of our most fundamental assumptions and beliefs.

Carol and John Steinhart
The Fires of Culture[7]

Visions of the Future

Growing is part of being human; it is part of being alive. Clearly, alternative concepts of the future cannot imply no growth at all. The thought of a changeless social and economic order is repugnant to men and women of the twentieth century because they sense they can create more-just social structures and enrich human existence. We can never say of our world, "It is perfect; we are completely satisfied."

Growth is value-laden. Desirable growth is not random change; it is directed to the future; it is personal, incorporating the hopes and aspirations of the one growing or directing growth. Every one of us has a vision of a future that is more or less global or individual, formalized or naïve, revolutionary or conservative, selfish or other-oriented.

A question worth considering is whether or not we are at a historic moment similar to the beginning of the scientific or industrial revolutions, when the collective human vision of the future receives fundamental redirection. Few observers deny the limited aspects of traditional energy sources; all recognize influences at work—but there agreement ends. Just what can rescue us? Technological optimists like Buckminster Fuller, Herman Kahn, and Edward Teller think technology can extricate us from problems faster than it creates them. On the other hand, E. F. Schumacher, Barry Commoner, and René Dubos believe that an incautious technology must be countered by nontechnical inputs.

Technological optimists place faith in the tools of human beings. The miracles of science will continue, they believe. They are at home with engineering competence, computer techniques, automation. Some of them conceive of nuclear power as the genie in Aladdin's lamp, a powerful and obedient servant when commanded by prudent scientists. They are convinced that scientists are unbiased and above the allurements of subjectivity.

Ecological realists, on the other hand, place their hopes in energy conservation, decentralized technologies, smaller and more responsive social structures, nonutilitarian education, and labor-intensive operations. They realize human limitations, including those of scientists. They are more likely to remember the story of the sorcerer's apprentice, whose experience showed that incomplete knowledge is dangerous. The apprentice knows the proper magic formula to get his broom-servant to draw and carry water, but is fuzzy on how to stop it. Knowing human limitations, ecological realists are more prone to proceed with caution, even when it delays some form of technological advance for a period of time.

We cannot deny that modern science and technology have wrought genuine benefits. But technology is not neutral. It depends on the values of its controllers—the scientists, politicians, and businesspeople whose visions of the future are limited. Realists are more aware of such limitations as the undeveloped condition of the new science "ecology," which does not yet grasp how the ecosystem's complex interrelationships work. Mindful of the limits of science and technology, we must steer a growth policy with caution.

Toward a Steady-state Economy

Many production inputs are drawn from nonrenewable resources; the by-products of this production must eventually be returned to the environment. Ecology describes limits beyond which the environment cannot tolerate these processes and still sustain itself. Disdain for the limits results in increasing depletion of resources and pollution of the environment. All social, economic, and cultural subsystems, as part of the ecosystem, must conform to these physical constraints and limits. This perspective has precipitated the notion of "steady-state" systems.[8]

Steady-state is fundamentally a thermodynamic concept, referring to the maintenance of a system by the interplay of certain chemical and physical forces. Here the concept is applied to economics and refers to a constant stock of people and a constant stock of physical capital. The *stocks* are maintained by a rate of renewal—birth and production—equal to the rate of expiration—death and consumption. This equilibrium of relatively common stocks can occur with either a high rate of *throughput* (movement) or a low one. For the population stock, a low rate of throughput—low birth rate and low death rate—means a high life expectancy. For the capital or wealth stock, a low rate of throughput—low production and low consumption—means longer lifetime or durability of goods. This should imply not only a long life of serviceability, but also ease in recycling (some goods such as single-metal containers are easier to recycle than bimetallic ones). It would appear that a low rate of throughput is preferable because fewer resources are needed and more can be reused with less effort and energy.

The throughput of stock helps produce *services* that satisfy human wants. Services represent benefits; throughput required for maintenance eventually results in costs of depletion and pollution. Herman Daly describes a relationship between these variables:

$$\frac{\text{Service}}{\text{Throughput}} = \frac{\text{Service}}{\text{Stock}} \times \frac{\text{Stock}}{\text{Throughput}}$$

The service/stock ratio measures *service efficiency* and is maximized by increasing services and decreasing the amount of stock used. The stock/throughput ratio measures *maintenance efficiency* and is maximized by lowering the throughput.[9] The ultimate efficiency of the system is measured by the service/throughput ratio.

Maintenance efficiencies are limited because everything

eventually wears out. On the other hand, it is possible for service efficiencies to increase indefinitely. The "production" of service is not achieved only through the consumption of goods; it is also a function of human creativity and intelligence—both "renewable" resources capable of fueling qualitative growth. As George Harrar, president of the Rockefeller Foundation, has stated:

> Our resources are not limitless, and when those that are non-renewable are consumed or transformed, they can never be replenished. . . . More attention should be devoted to services and to those areas of life that enrich the quality of human existence; cultural activities . . . , aesthetic improvements and human relationships.[10]

In a steady-state economy a low throughput places more emphasis on distribution than on flow of capital. The argument that everyone should be satisfied with increasing shares of an ever-growing wealth pie falls apart, for in a steady-state system the stock of wealth tends to be constant. An unequal distribution of wealth, given a constant total stock, is more difficult to justify. As Daly states, "The steady-state would make fewer demands on our environmental resources, but much greater demands on our moral resource."[11] He adds that if the steady-state system is to be any more equitable than the growth-oriented one, it must affirm the right of all to self-determination and access to resources necessary for a basic fulfilling existence. This affirmation requires citizen participation and community control of decentralized economic systems.

The ecological and human costs of a low throughput are related to the types of technology used. Large-scale, energy-intensive technologies that facilitate high rates of production and consumption cannot lead to a low rate of throughput. More important, these megatechnologies invariably disrupt the environment, human and otherwise.

A frequent question voiced today is how to make machines fit people, instead of making people conform to machines, as in current large-scale technologies. To answer this, the concept of *appropriate technology* (AT) has emerged. It is a technology responsive to the needs of ordinary people and suitable for a given operation or goal. AT makes human and environmental needs—not machines—the starting point for technical and economic discussion. It assumes that work is humanistic and a fulfillment in one's life. It generally—but not always—will be more localized, more labor-intensive, more decentralized, more apt to utilize renewable resources.

AT says that a rice farmer in Southeast Asia need not employ a 100-horsepower electric pump that is expensive and consumes oil. Nor should an urban dweller use electricity from nuclear power when much is wasted through inefficiencies. A more efficient waterwheel or an installed solar water heater are forms of technology that are more appropriate and respectful of human welfare and the environment. Movement toward AT is much more compatible with the ideal of low throughput than an overreliance on conventional large-scale technology. Many workers do not benefit from automation, restricted capital, or overly sophisticated technologies. Quite often their jobs are characterized as drudgery, boring and alienating, and all sense of fulfillment and satisfaction has evaporated—but these are the fortunate ones; the rest are too unskilled to find work in the limited field.

Appropriate technology is most often spoken of with respect to developing countries that attempt to imitate high-technology economies. But AT is also needed in the so-called developed countries as well. Our homes waste enormous amounts of heat. One remedy is to adapt "passive" building designs that use solar energy naturally, contain little mechanical hardware, require little or no energy themselves, and tend to be low in cost.[12] A number of techniques are suggested with approximate savings estimated: flexible ceiling partitions, zoned heating, solar window shutters, earth berm to windowsill or to roof eave, circular floor plan to conserve exterior wall area, orientation for natural ventilation, use of an atrium or south-facing glass façade.

Other AT techniques which are being developed or which make use of time-tested procedures from our past are found in food preparation and preservation (sun-drying, salting, and cool storage techniques), farming and gardening (composting, natural pesticides, greenhouses and hot beds), and clothing and consumer product use and reuse (textile choice, recycling of containers). In the areas of transportation and fuel use, AT can result in substantial savings.

A steady-state system emphasizes increased services in place of goods. For instance, more automobile repair work should be encouraged in place of new cars, to make them last longer and keep them operating. An improved quality of services from waiting table to tailoring would add a touch of humanness to our lives. Service-oriented economies continue to require the production of goods (education needs textbooks, medicine needs hospital supplies, environmental control needs detectors), but the quantity of these goods would be far less than in a goods-oriented economy like our own. In aiming for a middle way between materialistic heedlessness and traditional immobility we can, as Schumacher reminds us, discover a path of "right livelihood."[13] Such a path certainly must include AT techniques and emphasize human services in place of goods.

Equitable access to resources by all peoples is a prerequisite to stabilizing population growth rates. This accessibility may be better gained and preserved by means of a service-oriented, steady-state economy using AT principles of humanness, local control, and resource conservation. It is hoped that some of the human and environmental problems associated with material growth systems can then be reduced.

Guidelines to Ensure Qualitative Growth

According to Herman Daly, a major, though often neglected, criterion for evaluating an economic system is whether the system can adapt to the constraints imposed by environmental and human limitations. The economies of many Western nations certainly have not respected the integrity of the environment; in fact, the ability to draw upon the environment at little or no realized cost has contributed to an ever-increasing flow of goods and wastes. Nor have these economies as such respected people, who are often regarded as somewhat unnecessary and to be shunted aside when unprofitable.

The human desire to grow is not wrong, if properly

directed. The insatiable desire to become something more, to move forward, to strive beyond the present state is what drives explorers, scientists, and dreamers alike. St. Augustine calls it the basic quest for God. It is the hunger that is not satisfied in our present state of life. To fail to see the spiritual dimensions of this desire and, instead, to convert this quest into an insatiable appetite for material growth is self-destructive. The thrust should not be to restrict or discourage the human quest through growth, but to channel it properly. This is both challenge and risk, but one worth it if the positive good is the qualitative growth of the human species.

John Maynard Keynes states that the real *absolute* needs are those that can be satisfied. It is the *relative* needs based on "keeping up with the Joneses" or our materialistic whims that are materially insatiable. Attempts to satisfy nonessential *wants* on a material plane leads to a concatenation of more material wants far beyond the endurance of our environment and natural resources. We are experiencing, not just individuals, but entire peoples and nations with these materialistic drives.

The reflective environmentalist is challenged to convert whole peoples from material to more qualitative—spiritual, cultural, artistic, intellectual, human-care—wants, and thus channel the urge to grow into more personal and humanly fulfilling ways. In so doing, fewer natural resources will be expended, for it takes far fewer tons of steel and tons of coal to do artistic work than to build cars. More material things will be available for those needing basic essentials, and the redistribution of resources will lessen the demands for military defense and security services, which are heavy material consumers.

The challenge to growthmania demands a reordering of our social priorities, for it has supported the status quo of unequal wealth distribution. Have-nots have been led to believe that through harder work all can share in the wealth flow. By directing attention to this flow—however trivial—the wealthy have salved their own consciences and distracted the dispossessed.

An awakening consciousness among dispossessed peoples makes it harder to justify the practice of maximizing wealth flow. Henceforth, the insatiable appetite of human beings must be redirected away from territorial, population, material, and power growth to the drive for human rights, literacy and education, cultural and artistic advantages—in short to all that enhances social interrelationships. From what has been said, a general principle can be set forth:

Maximize social interrelationships and minimize physical resource expenditure.

The second part of the principle gives a conservationist no difficulty, but the first part might. For maximizing social interrelationships seems to fly in the face of strivings toward local control and self-sufficiency. However, to enhance one's education or expand one's vision need not be to the detriment of the locality. In fact, it may foster the drive to develop local controls in areas where technologies are less than human or more resource-intensive. Self-sufficiency in material resources is laudable, for it takes fewer resources to produce food or extract fuel close to home. But in our ever-shrinking world it is not better to isolate ourselves from others' concerns in the name of self-sufficiency and independence. Instead, we should become concerned about their own self-sufficiency in resources—and that is better done by expanding our communication, education, and political involvement (our "socialization").

To help find out whether this principle works in our own lives, a number of questions might be in order:

* Do we accept our limitations whether physical or psychological, whether our tools, our abilities, or our resources?
* At the same time, do we see our goals, our ideals, our strivings, and our desires as unlimited?
* Do we respect the right of people to control their own lives and work, and see the duty of society to be the employer of last resort?
* Do we see the need to determine how much damage has been caused by excessive material growth and who is to pay proper retribution?
* Do we see the need to foster a growth of human rights?

* Are we willing to participate in improving services for the elderly, infirm, and retarded, and in expanding adult and special educational privileges?

* Are basic foods available in our community at very low cost to the poor?

198   GROWING DURING A CONSERVATION ERA

REFERENCES

1. J. Holland, "Labor Day Reflections," *Center Focus* (Washington, D.C.: Center of Concern, Spring 1977), p. 1.
2. R. Grossman and G. Danker, *Jobs and Energy* (Washington, D.C.: Environmentalists for Full Employment, 1977), pp. 1–4.
3. E. F. Schumacher, *Small Is Beautiful* (New York: Harper and Row, 1973), pp. 138 ff.
4. Louisville *Courier-Journal*, Feb. 15, 1978.
5. Census Bureau report quoted in release by Ann Blackman of Associated Press, Nov. 20, 1978.
6. B. Commoner, address to 1977 Rural America Conference, Washington, D.C. (Dec. 6, 1977).
7. C. and J. Steinhart, *The Fires of Culture: Energy Yesterday and Today* (North Scituate, Mass.: Duxbury Press, 1974), p. 5.
8. H. Daly, Introduction to *Toward a Steady-State Economy*, H. Daly, ed. (San Francisco: W. H. Freeman, 1973), pp. 14–19.
9. H. Daly, "Steady-State Economy" testimony given in hearings before the Joint Economic Committee, U. S. Congress, Washington, D.C., 1976.
10. G. Harrar, as reported in *The End of the American Future*, P. Schrag, ed. (New York: Simon & Schuster, 1973), p. 353.
11. Daly, *Toward a Steady-State Economy*, pp. 14–19.
12. "Passive Design Ideas for the Energy Conscious Consumer" (Rockville, Md.: The National Solar Heating and Cooling Information Center, 1978), p. 2.
13. Schumacher, op. cit., pp. 256 ff.

For Further Reading

E. and D. Dodson-Gray and W. F. Martin. *Growth and Its Implications for the Future.* Branford, Conn.: The Dinosaur Press, 1975.
E. J. Mishan. *Technology and Growth: The Price We Pay.* New York: Praeger, 1969.
Ozark Institute. "A Special Report on Appropriate Technology." *Ozarka.* Eureka Springs, Ark. 72632: 1978.

VI

SIMPLER LIVING FOR ALL

Ironically, our inefficient use of energy, the improvident ends to which we have used it, and the increasing inefficiency of our institutions has resulted in our quality of life actually becoming in many ways lower than that of other nations consuming only a fraction of the energy we do, and having, by our standards, considerably less wealth.

Tom Bender
Sharing Smaller Pies

The transformation of our growth "ethic" from materialistic and institutional to service and personal goals must occur on both the social and the individual levels. Social activists may argue the primacy of institutional transformation, and many religiously oriented persons will champion the need for personal conversion and reform. But a third and perhaps more universally held position is that both levels must undergo change. Having mentioned some of the institutional changes in the last chapter, we will now concentrate on the personal changes of lifestyles.

Our lifestyles are the outward manifestation of exactly how much we have interiorized the growth ethic. When we are immersed in our consumer culture and uncritically accept materialistic goals, we find that our cars, clothes, food, and recreation reflect these values. When wasteful practices do not prick our consciences, then we accept energy inefficiency and ultimately environmental degradation—no matter what we say about ecology and sharing with the world's poor.

Lifestyles are more than symbols of what we are; they can become instruments for change. If we conscientiously attempt to simplify lifestyles through more use of public transportation, more natural and unprocessed foods, and fewer consumer purchases, we are helping to change our own attitudes and, it is hoped, those of people around us. But the urgency of responsible stewardship and the slowness of citizens to respond to the calls for individual conservation practices make us aware that more must be done. We must establish a justification for simple living, publicly giving reasons for others to change, and we must effect changes in institutional policies so that others are required to cease major wasteful practices and extravagant lifestyles.

BASIC DISTINCTIONS

A number of terms have been used within a materialistic growth ethic that are not necessarily restricted to quantitative meanings, and others can hardly be transformed. Since these are often loosely used, precision requires some discussion of their application here.

Conservation means protection from waste and loss. In reference to lifestyles, conservation is a way to simpler living, through practices that reduce energy and raw material wastes. Often, simpler living is measured by such quantifiables as the saving in nonrenewable energy (coal, gas, oil, and other fossil fuels), which can be readily calculated by proven methods.

After President Carter said that America needs to embrace the conservation ethic,[1] numerous civic and business organizations have taken up the message. Some impetus is due to money-saving efforts, some to a patriotic gesture, and some to use as a publicity gimmick. Whatever the motives, conservation has become respectable in only the last few years. However, corporate practices that encourage wasteful practices go hand in hand with acclaimed success stories of savings.

On a broader level, conservation is a form of stewardship that signifies faith in the earth's future, respect for all living creatures, acknowledgment of the finiteness of the earth's resources, and concern for needy human beings. It is other-directed and follows a principle of sharing from a limited pie, even when the individual saving is not applied directly to others in need. It reflects the belief that a good exists in modifying one's use of resources. This good might be a more healthy diet, less use of dangerous drugs and medicines, less dependence on institutions, a sense of communion with nature, and healing of ecological disharmonies of the earth.

Quality of life means the entire complex of factors that give value and meaning to human life and raise it above the level of mere subsistence. It includes health benefits; educa-

tional opportunites; medical facilities; recreational and leisure time; democratic government; chances for artistic and
spiritual growth; maximization of freedom for the greatest
number of individuals; clean air and water; adequate food
sources; balanced diet; sufficient clothing, including shoes;
adequate personal products; rapid and safe transportation;
rapid communication networks; proper outlets for talents;
safe occupational situations; community control of energy
and resource outlets; and adequate sewage, garbage, and
utility systems.

Quality of life is not necessarily measured by energy expenditure, consumer accessibility to goods, or gross national
product. In some instances a stable political system and balanced economic system are prerequisites for a good quality
of life. While these systems are subject to certain statistical
analyses, still "quality of life" is not a quantitative term, even
though our present culture presumes so. On one hand, some
resource use is needed to maintain an adequate quality of
life; enormous energy and resource use will, however, lower
this quality of life because of resulting pollution and inade-
quacies for the poorer portion of the population.

Standard of living is a quantitative measurement of the
living situation of different groups of human beings based on
such measurables as capital, time, salaries, service costs, and
materials. This standard is an economic term used to compare different regions or nations. Often the "standard of living" is derived from the gross national product (GNP), the
total national output of goods and services, and refers to the
per capita fraction of that GNP.

Standards of living are obviously not exact. A service
might cost little in money terms in one country but be of far
better quality than a similar service in a higher-priced nation,
yet the standard of living will reflect the second as being
higher and thus "better." Again, the standard of living is not
necessarily proportional to the amount of energy and raw
materials consumed. West Germany, for instance, has a
higher standard of living than the United States, yet it uses
about half the energy. Reduced resource use might lower the
need for drilling and transport equipment, yet it would also
mean reduced pollution and exploitation of resources. How-

ever, "standard of living" calculations never consider nega-
tive factors as such, except when the services required to
curb pollution and clean up environmental damage are
added to the total service output as a credit.

Lifestyle is an outward expression of the inner values held
by the individual. This outward expression embraces the entire complex of day-to-day living practices (food eaten,
clothes worn, toiletries used). It also embraces the friends we
choose, the type of shelter we live in, where and how we
worship and recreate, and the manner in which we prepare
for the future. A lifestyle is a form of human communication
to others of who one is and what one wants to become. It is a
way of life whether freely chosen or not.

Everyone has a lifestyle. To simply refuse to discuss an individual's way of living is to be uncritical; and when in a
wasteful society there is a chance of personal extravagance,
then such omissions are also irresponsible. People who shy
away from such discussions are often threatened by changing
lifestyle patterns—generally in marital or sexual relationships
—and fail to grasp the broader dimensions of the term.

Simplicity of life means absence of waste, luxury, and extravagance. It sometimes refers to plain living and unadorned
style. In the context of a conservation ethic, simplicity of life
means a quality of consciousness in which one is aware of resource use and maldistribution. A person committed to a simple life conserves natural and human resources, be they food,
fossil fuel, water, wildlife, or the physical and psychological
health of communities and individuals. Within this conservationist definition, concepts of being plain and unadorned
may or may not enter. For instance, wearing jewelry, deco-
rating the home, and using toiletries and perfume may be
done tastefully and in moderation by one living a simple lifestyle. Jewelry as such requires small resource expenditure in
production, for it is quite labor-intensive and the items may
be retained and used for centuries. We should remember that
precious metal and stone mining practices have included
exploited labor and the use of nonrenewable resources. Toiletries made from natural products are preferred, and we
should refrain from those with ingredients derived from endangered or other species, such as whales. Keep in mind that

all "primitive" people have simple lifestyles and yet use jewelry, decorations, and cosmetics. In any event, the isolation of the hermit is not intended here.

Simple living need not be rustic, but can involve prudent use of resources in urban and suburban areas as well. Examples of how concerned people with some modern vehicles, appliances, and consumer products can practice simple living include:

Type of Conservation	Specific Practice Areas
* Food	Consume less meat
* Fossil fuel	Encourage mass transit
* Materials	Ban the nonreturnable
* Water	Save water (in home practices)
* Community health	Fight environmental pollution
* Individual health	Do not abuse drugs
* Wildlife	Do not wear furs from endangered species[2]

Other whole areas of simplicity deserving of more attention are those of natural birth-control methods; natural childbirth techniques; natural infant feeding; reduced institutionalization of the sick, elderly, and handicapped; simple weddings and funerals; and free schools. These are not specifically conservationist in nature but do require fewer goods and more services by caring individuals.

Among the qualities of a simple lifestyle that is both conservationist and personal include the following: less waste, less fashion-orientation, less needless travel, less noise, less consumption of energy, less addiction to commercialism, more natural foods, more home cooking, more personalized gifts, more walking and jogging, more natural fibers, more community participation and control, more crafts and arts.

Lifestyle efficiency produces the highest quality of life for the most people while using the lowest quantity of energy and natural resources and emitting the lowest quantity of wastes. Efficiency in energy terms has commonly meant the ratio of work to energy input. "First-law efficiency" means the energy transfer (of a desired kind) achieved by a device or system divided by the energy input to the device or system. This includes the efficiency of an electric motor (mechanical work output divided by electric work input) or an air-conditioner (heat removed divided by electric work input).

"Second-law efficiency" is *task-*, not *device-*, oriented. For a given task such as heating a house or cooking a meal, it refers to the process needed to complete the task with the least energy expenditure. Second-law efficiency tells us that insulating one's house better is a more efficient way of keeping warm than sitting in front of an electric space heater. More broadly speaking, second-law efficiencies might suggest substituting small hydroelectric plants for fossil-fuel ones; substituting natural gas for electricity in home cooking; and comparing canning energy use in a large factory, a community cannery, and home practices. Substituting a machine that consumes "cheap" energy for a worker needing a job may be deemed "efficient" from a capitalistic viewpoint because it enhances profits, but it may prove grossly inefficient from a personal fulfillment standpoint.

Lifestyle efficiencies include not only *device* and *task* efficiencies but also *goal* efficiencies, which measure how effective various personal and social goals are in contributing to a desired quality of life. If the aim is putting vegetables of the highest quality on the table, then one compares backyard gardening, supermarket, and farmers' or cooperative produce markets. If the aim is choosing good clothing, then one must weigh the advantages of different products for washing requirements, length of wear, weight, and numerous other factors. In defining goals, the individual value judgments are of prime importance. For one person the satisfaction of growing vegetables or of comparing clothing materials may be enjoyable and add to the quality of life; for another who has other time demands, perhaps not.

From a conservationist view, less use of nonrenewable energy sources yields a higher quality of life, for waste materials in production and consumption are minimized. When second-law efficiency is low, and ordinary tasks are done with high-energy expenditure, pollution and resource depletion ensue and the quality of human life suffers. Entropy, or the measure of disorder in the universe, increases. Thus conservationists strive to maximize second-law efficiencies.

An environmental ethics has something to say about goals and about principles to use in reaching them. To introduce convenience products, laborsaving machines, or modern agricultural methods may not be desirable from a total ecological perspective. Many factors must be considered, among them the need for the product, status and quality of the labor force, nature of labor saved, use of time saved or lost, culture of the people, and energy demands to upkeep and operate the new device. Automation or modernization, causes of ecstasy for technological optimists, may be harmful when all social goals are included. A neglect of such considerations may result in resource depletion, increased pollution, instability in community economies, heavy dependence on outside repair systems, and lack of mobility in times of disaster or periods of hardship.

Principles for lifestyle efficiency choices include:

> *Principle of first-law efficiency*—When a device is used to obtain desired goals, that device should be operated at maximum efficiency. If I travel by car, I must make sure it is in top shape.
>
> *Principle of second-law efficiency*—When a task may be performed by more than one device or system, one should choose that which requires the least expenditure of nonrenewable resources and emits the smallest amount of toxic products. If I can walk to the store or drive, it is better to walk, all things considered.
>
> *Principle of goal efficiency*—When a goal may be reached by two or more equivalent operations, one should choose the means that provides the maximum good to the greatest number of people. I may go to give a talk by bus or train, but I find I can do a better job by using the latter.

Ideal lifestyles are those giving the highest quality of life to people and may vary with age, temperament, skills, health, occupation, expertise, and cultural background. Thus there is no ideal lifestyle suited to all, but rather as many as there are people. Finding one's ideal lifestyle is a major undertaking worthy of serious personal discernment. It cannot be an individual choice made in isolation from the social needs of persons around us.

Our ideal individual lifestyle should include the following characteristics:

* Caring for one's health—eating proper food in moderation; not overusing alcoholic beverages, tobacco, or drugs; getting proper exercise; practicing good hygiene.

* Developing talents—finding new outlets for energy in music, crafts, and hobbies; learning to budget time and disciplining oneself.

* Maximizing freedom—freeing oneself from the pressures to consume and gain material possessions; freeing oneself for others.

* Opening to qualitative growth—developing spiritually, educationally, and socially.

* Harmonizing with nature—gaining an awareness of the wastes of overconsumption; doing more things out of doors; reflection on the beauty and joys of nature.

* Being conservative of resources—learning that conserving is actually both economic and helpful for self and others.

* Using renewable resources—adopting solar and wind systems as opposed to using fossil fuels and nuclear power.

* Becoming an example for others—becoming a prophet and testifying to the joys of simple living.

* Enhancing social involvement—finding it easier to communicate with the poor and needy people around us; sharing with and assisting them.

* Taking an interest in other people within the community—becoming involved in community issues.

* Working for social reform—freeing oneself from the institutional enticements of our economic system; becoming critical of corporate irresponsibility and doing something about it.

* Taking on a global view—seeing the imperative to adapt in an age of scarcity.

Lifestyle index is a system for determining one's lifestyle efficiency by focusing on the expenditure of nonrenewable energy (fossil fuels). While no single quantifiable measure is sufficient, still most consumers could profit from knowing their energy use (gasoline, home heating and cooling, energy contained in daily services and consumer products). The measuring system assumes that all energy in this country is directed to individual consumers, and thus divides industrial, commercial, and transportation energy use according to the end uses individual consumers make of them. Social services are sometimes restricted by availability (people without sewers are not charged this social service). On the other hand, whether citizens approve of federal or military expenditures, these expenditures are apportioned equally among all.

This consumer energy audit needs constant updating as better data become available, but in its current form it gives a good approximation of one's annual energy use. It includes the following basic operations:

* Home energy use (heating, cooling, ventilating, refrigerating, lighting, and other appliance operation, plus manufacturing expenditures).
* Food consumption (agricultural production, transportation to and from processing plants, marketing, machinery production, processing, sales, and preparation) and food containers.
* Personal items (clothing, footwear, tobacco products, soaps, cleaners, beauty products, and medicine).
* Recreation (spectator and participative sports, cultural events, hobbies, crafts, and other relaxation energy use such as vacation travel).
* Transportation (energy expenditure going to and from work and for basic social services, plus manufacturing costs of vehicles).
* Social services (health, education, religious, personal—such as barbering, governmental expenditures in-

cluding weapons manufacture, and communications and financing services).

In each part of the consumer's life there is energy expenditure, but most do not know what it is. How much energy is expended on an average to run one movie for one customer? This includes the operation of projector, lights, heating of building, and processing of film. Calculations show that the amount is one "energy unit" per consumer-showing.[3] Added to this is the fact that average Americans go to eight or nine movies per year. With these two sets of data one is able both to calculate personal use and to compare it with what other consumers are using in the United States.

By repeating the audit for all foods, consumer products, appliance use, and so on, the individual consumer knows where he or she stands with respect to other consumers in nonrenewable energy use. Many areas often overlooked are exposed. The index is pedagogical in nature; it teaches consumers where energy is used and where potentially the greatest savings may be made.

A difficulty arises when counting energy use against oneself (energy for me) or dividing it among a number of consumers. I occupy a house with other people and thus share the energy use in heating and cooling. A lecturer may count energy for travel against the audience as receivers of the words being delivered; the audience may include those not wishing to account the energy to their own expenditure, thinking the lecture not worth the effort. In any case, dividing energy use or apportioning it to certain consumers leads to approximations because of different interpretations of who is the ultimate user.

All in all, auditing energy use through a systematic index gives some understanding of where wastes occur and how savings may be performed. Our own goal efficiency requires proper justification through discernment. The following are some questions that may help in determining one's justification for energy use:

* For whom do I use the energy? For myself or others?

° Can I do the same task or operation using less nonrenewable energy?

° Is time required for labor-intensive alternatives better spent in other ways? Perhaps I cook less because my volunteer hospital work exhausts me.

° Is the energy use for others directed to the poor or the affluent?

° Do I understand that energy use for relaxation is necessary for my service to family, friends, and others?

° Do I recognize the needs of others in home conservation practices, or is the decision made by me alone? In food use? In transportation?

° Does the decision allow all to grow as better persons?

Lifestyle choices are the areas of freedom that give individual character to one's lifestyle. Even in repressive societies, lifestyles are individualized. They may be described as comfortable, harsh, relaxed, rigid, cultured, barbaric, socially oriented, egocentric, luxurious, frugal, uplifting, depressing, elitist, egalitarian, elegant, plain, tasteful, gauche, and so on. The multitude of descriptive adjectives reveals room for individual choice. Exercising one's freedom to choose is part of a higher quality of life. As in the exercise of any freedom, however, limits exist beyond which either the individual suffers for want of necessities, or others suffer through the individual's excess.

Lifestyle choice depends on underlying values. All lifestyles have an impact on the environment, but in varying degree. The challenge is to create a suitable lifestyle that minimizes this impact and yet enhances our interrelationships with others. Ideally, a person should strive to maximize social interrelationships and minimize physical resource expenditure. The challenge extends to affluent people restricted by the pressures of peer group conformity, and to the less affluent who attempt to strive for self-sufficiency. It raises the question whether interdependence is not a better goal than independence, while recognizing the weakness of physical dependence on others for vital resources.

Energy and resource budgets might be ways of sharing resources but allotting to all individual consumers certain limits on expenditure with some room for exceptions such as for the sick, disabled, disadvantaged, and professional people. Whether such a system of rationing could be imposed on a nation or on the world without some crisis situation is quite problematic. How much expenditure should be at the discretion of the individual and how much socially regulated is also an issue. Individual budgeting has many pitfalls and oversights; so do socially imposed rationing schemes where black-marketeering and lobbying for exemptions are most tempting. Resource audits are not meant to discipline or coerce, but should enhance one's freedom in making lifestyle choices.

A *lifestyle scale* is a measure of the room between extreme destitution and overconsumption in which individual lifestyle choices might occur.

LIFESTYLE SCALE

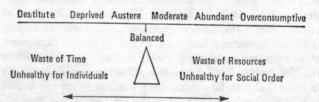

It includes making choices that recognize limited world resources, resource expenditure of various alternatives, and the individual and social impacts of too little or too much.

Absolute resource data cannot be obtained for the above scale, for they are conditioned by culture and time. For instance, a "primitive" person may work close to home and have a building requiring little indoor heating. People living in rural areas may grow and prepare their own food and use wood for heating. On the other hand, even an austere urban lifestyle may require food and fuel processed and transported over a long distance.

Balanced lifestyles must compare time expended in personal labor with resources expended in energy-intensive operations. Imbalances result when resource use is disproportionate to time saved, and when goals sought are not in harmony with the needs of others. As a sense of global consciousness grows—an interdependence on global resources—more reasonable goals that respect resource limitation will be brought forth.

TWELVE REASONS FOR A SIMPLE LIFESTYLE

If we are to convert others to a conservation ethic we need moral justification. Since lifestyle change is difficult, a variety of motivating reasons—some noble and some mundane—is needed. This apologetic must address both individuals and social institutions, so that conservation can really work in improving our quality of life and can lead to a more equitable distribution of global resources. Likewise it must be forceful enough to demonstrate to a wide variety of persons that simpler living is the most effective means of fulfilling the conservation ethic and improving the environment.

The following reasons are arranged from those appropriate on a more individual level to those appropriate on a more social one. Some people are deeply concerned about health and safety; others have a more developed awareness of social justice. This series does not presume the noblest motivation as a starting point, but only openness and good will. While lulled by consumer enticements, still we experience a growing sense of need for change which is costly to the individual in respect to convenience, but promising in terms of personal growth and freedom.

Simple living needs an apologia. If little has been said or written on this matter, it may be due to a number of factors: a lack of a discipline or systematic reflection on simple lifestyles; a basic distrust of certain lifestyle practices; a reluctance by practitioners to publicize their way of living; and a failure to reach the general public.

Individual Health

The complex modern lifestyles of many citizens are filled with health hazards—food additives, excessive drugs, household chemical products, gasoline additives, lead-based paints, overly processed foods, polluted air and water, PCB's, DDT, DES. . . . The list goes on and on. Some citizens hope that curbing the known hazards while they remain big consumers will remove the problem. They look for a public-interest guru who can point out what to avoid, provided the consumer culture is not disturbed.

Simpler living affords an answer on another dimension— the change of the total pattern of use of products, not just selective prohibitions and bans. It encourages balanced diets and improved nutrition, not selective dieting; relief of tension without drugs, not more and more potent ones; less travel by auto, not faster and more expensive autos. It emphasizes physical fitness and proper exercise, partly by a reemphasis on labor-intensive operations. Simpler living helps foster psychic health, inner harmony, and a balanced "internal" ecology. Lower driving speeds, more time for relaxation, and a balance of work and leisure are all part of the ingredients of simpler living.

People are ready for this reason. Health is one of their leading concerns, their experience of family and personal problems is close at hand, medical costs are rising, and there has been considerable discussion of modern health dangers in the world around them. The dramatic interest in natural foods, the dangers of air pollution and toxic chemicals, and the rise in cancer rates all add to an atmosphere where people are receptive to some change in their lifestyle practices.

Discipline

Most people want to stay young and to develop their own talents in new and interesting ways: music, crafts, hobbies, and intellectual disciplines. But they know that it takes effort to learn something new. It requires people to budget time and to undergo training and exercise. Spartan discipline is required for all major physical ventures—long journeys; underwater, cave, or mountain explorations; revolutions. Acquiring new talents modifies one's lifestyle. Most citizens admire others disciplined in sports, theater, dancing, and so on. Underneath, they most likely desire more discipline for themselves. Simple living creates the atmosphere for such personal exercise, for it strengthens the will to say no to consumer allurements.

Liberation

The practical and independent side of us is part of the hallmark of First World leadership. We believe in individual freedom; we believe that it has been acquired at a high price and that it requires ongoing effort for preservation. Many of us place higher values on lifestyles that enhance our freedom. Freeing ourselves *from* the pressures of the marketplace and *for* our fellow human beings is part of that exercise of freedom that we cherish. It can be done better by certain lifestyles than others.

Citizens who desire to influence and change our politico-economic system for the better know that it takes time and money. Those holding the purse strings know it also, and often withhold funds from threatening innovators while rewarding those thinking with the system with generous funding. As long as the social innovators need more money, the funders may exercise their control by dictating current policy. Only a liberation of innovators from such dependence will break the cycle. Simpler living is one such way.

Freedom is not something completed once and for all. It is a continuing struggle. To loose ourselves from modern conveniences such as boats, expensive homes, or automobiles takes effort; to see such a negation as liberating us—from repair and maintenance costs, from operating expenses, and from pressures to change with fashion—requires insight. It is also necessary that the champions of freedom continue to purify their understanding of it: that freedom is a social as well as an individual exercise, and that our freedom is enhanced by the liberation of all.

Spirituality

Many people deeply wish to develop interiorly and seek a meaningful spiritual experience. They find the current culture lacking and blame broken homes, overuse of drugs, crime, and rampant commercialism on the loss of spiritual values. They search for new and different religious experiences. Many eventually arrive at a simpler lifestyle as a way to inner peace, for it affords time for reflection and contemplation. It allows self-mastery; it affords models to follow in simple living—Jesus Christ, Francis of Assisi, Buddha, Gandhi, and a host of Eastern and Western mystics. It negates materialism and opens the way to a quest for deeper values; it speaks of a more just way of living and a communion and solidarity with others on this planet. It adds a new dimension to the reality of human relations; it rejects worldly values and sets people in opposition to superficially established goals of comfort, convenience, and power.

Other people seek qualitative growth through education and personal development fostered by simpler lifestyles. The sense of self-fulfillment and personal growth through interpersonal relationships advanced by means of simpler living—helping others do simple tasks such as growing vegetables or baking—can be fostered in a more labor-intensive and less energy- and resource-intensive lifestyle.

Nature

To speak truly, few adult persons can see nature. Most persons do not see the sun. At least, they have a very superficial seeing.

Ralph Waldo Emerson
The Romantic Philosophy of Nature

To see nature and enjoy it requires a certain state of mind, a commitment, a communication with it. This atmosphere and mind-set is lacking in a culture that becomes removed from nature and builds a wall of artificiality between people and the world around them. By living simply, we have time and psychic energy to begin seeing the simpler things around us and to appreciate the harmony in nature, which includes us. We become immersed; we see, touch, smell, and taste a total environment that is often overlooked and ignored. We sense a world of nature around us—flowers, weather, clouds, birds, insects, wild foods. We appreciate the delicate and sensitive changes of the various seasons. We learn the importance of silence and reflection. By communicating with nature we are more able to appreciate simplicity in other people.

The enormous growth of such exercises and sports as jogging, camping, hiking, cross-country skiing and mountain climbing all reveal the sense of coming nearer to nature that lies deep within our cultural heritage. Our distance from the rural life is now traversed by a multitude of people seeking natural outlets in mountains, lakes, and forests throughout this land. With a growth in awareness of nature's beauty there comes a growing abhorrence for litter and environmental degradation.

Conservation and Economics

People pay attention to ways to save money, and simpler lifestyles are money savers. There's less need for money—smaller cars and thus lower fuel bills, less-processed food and lower food budgets, less emphasis on clothing fashions and more on durability. Simpler lifestyles require the earning of less money to sustain oneself, and thus bring the added benefit of less tension in work and less striving for higher-paying jobs.

The movement toward a conservationist philosophy appeals to an older generation that experienced the belt-tightening days of the Great Depression and World War II. Often they are people who are now feeling the pinch of inflation and higher taxes, since many live on fixed incomes. To such people economic arguments for simpler living have a great appeal.

Ecology

Simpler living champions the use of solar and wind power as opposed to currently used fossil fuels and nuclear power (nonrenewable types). A surge of interest is being shown in a return to wood heating and to other forms of renewable energy sources such as methane generation from biological wastes and geothermal energy. A more pronounced movement toward these other energy sources will save natural resources; lower dependence on foreign oil and gas; reduce air, water, and soil pollution; and reduce waste heat emission. There are theoretical limits to the amount of waste heat this environment can hold. Regardless of energy source, there are limits on energy generation, and much of current energy use is for consumption patterns completely at odds with simpler living. The thermodynamic limits to energy use tell us that there are limits to increasing energy-intensive lifestyles. Simpler living permits a slower growth rate and even a decline in energy use, thus enhancing the environmental health of this planet.

While many desire a better environment, they are still not

willing to see dramatic changes in the energy-based economy. They talk of employment reduction and loss. They forget that job fluctuations have occurred throughout our history. It is imperative that governments enter the picture and mitigate these circumstances. Actual job losses can be offset—even overcompensated for—by increases in services, but this may not soften opposition to lifestyle changes from corporations and labor unions producing autos, containers, and steel.

Example and Prophecy

The call for a conservation consciousness requires that people bear witness to it. Credibility is of utmost importance. If we live wasteful lifestyles we cannot but be hypocrites, saying one thing and doing another. Thus a national conservation program requires that we reexamine our individual lifestyles and find where wastes occur. Developing and needy nations are already quite critical of Western hypocrisy, and simpler living is a sure way of overcoming this attitude and compensating for our cultural shortcomings. In so doing we can establish a solidarity with the world's poor, who often embrace simpler lifestyles by necessity, not by choice.

Lifestyles reveal our inner selves, and so changes of lifestyles tell people where we are going. They are prophetic messages. Prophecy deals with future events insofar as these possible occurrences are realistic projections of what will happen if people continue to live in a reprehensible manner. Prophecy is clear insight into a *present* situation and explains what will surely follow in the future unless corrective measures are taken. Simpler lifestyles are admonitions to our people to convert from practices of exploitation of world resources for luxurious living while many peoples subsist on bare essentials.

Society

People want to get involved but often don't know how. However, a hidden obstacle is the lack of urgency and of procedures for going out to others, sharing with them, and joining forces with socially oriented citizens. Simpler living may lead to more individualistic endeavors or it may make persons more socially oriented. By simple living we become more aware of environmental degradation and wasteful practices. We sense the need for everyone to pitch in and join community conservation programs. We sense the pressures in our society that discourage conservation, and we may become angry.

Awareness without a social outlet leads to frustration, which betrays the limits of individual actions taken alone. For instance, a conservationist becomes enthusiastic about recycling programs, but soon sees that bringing paper and cans to a center is not enough. If no market for secondary materials exists, the center soon becomes a junkyard. Frustrated recyclers seek deeper solutions and look to the irresponsible corporations that create the throwaways and profit by abandoning them at the consumer communities. A moment of decision arrives. Simple-living people may either turn inward and retreat to individual concerns, or see the frustrating situation as a chance to go out and unite with others interested in meaningful change.

Community Building

To live simply means that we live with others and share more with them many common daily tasks—washing dishes, cleaning rooms, cooking, growing vegetables, home repairs. Time spent working together is time spent developing community. Sharing helps each individual see the talents and weaknesses of the others, become more tolerant of others, and open the way for a certain specialization of duties and work. However, while it might be nice for the better cook to prepare the more festive meal or the better writer to develop promotional material, still there is true value in all undertaking a great variety of tasks and duties such as learning to cook or write. Overspecialization has created a world of crippled people unable to venture out into new undertakings. Limited specialization may, on the other hand, allow certain talents to develop more fully; how much a community will encourage depends on the openness of all to the talents of others.

Simple living demands more time spent on the mechanics of living. But these mechanics include objectionable tasks that no one really likes. Gandhi would take time from his

busy schedule and offer to clean the toilets of his guests. The
community coalesces and finds inner harmony when it recognizes that all the unpleasant tasks must be shared. While
some community specialization is necessary, every able-
bodied person regardless of sex or learning must assume
maintenance tasks, as well as giving time to make creative
contributions.

Institutions

Simpler lifestyles require less of a consumer-oriented men-
tality; there is less need for the products made by larger corporations and the multinationals: gasoline, autos, packaged
food, fashionable clothing, and so on. Thus there is a greater
independence from those institutions and more dependence
on the products of local industry and crafts. People can
afford to become critical of institutions that encourage neoco-
lonialism and resource-intensive practices.

Internationalism—Imperative in an Age of Scarcity

While the preceding reasons are somewhat optional, this
one stresses the moral imperative to change, to expand our
vision and concern, and to adjust ourselves to a world of limited resources. Only the very wealthy and insensitive can attempt to live a luxuriant lifestyle (see next section). To permit a totally free choice of simple versus affluent lifestyle is
to accept unlimited affluence as a good. Only the rich now
have such a choice. Poor people in India, Brazil, and Appalachia do not.

To truly become international in lifestyle attitudes means
that we transmit concern for the world's poor into action.
The United States is a land with 5.4 percent of the world's
people and yet it uses between 25 and 30 percent of the
world's goods. Many moral leaders from needy lands call
upon the affluent to curb waste and share with the poor of
their lands.

The reality and the depth of the problem arises because
the man who is rich has power over the lives of those
who are poor. And the rich nation has power over the
policies of those who are not rich. And even more important is that a social and economic system nationally

and internationally, supports those divisions and constantly increases them so that the rich get ever richer and more powerful, while the poor get relatively ever poorer and less able to control their own future.[4]

President Julius Nyerere of Tanzania

Living simply makes one sensitive to the connection between modern lifestyles and global poverty. By placing demands on limited world resources, the rich indirectly control the lives of Third World people; by our reduction of these demands we show concern for the poor, regardless of how small total resource savings are due to individual actions. By uniting our actions with those of like-minded people we are able to expand our consciousness to include the needy in other lands.

MANDATORY OR OPTIONAL LIFESTYLE CHANGES

Little serious thought has been given to lifestyle change. Perhaps this is partly owing to conceiving of lifestyle as being totally within the realm of personal choices, something akin to freedom of speech or of assembly. However, rapid depletion of global resources through individual lifestyle choices—albeit institutionally induced—make it imperative to reexamine the optional aspects of lifestyles. How can we preserve our precious individual freedom, which is demanded for a higher quality of life, and yet become restrictive about certain lifestyle practices? And more important, when can we say no to excessive lifestyle practices or engage in selective restrictions on individuals for the sake of the common good?

People in the Western world know that individual freedom is delicate and can be easily lost. It needs time to grow; a complex of laws must be formulated to defend and nourish it. It needs to seep in and find personal expression in our lives. In describing and defining freedom, lifestyles stand in contrast to verbal utterances. They answer the call for actions, not words; they are a deep and personal communication of human freedom. They reflect our goals, aspirations, and general concern for our neighbors. They even express the fact that some precious moments of life are being squandered.

If living one's lifestyle is a communication, a change of lifestyle is even better. Change is implied in growth, and the imperative to grow is part of being human. To grow better is part of our acceptance of the call to freedom. Change in lifestyle can manifest that freedom is not yet attained but is an ongoing process. It means that we are alive and ready to adapt to the new conditions of our world. A public commitment to lifestyle change tells the world that privileged people freely want to share and grow with less fortunate people in a world of scarcity. Thus commitment to change is a liberating moment, even when this commitment might entail the risk of restricting our use of resources.

What can be said of an individual's lifestyle can also be said of the community's, for lifestyle changes have a social dimension. This social quality, however, is not generally recognized even though many ecological and economic imbalances are. An axiom stated in the previous chapter applies here: maximize social interrelationships and minimize physical resource expenditure. Just as a high-volume microphone does not necessarily convey the best communication, so a personal or communal lifestyle that uses the most resources is not the best.

A lifestyle must communicate harmony and inner peace, but this can hardly be done when the environment is disrupted to sustain it, or human injustices exist to support it. And if this harmony is to be complete, both the individual and community are part of it, and both must work together to create an atmosphere wherein suitable lifestyles might coexist. However, some lifestyles by their very extravagance are disharmonious and create division in the global community. Thus the common good raises the possibility of lifestyle regulation and society's restriction on excesses. Could not community freedom be enhanced when the license of a few individuals is curbed? The above axiom might be modified— maximize personal and communal freedom while minimizing resource depletion and misuse.

Environmental regulations often clash with individual

practices, and so it might also be with lifestyles. For instance, noise on a resort lake is restricted by allowing motor boats to operate only during certain times; the good of a number of sleepers is considered by the regulation. The "freedom" to operate a motor boat any hour of day or night is restricted so that a greater freedom—the community's sleep —might not be impaired.

From a global perspective, one may argue that a privileged 10 percent of the world's people using about half of the world's resources is stifling a diversity of lifestyle among a large portion of the world's people. Thus freedom to seek a higher quality of life is restricted for the multitudes who cannot rise above the struggle for the basics of life. Even among the affluent, economic and social pressures can deaden free will and even, ironically, narrow lifestyle choices. Thus society must set the groundwork for a more just distribution of resources needed for lifestyle expression and foster creativity for the greater number. A truly human and environmental ethics should encourage concerned citizens to initiate actions —whether political, legal, economic, or even physical—that place roadblocks in front of excessive lifestyle. Society may restrict the use of fuel for recreational vehicles, challenge the manufacture of gas guzzlers or inefficient electric appliances, or demonstrate against a nuclear power plant. To restrict institutional and individual excess is to expand the lifestyle choices of the entire human community.

Societal regulation need not mean regimentation; citizens may opt for a wide variety of lifestyle differences within certain bounds. Necessity (imposing regulation to preserve limited resources) may again become the mother of invention. A host of simpler and more appropriate technologies deserve implementation; a richer variety of flavorful and nutritious vegetarian dishes might replace energy-intensive meat and fish dishes; faster, cleaner, and more efficient modes of public transportation might be used. The diversity of lifestyle expressions might be as varied as the peoples on Earth.

The duty of society to restrict certain behavior is not in question theoretically, but in practice it may be. We recognize the need to restrict the antisocial and to prohibit certain actions by them, such as robbery, murder, or rape. Robbers are not free to act at will. But does not excessive use of resources border on robbery; and if so, may we deinstitutionize the ecological crime and consider even the excessive lifestyle practitioner responsible? If one accepts the need for lifestyle restrictions, then a group of working principles dealing with individual and communal lifestyle changes is in order:

Individual Voluntary Action Principle

I *may* make voluntary lifestyle changes when I sense the need for such action, desiring to convey meaning and value through explicit change, and when my personal growth will result from this particular action. An example is that I am aware of food scarcity and so refrain from eating meat on certain days or at certain periods.

Individual Mandatory Action Principle

I *must* make lifestyle changes when I am convinced that this action is necessary to express the harmful aspects of current lifestyle practices that infringe on the rights of my neighbors (domestic or foreign) and that the possible success of this action is real. I should stop using aerosol sprays because they are quite likely harmful to the environment and may harm other people. My practice actually contributes to the decrease of ozone in the upper atmosphere, and my change of lifestyle practice will help halt this deterioration.

Social Voluntary Action Principle

We *may* make communal lifestyle changes when the collective consciousness is aware of a harmful social practice but there is uncertainty about the success of the strategy to counter it, when there is some possibility that the group action has value and meaning, and when this particular action suits the group's resources and temperament. A group will boycott a multinational corporation that practices economic repression of others and refrain from use of products—thus changing a lifestyle in the process.

Social Mandatory Action Principle

We *must* make communal lifestyle changes when the need for action is critical and inaction will further infringe on the rights of our neighbors, when the action has some likelihood of success, and when the lack of action will lead to irretrievable harm to the human and/or physical environment. We must cease using natural gas for certain practices that are clearly wasteful, such as outdoor ornamental lighting.

These four operative principles acknowledge the possibility of both individual and social or communal lifestyle changes, designate circumstances and conditions for when these are optional or obligatory, recognize the "witness" value of lifestyle change, and indicate how anticipated practical results might help determine or condition methods used for effecting change. What is left unsaid is the agent of change—peer pressure, educational program, individual conscience, governmental regulation, or other forces.

POSSIBLE GUIDELINES AND POLICY IMPLICATIONS

Enforced social lifestyle changes are not novel, but for many of us the prospect is disconcerting. What only a generation ago would have been unthinkable—cutting highway speed limits nationwide by one fifth—is now accepted. Granted, truckers still complain and even argue that they could save fuel by faster travel. In some states police and motorists even ignore the limits. But speed limits have been cut overall and traffic deaths have been reduced 11 percent between 1973 and 1977. A universal lifestyle change has been instituted with little prior education or nationwide coverage, and the "freedom" to speed is over.

Perhaps a far harder task than imposition of universal regulations on all of our lifestyles is the selective restriction of excessive lifestyles. In some countries, such as France, public officials enter and check thermostats in private residences. It seems that economics alone is succeeding in eliminating highly energy-intensive ocean cruises. But numerous other excesses, from private aircraft to yachting, still remain. Some argue to let the economy take care of the situation. But the rich always find money for the exotic. A fairer method—across-the-board restrictions—avoids the risk of further depletion of valuable resources. Merely taxing those with luxurious tastes may not halt the drive by many to become like the very rich. Special-interest groups are adept at tax loopholes, allowances, and redefining luxuries into business expenses.

Ethical analysis can point out the unfairness of such abuses and the need for developing a social responsibility with regard to lifestyle practices.

One wasteful lifestyle practice does not make much difference on the global scene, but a large number of individual actions do. At a luncheon for five at which all have thrown in a few dollars, if one should help himself or herself to an enormous meal, all the others would perhaps be incensed. The percentage enjoying the meal would be less at a luncheon for fifty persons and far less at one for five hundred or five thousand. Our environmental social actions and wasteful practices involve millions, some of whom help themselves to the earth's resources far in excess of their own share, and they fortify their conduct by power plays to retain the things grabbed.

How do we raise that sense of social consciousness, wherein our lifestyles reflect responsible action? A libertarian might champion educational and voluntary approaches. If external pressures are to be applied, let them be done in the free marketplace where the demand for better action and products serves as its own corrective. Excesses soon become higher-priced because of growing scarcity. All in all, individual liberty and free choice are preserved.

A more utilitarian approach seeks to formulate public policies so that they maximize the greatest happiness to the greatest number. It usually judges voluntary and economic approaches as insufficient but recognizes an educational role in information dissemination. If many people are enlightened, then changes will occur. When these people are perverted by pressures in a consumer culture or when certain special-interest groups dictate lifestyles, then regulations must be used such as advertising restrictions, taxes, and conservation measures.

A more radical position is that what is required for a better world is not single-measure lifestyle changes but rather a fundamental restructuring of our society. Public-interest measures are mere Band-Aids on a sick society; modern lifestyles are symptomatic of deeper ills not solved by curbing car speeds or teaching energy conservation. Appropriate technology innovations may primarily benefit the wealthy, who are skillful at obtaining governmental subsidies and can gain immediate benefits from investment in solar and wind power. Changes are needed in the political system, which fosters the consumerist culture, which in turn depletes world resources. New energy programs must be tied to reapportionment of power and influence.

All three positions admit of shades of difference, yet proponents of each would say they favor greater freedom ranging from individual to social varieties. An environmental ethical treatment, while attempting to remain nonpartisan, might develop values and principles that displease one or another group. To the radical, freedom grows as more social participation occurs; but historically it occurs gradually and seldom by violent means. Freedom grows through education, but some people still waste resources. Individual freedom must be cherished, but so must the need for social pressures.

Being mindful of preserving individual freedom and the need for an effective control over excessive lifestyles, we might be better prepared to implement the social and political goals that have emerged throughout the book: a decentralized economy; local citizen control where possible; a need for qualitative growth through encouragement of services; specific air, water, and land environmental regulations. A reasonable lifestyle leading to these goals must have the characteristics already mentioned and must also be open to change, use resources efficiently, and not exist at the expense of others.[5]

Restrictions on excesses must be fair and applied both to manufacturers and consumers; they must be enforced with proper penalties; they must be able to point the way to more suitable alternatives; they must be global so that the affluent will not escape to other places to pursue their practices; they must be accompanied by an atmosphere of greater freedom to live within our resource limits.

REFERENCES

1. *The National Energy Plan,* Executive Office of the President (Apr. 29, 1977), p. 35.
2. Center for Science in Public Interest and A. Fritsch, ed., *99 Ways to a Simple Lifestyle* (Garden City, N.Y.: Doubleday/Anchor, 1977), pp. xii–xiii.
3. A. Pierotti and A. Fritsch, "Lifestyle Index," Citizens' Energy Project, 1978.
4. President J. K. Nyerere, *Maryknoll* (June 1971), pp. 34–35.
5. A Fritsch, *The Contrasumers* (Praeger Publishers, 1974), pp. 79–80.

For Further Reading

Periodicals

Creative Simplicity. Shakertown Pledge Group, W. 44th and York Ave. S., Minneapolis, Minn. 55410.
Simple Living. Simple Living Collective, American Friends Service Committee, 2160 Lake St., San Francisco, Calif. 94121.
Mother Earth News. P.O. Box 70, Hendersonville, N.C. 28739.
Green Revolution. School of Living, P.O. Box 3233, York, Pa. 17402.
People and Energy. Citizens' Energy Project, 1111 Sixth St. N.W., Washington, D.C. 20001.
Doing It. Urban Alternative Group, P.O. Box 303, Worthington, Ohio 43085.
The Workbook. Southwest Research and Information Group, P.O. Box 4524, Albuquerque, N. Mex. 87106.
Alternative Sources of Energy. Route 2, Milaca, Minn. 56353.
Self-Reliance. The Institute for Local Self-Reliance, 1717 18th St. N.W., Washington, D.C. 20009.
Rain. 2270 N.W. Irving, Portland, Oreg. 97210.
AERO Sun-Times. Alternative Energy Resources Organization, 435 Stapleton Bldg., Billings, Mont. 59101.
Natural Living. Jarvis, Ontario, Canada.
Co-Evolution Quarterly. Box 428, Sausalito, Calif. 94965.

Books and Booklets

T. Bender. *Living Lightly: Energy Conservation in Housing.* Portland, Oreg.: RAIN, 1973.
———. *Sharing Smaller Pies.* Portland, Oreg.: RAIN, 1975.
Movement for a New Society. *Macro-analysis Manual.* c/o Philadelphia Macro-analysis Collective, 4719 Cedar Ave., Philadelphia, Pa. 19143.
E. F. Schumacher. *Small Is Beautiful: Economics as if People Mattered.* New York: Harper & Row, 1973.

Simple Living Collective, AFSC. *Taking Charge!* New York: Bantam, 1977.

E. Wigginton, ed. *The Foxfire Book* (Volumes I through IV). Garden City, N.Y.: Doubleday & Co., 1972, 1973, 1975, 1977.

Catalogs

Whole Earth Catalogue, Last Whole Earth Catalogue, Whole Earth Epilogue. Whole Earth Truck Store, Menlo Park, Calif. 94025.

Rodale Press. 33 E. Minor St., Emmaus, Pa. 18049.

Garden Way Publishers. 47 Maple St., Burlington, Vt. 05401.

VII

THEOLOGICAL FOUNDATIONS FOR AN ENVIRONMENTAL ETHICS

> The wolf lives with the lamb,
> the panther lies down with the kid,
> calf and lion cub feed together
> with a little boy to lead them.
> The cow and the bear make friends,
> their young lie down together.
> The lion eats straw like the ox.
> Isaiah 11:6–7

The Judeo-Christian tradition is the cornerstone of Western civilization and has furnished the foundations of the ethical conduct of that culture. The scientific and technological revolutions of the past few centuries were stepchildren of the tradition, thus implicating it as a cause of the current environmental crisis. A much quoted essay by Lynn White, Jr., concludes that "we shall continue to have a worsening ecologic crisis until we reject the Christian axiom that nature has no reason for existence save to serve man."[1] Many others have joined in the debate. Lewis Moncrief holds that the Judeo-Christian tradition is only one of many cultural factors contributing to the environmental crisis.[2] Others contend that it is a perversion of that tradition which has precipitated the present crisis.[3]

This book is not the place to continue the debate; an environmental ethics should attempt to search out in this tradition both the meaning of our actions and ways of correcting the faults committed. Several points stand out when looking into the sacred Scriptures and the living experience of people steeped in the Judeo-Christian tradition: a prophetic witness to the need to reform; exemplary lifestyles demonstrating the need for harmony with the earth; and a stewardship that stresses the major elements of environmental conservation. Perhaps there are many more such points that theologians could fruitfully develop, some of which were only germinally operative in biblical times.

PROPHETIC WITNESS

The spirit of the Lord has been given to me,
for he has anointed me.
He has sent me to bring the good news to the poor,
to proclaim liberty to captives
and to the blind new sight,
to set the downtrodden free,
to proclaim the Lord's year of favour.

Luke 4:18–19

The prophetic voice constantly sounds throughout the Judeo-Christian tradition, awakening people to their wrongdoings, pointing out the dire consequences of continuing in their ways, and calling them to reform and give justice to the oppressed. When heard, this voice often sparks resistance from the established order; when listened to, it produces a *metanoia*, or change of heart. When it is not heeded, the predictions come true. The prophetic voice is public, to be heard by all; it often runs counter to a prevailing culture and lifestyle; it offers an option for change. It is direct and concrete:

You are the ones who destroy the vineyard
and conceal what you have stolen from the poor.

Isaiah 3:14

It attacks not just violence but also idolatry, or the act of giving undue attention or value to the material things around us (Isaiah 40:18–20 or Jeremiah 10:1–9). The consequences of continuing such practices are shown:

A workman made the thing,
this cannot be God!
Yes, the calf of Samaria shall go up in flames.
They sow the wind, they will reap the whirlwind.

Hosea 8:6–7

However, the invitation is also present:

> Sow integrity for yourselves,
> reap a harvest of kindness.

> Hosea 10:12

Positive acts of violence and wrongdoing are not the only prophetic issues:

> Woe to those who add house to house
> and join field to field
> until everywhere belongs to them
> and they are the sole inhabitants of the land.

> Isaiah 5:8

The modern prophetic voice continues as part of that tradition, speaking for human rights and against greed and avarice. It is direct and balanced; it is often dire in that it paints the world as it is—if change is not made, something worse will happen; it is filled with hope by pointing out the possibility of that change. That voice extends to consumer and environmental matters, exposing the glorification of modern idols such as automobiles and aerosol sprays and the waste of natural resources.

A prophetic voice does not speak in the abstract or generalities;[4] it is concrete and relevant and addresses issues of major moment to people, such as nuclear power and human rights. For example:

> As a result of these inherent properties of the plutonium and other materials associated with the nuclear fuel cycle, use of this source gives rise to several fundamental problems:
> —The potentially catastrophic releases of plutonium and nuclear wastes . . .
> —The diversion of nuclear fuel . . . by criminal elements . . .
> —The necessity for perpetual, reliable containment of the nuclear wastes. . . .[5]

Another example is:

> The right to have a share of earthly goods sufficient for
> oneself and one's family belongs to everyone. . . . If a
> person is in extreme necessity, he has the right to take
> from the riches of others what he himself needs.[6]

While the environmental crisis began in the West, it is the
religious tradition of these lands that influenced such international meetings as the Stockholm UN Conference on the Environment in 1972 and the Vancouver UN Habitat Conference in 1976. At these meetings key people included Barbara
Ward, René Dubos, and Margaret Mead, also steeped in the
Judeo-Christian tradition.

Perhaps the unique contribution of the prophetic voice
today is in the continuity between ecojustice (justice for the
whole order of created things and beings) and social justice.
It cautions that a national energy plan must be one where
none make an unfair sacrifice and none reap an unfair
benefit;[7] but it adds that this is impossible while inequities
exist among those who control the supply and information.
Vested interests make any fairness principle a sham.

Prophetic voices say that all have a right to the basic necessities and that the needy have a right to take from the
rich. One of these necessities is fuel for cooking and heat,
which is often obtained from nonrenewable resources. But
matters do not rest with the utterance of rights. It follows
that in some way the resources must belong to all, and thus
some form of control different from what is commonly accepted must be recognized. Thus the message calls for a fundamental rethinking of social and economic structures, so
that worse consequences will not follow. The prophetic
voices give to environmental ethics urgency, vision, and
promise of rational solutions.

EXEMPLARY COMMUNITY

The tradition that fostered the prophetic word realizes that
it must be coupled with deed. But the deed does not necessarily have to be confrontation. It may be the lived experi-

ence of peace, harmony, promise, and joy that is held out as a rational alternative to the present state of affairs.

> The faithful all lived together and owned everything in common; they sold their goods and possessions and shared out the proceeds among themselves according to what each one needed.
>
> Acts 2:44-45

The short-lived early Christian communistic community included faithfulness to the word of God; common life, which enhances self-discipline; ownership in *common*, which generally takes the form of simpler lifestyle; getting rid of excesses to be freer for service; and sharing proceeds with the needy. The religious community life has been expressed in a multitude of forms through the centuries such as the Essene community, desert hermitage, monastery, convent, rural commune, or settlement house. Some forms have explicit religious traditions, while a great number in our day—though guided by religious principles—are actually secular in character. Others, like the Taizé community in France, try to blend the rich expressions of the tradition into ecumenical life.

The variety of communities complements the ongoing prophetic witness; when authentic the community shows love in action—see how the members love one another! The community symbolizes what the entire human family is seeking; it attracts those searching for a ground for belief or a haven; it presents concrete examples of a balanced spiritual "ecology," where all parts work together.

This harmony of all the parts—which include plants, animals, and all of creation together with human beings—is expressed in many ways:

as brotherhood: How good, how delightful it is
                  for all to live together like brothers.
                                    Psalm 133:1

as shalom: Great is Yahweh
                  who likes to see his servant at peace!
                                    Psalm 35:27

as messianic age: The wolf lives with the lamb,
                   the panther lies down with the kid,
                   calf and lion cub feed together
                   with a little boy to lead them.

                                            Isaiah 11:6

as joy: O soil, do not be afraid;
                   be glad, rejoice,
                   for Yahweh has done great things.

                   Beast of the field, do not be afraid;
                   the pastures on the heath are green again,
                   the trees bear fruit,
                   vine and fig tree yield abundantly.

                                            Joel 2:21–22

The harmony or peace does not consist in mere prosperity and well-being, but essentially in righteousness.[8] It is a completeness, perfection, a condition in which nothing is lacking. The oneness of all creation can be thus reflected in a community of persons who practice righteousness together. It is prophetic word through lived experience. It presents a model of what our earth must become so that a balanced environment might prevail.

The exemplary community exudes power, but not power in physical or ordinary political terms. While not denying a power expressed in such ways as "sons of God," "Christ-in-power," "re-creating the earth," "transforming bread and wine," the community still views that power and dominion (Genesis 1:28) in terms of loving service to those within and outside of its boundaries.

You call me Master and Lord, and rightly; so I am. If I, then, the Lord and Master, have washed your feet, you should wash each other's feet. I have given you an example so that you may copy what I have done to you.

                                            John 13:13–15

While the power of human beings working in community is very real, it still demands constant self-examination and self-discipline. And this is precisely the importance of a community-in-faith during the heady times of a technological revolution. Examination shows us where we have drifted from our beginning commitment; discipline helps us continue in a spirit of humility and freedom. The community becomes the instrument for maintaining commitment and humble and loving service as keystones in the exercise of a spiritual power of the children of God. Without commitment, the vital symbol of God-always-faithful-to-his-people is lost; without humility, power degrades into pride, haughtiness, insensitivity, and disrespect for God, fellow human beings, and all of creation. Individuals who break with their Judeo-Christian tradition and leave a self-correcting community soon cast about for meaning and value; their system of checks and balances is often lacking, and they replace loving service with cynicism and pointless action.

TOWARD UNDERSTANDING STEWARDSHIP

Always consider the other person to be better than yourself, so that nobody thinks of his own interests first but everybody thinks of other people's interests instead.

Philippians 2:3–4

Bruce Birch says the key to a biblical understanding of humanity and nature is relationship.[9] God, humanity, and nature are to be in harmonious relationship, with nature itself having intrinsic worth before God (Psalm 24:1) and being witness to God's work. Humanity is at one with nature in our standing before God in a harmony characterized in the Old Testament as *wholeness*, or shalom. For this perspective of harmony and interdependence, Birch says a greater stress is placed on the realization of human limitation, of humanity's rootedness in creation, on sin as relational, and on the redemptive task as including both human and nonhuman creation.

As human beings, we recognize our interdependence with other creatures on this earth. We are from dust and are what we are because of our earthly origins. Our relationship both with the Creator and with other creatures is weakened and even broken through sin, which is an act of disharmony. However, our limitations and weaknesses can be overcome and we can be filled by the power to take on our human responsibilities to other creatures and the environment. But this power is a delegated power, for we are stewards and not owners of the thing of creation (Deuteronomy 8:7–19). If on the one hand we are part of creation, on the other we are empowered to give Christlike service to other creatures. Periodically, the prophetic word recalls us to the responsibility of being creatures-with-power; the faithful communities offer ongoing checks on our practices; the Bible gives us clues to how to exercise stewardship properly.

Sparing the Earth

Many of the basic notions of how to treat nonhuman creatures come from the Book of Genesis. The Genesis account shows:

—God is the Creator of all things of the earth. (1:1–25)

—Earth is good and enters into the whole of human history. (1:26–31)

—Men and women are created in the image of God. (1:27)

—Everything God makes is good. (1:31)

—Humanity has dominion over the things of earth. (1:28)

—Humanity is placed on earth to cultivate and take care of it. (2:15)

—Humanity has power over creatures in the act of naming the animals. (2:20)

—Humanity is obliged to refrain from excessive use (tree of good and evil). (2:16–17)

The Genesis passage shows our relationship with both God and the rest of creation. Creation is in no way evil; it is to be lived with, cultivated, developed, and spared. None of these actions gives us as much trouble as that of "dominion" over the creatures. In this passage may come a philosophy of unwarranted environmental damage. But our human dominance must involve exercising a power of ministry to protect, guard, and enhance creation. Even our way of "dominating" is subject to growth and development.

A false or political notion of dominance can be harmful to those exercising the power. For if humanity is part of this earth and needing to be in harmony with it, then harm to the earth is harm to human beings. Autocratic dominance can lead to damage or destruction to those parts of creation which we might think we have a right to use, consume, or damage. Whether we perceive of reverence and respect for creation as flowing from reverence for God and/or humanity, or even from something within nature itself, it contains a homocentric or self-preservational element.

The cardinal precept not to eat the seed grain, no matter how hard the times, also holds for our relationship to natural resources in general and to all other living species. These are the seeds of life to future generations. Humanity's venture into the future is conditioned by a healthy and varied environment, which in turn is dependent upon many of our present actions. Destruction of parts of the environment is as suicidal as imposing grave risks on future generations; it is a desecration and an act of irreverence to both God and creation. From the biblical account we sense our power to build and to destroy, for contained in our power are both promise and peril.

Recognizing the ambiguous nature of this power is paramount. Here the need for self-discipline is quite important, for power used properly can build, but misused can destroy. Disciplining oneself can often be best done by refraining from use of certain good things, whether these be food, drink, or natural resources. The operative principle *Use resources sparingly* is a way to control our human power and a beginning point of spiritual growth and development.

> Hence, one is to make use of them [created things] in as far as they help him in the attainment of his end, and he must rid himself of them in as far as they prove a hindrance to him.[10]

The practice of sparing resources shows our own commitment to the future. We believe in a tomorrow when another generation will have authentic needs. We are opposed to the philosophy "Let us eat and drink today; tomorrow we shall be dead." (I Corinthians 15:33) An all-absorbing activity of sequestering goods and accumulating wealth is counter to the sparing principle—for after the barns are filled "this very night the demand will be made for your soul." (Luke 12:20)

With the rise of modern technology, people acquired the ability to dominate in ways never before dreamed of, such as through drugs, computer information retrieval, television commercials, and the obvious array of modern weaponry. Thus the need to become self-disciplined and to spare resources has become more evident. A profound ethical issue arises: exactly how much is needed for attaining human goals? Needs may be relative, for the luxuries of one generation may become the necessities of another. Constant reexamination is required lest the list of needs continue to grow.

> Do not weary yourself with getting rich,
> and have nothing to do with dishonest gain.
>
> Proverbs 23:4

A quantitative limit to what should be gathered for one's living is shown by a generous, providing God:

> Everyone must gather enough of it [the manna in the desert] for his needs, one omer a head, according to the number of persons in your families.
>
> Exodus 16:16

But enough is sufficient, and keeps the gatherers from becoming greedy.

The concept of sparing the earth's resources is further seen in the following:

> Land must not be sold in perpetuity, for the land belongs to me [God], and to me you are only strangers and guests.
>
> Leviticus 25:23

God had absolute ownership of the Holy Land, and the Chosen People were guests on the land. Thus the resources of the land were not theirs to squander. They were periodically to remember their situation, and even give the soil a rest. "But in the seventh year the land is to have its rest." (Leviticus 25:4) Not only did this sabbatical for the land reflect the need for self-discipline and respect for the bounty God had given, it was also good agricultural practice.

In the jubilee year (every fifty years) a liberation of slaves was enforced, along with a general enfranchisement of people and goods—rejoining clans and recovery of ancestral property (Leviticus 25:24–31). It was a way of redistributing wealth and controlling individual greed. The fact of the matter is that such operations seldom occurred, but the basic principle of sparing resources was set forth.

Repairing the Earth

The constant call for restraint and self-discipline in the Bible has a very sound reason: the human inclination to sin and exceed bounds. The relationship of harmony with God and creatures is broken by human misconduct; the sinner is driven from the primitive state of innocence and obliged to toil for a living (Genesis 3:23). An environmental catastrophe results in the form of a flood (Genesis 6–9), but God saves his faithful remnant and makes a covenant with all of us:

> Here is the sign of the Covenant I make between myself and you and every living creature with you for all generations.
>
> Genesis 9:12; see also 9:16

When human beings sin, the earth is wounded; when God forgives, the earth is healed—for humanity and earth form a single unity.

> From the beginning till now the entire creation, as we know, has been groaning in one great act of giving birth.
>
> Romans 8:22

But part of human fidelity to a forgiving God involves repairing the damage done through sinfulness. Sin creates a disharmony, but repentance reestablishes wholeness, or environmental balance.

Thus we might develop a second operative principle: *Repair environmental damage*. We each have both a social and an individual responsibility to make restitution for damages done. If we disturb the earth, we are responsible both to human beings and to all of creation.

> Fathers may not be put to death for their sons, nor sons for fathers. Each is to be put to death for his own sin.

Deuteronomy 24:16

The concept of personal responsibility was slow to develop in human history. And in environmental matters further development is necessary, not only for the many who litter and pollute, but for the corporate "persons" who potentially are able to do far greater damage than individual consumers. Polluters commit a "social" sin, a disharmony that damages the entire social fabric. Often, the perpetrators—groups of individuals or institutions—do not realize their wrongdoing. In such cases, once the wrongdoing is recognized, the culprit—not a governmental agency or the citizenry as a whole—should be made to repair the damage. Corporate executives should bear the responsibility for ecological crimes as much as should individual litterers, and that might even include jail sentences.

Scripture tells us that with repair come forgiveness and reestablishment of harmony with the earth and the Creator. A fragile ecology demands rapid repair, so that the earth also might be quick to forgive. The repentant sinner returns to a land flowing with milk and honey, and therein lies a promise that the earth is resilient and can be repaired, though not returned to a state of ecological purity. The wrongdoer can learn through repairing damage to live closer to nature.

Caring for the Earth

Involved in social sin, we must recognize the obligation to preserve the earth for future generations (Yahweh is the God of Abraham, Isaac, and Jacob—an enduring God), the fragile nature of this finite earth, and our capacity to damage and destroy this earth-gift. Infidelity is forgetfulness of the Creator, of human responsibility, and of the earth itself. Caring for the earth includes a social responsibility for this and future generations and for the earth's resources. To care is to show concern, especially when our neighbor fails to make necessary repairs. For each environmental abuse is a social sin and hurts the entire ecological structure. But social responsibility is never equally shared by all people. Thus we must imitate Christ and take on ourselves the social sin and make restitution through care and concern.

> ". . . and in my own body to do what I can to make up all that has still to be undergone by Christ for the sake of his body, the Church."

> Colossians 1:24

Caring is part of the duty of the entire human family. The caring person must be observant of where and when damages arise, prompt at responding to the damage, and willing to go out of the way to make restitution. The third operative principle is: *Caring for the earth is the concern of all.* This concern is not just for the culprit but is a common responsibility. Damage is always greater than what can be allocated to individual perpetrators. Thus concern must be greater. An energy waster or an extravagant person is wasting our resources, and a realization of the common heritage of those resources makes us act firmly and promptly to expose and punish the culprit. By our neglect and silence we become accomplices in the social crime.

Fidelity to the Judeo-Christian tradition includes a number of actions such as: reporting polluters of air, water, or land; sponsoring ordinances that restrict noise pollution; demanding proper labeling of indoor pollutants; teaching the family not to litter. Silence in the face of wrongdoing is an expression of infidelity; it denies the prophetic call; it weakens the community.

Sharing the Earth

The earth does not belong to us absolutely. We receive a trust for a specified time, and then we pass on like the withering grass, but the earth remains. Tillers of the soil, who are in communion with it, understand the transitory nature of crops and even eroding soil—it takes a century to make an inch of soil and a moment to lose it.

Some of us have greater trusts than others, through either birth, acquisition, gift, or accident. Those with less deserve more in justice, not charity. Thus we have an imperative to share both in time (with future generations) and in space (with less fortunate human beings). Furthermore, we must share our earth with the other living cohabitants. A fourth principle emerges: *Share the fruits of the earth with the less fortunate.*

Scripture says that *all* human beings are created in the image of God, not just those of one's family, social group, religion, or nation. The Good Samaritan parable extends neighborhood from backyard to the ends of the earth. Modern communications make this awareness even more acute, but even in St. Paul's day there was a sense of sharing with distant people; he asked Christians in Greece to support the church of Jerusalem.

The Scriptures contain many examples of the need to share. The parable of Dives and Lazarus in Luke 16:19–31 speaks of punishment for failing to give to the poor. Exhortations to share with others abound:

> When reaping the harvest in your field, if you have overlooked a sheaf in that field, do not go back for it. Leave it for the stranger, the orphan and the widow, so that Yahweh your God may bless you in all your undertakings.

> Deuteronomy 24:19; see also 24:20–21

> If one of the brothers or one of the sisters is in need of clothes and has not enough food to live on, and one of you says to them, "I wish you well; keep yourself warm and eat plenty," without giving them these bare necessi-

ties of life, then what good is that? Faith is like that: if good works do not go with it, it is quite dead.

James 2:15–16

Tell them that they are to do good, and be rich in good works, to be generous and willing to share.

I Timothy 6:18

If your brother who is living with you falls on evil days and is unable to support himself with you, you must support him as you would a stranger or a guest, and he must continue to live with you.

Leviticus 25:35

Sharing is an integral part of the biblical message, and many passages show God's favor to those who imitate the God who shares with his people. Sharing concretizes the unity of faith and justice, wherein believers show fidelity to a generous God and manifest it by establishing justice for their neighbors throughout the world. Sharing is closely associated with sparing the earth, for to share is to require less for more people; sharing taps the human resources that are wasted by those scratching for the bare essentials of life, and gives them an opportunity to develop talents and further the glorification of God's creation. Sharing is a form of communication—the best form within the Judeo-Christian tradition—between those who have something to give and those who are in need.

Responding to the question that Christ will be asked: "When did we see you hungry and feed you?" (Matthew 25:37) means giving in charity to the needy. But there is perhaps more—a hunger for justice that must be fulfilled. *Ecojustice*, or the need to deal justly with the environment, is not removed from the problem of justice and human rights that is felt throughout the world. For humanity and earth are united, and what is a disharmony for one is so for the other. So to share with the oppressed in such a way that they are empowered is really to give and share something with human beings and the earth itself. Thus the ultimate sharing that we can do is to help the oppressed gain control over their own lives and community, and, in our so doing, both the social and physical environment will surely benefit.

DEVELOPING THE CONCEPT OF STEWARDSHIP

Stewardship in its rudimentary meaning refers to management, a management which uses no more of the available resources than needed (a sparing), which does not allow damage to go unattended (repairing), which includes a proper dominion (caring), and which looks out for others' needs (sharing). Wealth, power, or resources are held in trust and include serious social responsibilities.

> What is expected of stewards is that each one should be found worthy of his trust.
>
> I Corinthians 4:2

Stewardship need not be considered only in economic terms but embraces the entire complexus of human living in our environment. As William Byron says, stewardship means wise use, and this can also apply to the ideas needed to develop renewable energy alternatives.[11] Max Stackhouse extends stewardship to include three areas: care for persons, care for spirituality, and care for social institutions.[12]

The oldest Christian traditions understood the use of property to be in common, with private ownership being a concession to human weakness.[13] Holding things in common was an ideal of the early Christian community (Acts 2 and 4), and the tradition was followed in subsequent ages in religious communities and even down to this day. To use things in common has a direct bearing on our environment, for air and water and energy resources are held by all and are not for the exclusive use of a few. So those who damage the water quality or pollute the air or waste energy are really taking from what belongs to a common heritage, and in some way are stealing from their fellow human beings.

Christians have struggled with the concept of economic activity as either a reluctantly tolerated necessity or a potentially positive activity to be integrated into everyday living. Stackhouse says the early Church recognized the tension be-

HISTORICAL DEVELOPMENT OF STEWARDSHIP CONCEPT

Century	Historical Situation	Ideal Christian Ethical Response
1st–4th	Hostility of pagan Empire	Learn to live in persecuted circumstances and to conserve spiritual resources
5th–7th	Barbarian invasions of West	Adopt flexible educational method (monasteries) in order to civilize and retain culture
8th–12th	Arab and Turkish conflicts	Integrate ancient philosophy and literature into current Christian thought
13th–15th	Trading with the East	Expand vision of the West to entirely new and respected cultures
16th	Circumnavigation of globe	Accept the concept of a finite globe on which a limited number of people live
17th and 18th	Scientific revolution	Develop cosmic consciousness, with the earth as one part of the universe
18th–20th	Industrial revolution	Conserve human labor and make the machine the slave for human betterment
19th	Evolutionary theory	Be aware of the vast expanse of time to develop the species
20th and on	Age of scarcity	Become aware of the need to share resources and power with less fortunate members of the human family

tween Christianity and private property by requiring the vow of poverty from the clergy while allowing the ordinary believer to own property. The later Middle Ages showed great suspicion of economic activity, considering money both unnatural and unspiritual.[14] Stackhouse believes that "this two-level morality and anti-material spirituality was broken by the Reformation, which generated new economic attitudes and institutions, but no new clear and sustained economic ethic."

The understanding of stewardship has evolved during the Christian era, with much effort centered on the use of money and, to a lesser extent, real property. Often internal church discipline was the reason, but by no means the only one. In fact various historical conditions and events are responsible for expanding the Christian's self-understanding of being a steward and the Church's consciousness in developing and fostering proper stewardship. While the Church's awareness of its role was not perfect, it does advance beyond biblical times, as indicated on the preceding chart.

With a growing understanding of stewardship, one may expect improved personal attitudes about the environment: less waste, more reclamation, better plant and animal protection, more sharing of resources. But with this change of heart must come the fullness of the message of the Tradition, and that is the vision of a "new heaven and a new earth" (Isaiah 65:17; Revelation 21:1). The old is not good enough, even though creation was good. The creative act is an ongoing process, and the believers partake in that act. It is part of nature that improvement occurs, and it is part of human nature to help bring plants and animals as well as other people to a better quality of life.

Qualitative growth has often been viewed within the religious community as self-improvement. By becoming better we become more firm in faith, more moral in action, more respectful of our neighbor. In fact, the heavy concentration on personal conversion, on devotions and revivals and spiritual retreats, and on individual moral acts might lead one to think that this is the sole thrust of improvement. But experience teaches that an individual improvement without a social consciousness is quite hollow and not faithful to the prophetic word found in that Tradition which beckons the believer to do justice for others.

Faith is more than a personal experience; it is the community believing. The neophyte is received into a believing community; the community grows as a unit; the members become a pilgrim and covenanting people; they are a people in need of reflection and repentance; they are liberated and led as a people to a new land; they reach out to, touch, and influence their neighbors. Their actions are social in nature.

Growth in the individual and community goes beyond itself. As self-consciousness and self-worth grows, so is the sense that we are a social and historic people, rooted in our earth and having our origins here. We are more than dust; we have a power to touch earth, not just for the worse, but for the better. The earth of which we are part is composed of other creatures with whom we form a community, a fellowship, a common destiny. Redemption extends to the entire creation, which "has been groaning in one great act of giving birth" (Romans 8:22). Thus spiritual growth—the growth of the believing community's quality of life—is not merely individual or even social in character; it is ecological.

Human beings look to the future. Though sometimes diverted by the struggle for survival or the distractions of material amenities, we still look in faith to a better world. We crave improvement, for we are more than sparers, repairers, carers for, and sharers of the earth's resources; we are builders of a new heaven and a new earth. We have a destiny imprinted on our brains and woven into our spirits to add something to nature. We sense the incompleteness of the world around us—not just a world wounded by misdeeds, but a creation not yet fully created and awaiting the touch of *Homo sapiens*. From life we give life; from power—albeit awesome and often misused—we improve our earth.

Part of this sense of growth and improvement comes from the Christian tradition's belief in resurrection, of the power of life over death, of the capacity to give hope to others. Both faith and hope spring from an ecological community and both help transform power from overlordship to loving service. Thus environmental improvement becomes a sacrifice that believers assume through the hope in a new earth. It is more than refraining from destroying our ecosystem, more than distributing the earth's fruits to all people; it is a definite commitment to the task of rebuilding the earth, of giving all creatures a higher quality of life. Even within the environmental sin of pollution and waste, we can find redemption and a resiliency in an improvable earth.

The energy and optimism that are needed for improving the earth are spiritual; the planning and developing required are rational, systematic, and scientific. The genius of such a noted environmentalist as René Dubos is found in that delicate balance of spirit and rationality which calls for improvement of the earth. Professor Dubos has defended the power of human intervention in the environment.[15] He says:

I have an optimistic attitude about human intervention into the environment. I was raised about 30 miles north of Paris. This is a country which from the natural point of view was completely covered by forest and marshes until about 4,000 years ago. At that time Neolithic man settled in it and began clearing the land. Since then it has been under heavy agriculture with a very high population density. And yet today, many people think it is one of the most enchanting kinds of European landscapes, much like English East Anglia which also was forest and marshes before the advent of man.

Human beings can intervene into nature and transform it, provided they do it with ecological wisdom. Ecological wisdom in the past was purely empirical. People did certain things without knowing why, but now we have enough knowledge that we can change the landscape without destroying it.[16]

Theological reflection on what we are doing and what we should do helps us become active participants in the creative act. We can no longer remain satisfied with being merely passive observers on a cosmic scene. Such activism requires that we be grounded in our community activities and concerns and that we become involved in national and global energy and resource policies, monitoring of pollutants, research on natural habitats, proper land use and urbanization practices, and world food and raw material distribution systems.

Among questions raised in the preceding chapters that have theological import are these:

* Does liberation theology say something to us about our treatment of plants and animals?
* Must we dismantle all nuclear power operations to ensure world peace and security?
* Is conservation a permanent or a temporary attitude dictated by our current dependence on nonrenewable resource?
* Should enlightened people impose their insights and will on other citizens' free use of toxic materials?
* Must we create social and political mechanisms wherein the affluent must *share* with the poor? Must we reject the profit motive? Can we tolerate a world half-needy and half-satisfied?
* Do we need a radically new economic order for the profound lifestyle changes required in an age of scarcity?

For see, winter is past,
the rains are over and gone.
The flowers appear on the earth.
The season of glad songs has come,
the cooing of the turtledove is heard
in our land.
The fig tree is forming its first figs
and the blossoming vines give out their fragrance.
                    Song of Songs 2:11–13

REFERENCES

1. L. White, Jr., "The Historical Roots of Our Ecologic Crisis," *Science* 155 (1967), p. 1207.
2. L. W. Moncrief, "The Cultural Basis for Our Environmental Crisis," *Science* 170 (1970), p. 508.
3. A. Fritsch, *Theology of the Earth* (Washington, D.C.: CLB Publishers, 1972).
4. "This Land Is Home to Me: A Pastoral Letter on Powerlessness in Appalachia by the Catholic Bishops of the Region" (Prestonsburg, Ky., 1974), p. 5.
5. "The Plutonium Economy, Study Material for the Proposed Policy Statement," National Council of the Churches of Christ in the USA (New York, 1976), p. 2.
6. *Documents of Vatican II:* No. 69, "The Church Today," W. M. Abbott, ed. (New York: Guild Press, 1966), p. 278.
7. President Jimmy Carter, "Preface to The National Energy Plan" (April 29, 1977), Washington, D.C., pp. x–xi.
8. J. L. McKenzie, *Dictionary of the Bible* (Milwaukee: Bruce Publishing Co., 1965), p. 651.
9. B. C. Birch, "Nature, Humanity and God," Subcommittee on Energy Ethics, National Council of Churches Taskforce (May 21, 1977), p. 14.
10. L. J. Puhl, *The Spiritual Exercises of St. Ignatius* (Westminster, Md.: Newman Press, 1954), p. 12.
11. W. Byron, *Toward Stewardship: An Interim Ethic of Poverty, Pollution and Power* (New York: Paulist Press, 1975), p. 14.
12. M. L. Stackhouse, "Toward a Stewardship Ethics," *Theology Digest* 22 (Autumn 1974), p. 231.
13. W. Byron, op. cit., p. 16.
14. M. L. Stackhouse, op. cit., p. 229.
15. R. Dubos, *The God Within* (New York: Charles Scribner's Sons, 1972).
16. R. Dubos, "Think Globally, Act Locally," *Environmental News* (Boston, Mass.: U. S. Environmental Protection Agency, New England Regional Office, May 1978), p. 11.

VIII

MOVING FROM REFLECTION
TO ACTION

> Pretending that we can go on as we are
> will only make the eventual adjustment more painful.
>
> Anthony Lewis

The preceding chapters have dealt with a series of factors contributing to the environmental crisis and also with underlying and conflicting values in specific problem areas. We want to interweave here the common threads of the various treatments to construct criteria for environmental action and to apply them specifically to the seven problem areas addressed. Discussions up to now have been drawn from ecology, chemistry, physics, environmental health and law, engineering, history, economics, social science, and theology. As we move from reflection to action, the emphasis here is on advocacy, political action, and other public-interest techniques required to effect change.

Akin to each of the seven problem areas contributing to environmental degradation are the following responses or action criteria:

Problem Areas	Action Criteria
Disregard for life	Environmental protection
Uncontrolled technology	Exercising full responsibility
Disregard for natural resource limitation	Sharing resources
Overuse and waste of materials	Prudent use
Failure to include all environmental costs	Making a human environment
Exaggerated freedom in lifestyle choices	Building community
Failure to prepare for the future	Environmental improvement

The sets of criteria spring in part from our understanding and development of the concept of stewardship (sparing, repairing, caring for, and sharing the earth; growth in quality of life; community witness; and creative service). As part of the elements that make up our Western culture, they enter into the character of our environmental action. Before reviewing these action criteria in turn, it helps to mention some of the underlying basic rights and responsibilities that pertain to our environment.

BASIC ENVIRONMENTAL RIGHTS AND RESPONSIBILITIES

We are related to our environment and as such have certain rights that must be respected so that we live and grow and fulfill ourselves. The United Nations Conference on the Environment at Stockholm (1972) has developed a Declaration of Principles (DP; see Appendix IV for complete text), which opens by saying that we human beings have "the fundamental right to freedom, equality and adequate conditions of life, in an environment of a quality which permits a life of dignity and well-being" (DP #1).

This set of environmental rights would have to include the following:

* Clean air and water
* Healthy living space
* Essentials of life (food, clothing, and shelter)
* Job opportunity
* A healthy occupational setting
* World resource sharing
* Knowledge about environmental threats

These rights are self-evident once we have discussed the fundamental components of a quality environment, both social and physical. Other rights somewhat less clear and more disputed might include the right to join social and political groups aimed at deciding how to control energy and natural resources and the right to damages occurring from the extravagance of others. The spelling out of the boundaries of these rights can become somewhat difficult. Just how clean must the air and water be? How healthy the living space? What constitutes essentials? How many should receive what type of jobs? How healthy should the occupational situation be, especially when some are inherently dangerous? How do we share resources? How much knowledge is needed about environmental threats?

Besides the difficulties in spelling out these boundaries, there is also the whole complex problem of infringement on the social and political rights of people, which has detrimental effects on the entire environment. This is why the Declaration of Principles states:

> . . . policies promoting or perpetuating apartheid, racial segregation, discrimination, colonial and other forms of oppression and foreign domination stand condemned and must be eliminated.
>
> (DP #1)

Along with basic environmental rights go such associated responsibilities as the maintenance of air and water purity; creation of healthy living space; provision for the essentials of life; job opportunities development; preserving a healthy occupational environment; sharing global resources; and environmental information dissemination. Again, there are associated responsibilities that are somewhat less clear, such as the duties of a citizen in the decision-making process and the amount of repair needed for damage due to environmental insult.

Part of our responsibility is individually based and part is social. It appears that we should make responsible changes in our lifestyle when they are needed, to communicate to others the harm that has been done by individual actions, or when group actions infringe on the rights of our neighbors. This group responsibility might be that of a local community, or of a state or region, or of the national governmental agency or an international body. Referring to nations bearing environmental responsibilities, the Declaration of Principles says that they are to "insure that activities within their jurisdiction or control do not cause damage to the environment of other states or of areas beyond the limits of national jurisdiction" (DP #21).

A thorough discussion of these environmental rights and
responsibilities is beyond the scope of this book, but we will
attempt in the following sections to mention a large number
of them in treating environmental action criteria.

ENVIRONMENTAL PROTECTION

Anything that is fragile and valuable needs protection and
care. We give extra protection to our young, aged, infirm,
and handicapped. We must also give special protection to
our global environment, which is a fragile oasis of vitality in
an infinity of cosmic space. We must therefore guard the sacred trust given to us—our ecological heritage.

> The natural resources of the earth including the air,
> water, land, flora and fauna and especially repre
> sentative samples of natural ecosystems must be safe
> guarded for the benefit of present and future genera
> tions through careful planning or management as
> appropriate.
>
> (DP #2)

This heritage extends to our wildlife and its habitat (DP
#4), nonrenewable resources (DP #5), and seas (DP #7),
all threatened in ways undreamed of in the past. Ecologically
concerned citizens must take steps as individuals or in groups
to extend this protection in numerous ways.

* Protect wildlife—The United States is the leading consumer of wildlife (pets, ivory, skins, and an array of products) from other nations. It is necessary to strengthen the
U. S. Fish and Wildlife Service so that it will stop illegal
smuggling of animal products into this country and stop the
depletion of the world's wildlife. Ask your congressional representative to see that that agency is strengthened.

* Protect citizens—One of the best protections is to have
civil defense systems activated. Almost none are in a condition to be effective in case of a major disaster. See to it that
the local unit is alerted to the possibility of a nuclear power

plant disaster or an accident involving the transportation of radioactive materials.

* *Protect our land*—Care must be taken to develop proper land-use programs, many of which are related to fossil fuel extraction. The U. S. Office of Surface Mining is currently working on a long-term project to draw up guidelines on procedures for selecting lands unsuitable for strip mining. Citizens with strong environmental and ethical concerns should deliver testimony on what lands should be declared unsuitable and why.

* *Protect consumers*—Often short-lived and inferior products are a heavy drain on natural resources, so consumer and environmental protection generally coincide. Give support to the local, regional, or national groups working to strengthen existing laws. Write to companies that make inferior consumer products and complain and get reimbursed. Make sure to send copies of the correspondence to the Better Business Bureau.

* *Protect workers*—Occupational health is a major indicator of the quality of life for millions of people. The threats to that health are often environmental pollutants. Most workers do not recognize dangers. Each concerned citizen could hardly spend better time than to discuss working conditions with laborers. Often the casual conversation will open up abuses that a worker never knew of, and the first steps toward a remedy will be taken.

* *Protect our heritage*—Our communities generally contain a number of historic and cultural landmarks, some of which are unmarked. Help initiate steps to see that these are protected from greedy developers. Our historic sites always need a helping hand, as do cemeteries and gardens near such sites.

EXERCISING FULL RESPONSIBILITY

Being responsible human beings implies that we are accountable for our own mistakes and that we make repairs and restitution for damage. In environmental matters, a recognition of our fallible human nature is exemplified by cleaning up litter, restoring polluted rivers to their former state, or paying for damage done by oil spills. Sometimes being responsible means that we take an action before the damage is done:

> States must strive to reach prompt agreement, in the relevant international organs, on the elimination and complete destruction of [nuclear] weapons.
>
> (DP #26)

Some of these prior actions might include: banning the use of furs and commercial products from endangered species; calling for a moratorium on nuclear power generation; restricting the commercial production of chemicals, biological substances, and technologies that cannot be safely used or transferred; limiting economic development that results in irreversible ecological degradation or critically disrupts land, culture, family, and lives of people; and forbidding lifestyle practices that might result in irreparable harm to the ecosystem, such as fluorocarbons in aerosol sprays.

> The discharge of toxic substances or of other substances and the release of heat, in such quantities or concentrations as to exceed the capacity of the environment to render them harmless, must be halted in order to insure that serious or irreversible damage is not inflicted upon ecosystems.
>
> (DP #6)

Over and above curbing existing harmful practices, some form of positive repair mechanism must be set up to assist injured persons or restore a damaged ecosystem.

> The capacity of the earth to produce vital renewable resources must be maintained and wherever practicable restored and improved.
>
> (DP #3)

States shall cooperate to develop further the international law regarding liability and compensation for the victim of pollution and other environmental damage caused by activities within the jurisdiction or control of such states to areas beyond their jurisdiction.

(DP #22)

* *Restore threatened species*—It is not enough to protect and preserve wildlife through regulations against hunting or creation of refuges. At some critical points the resilience of the species has been jeopardized. Thus positive steps have to be taken, as, for instance, to bring the bald eagle back to restored numbers. Governmental agencies and individuals may have to assist in creating nesting areas, augmenting natural feeding supplies, removing predators, and building and equipping breeding grounds. Help might be more individualized, like washing off sea gulls after an oil spill or caring for an injured deer until such time that it might return to the wild.

* *Make nuclear plants insure themselves*—Whoever is in charge must be responsible as well. The government should not have to be the ultimate insurer of overly expensive and risky nuclear power plants. If the process is profitable, insurance must be demanded from the one making the profit; if this is too risky, then maybe it is a sign nuclear plants should be avoided. Presently the U.S. federal government insures nuclear power plants against major disaster.

* *Compensate injured citizens*—Residents near mining and power plant operations suffer from use of blasting materials, land disturbances, road deterioration, and pollution emissions, to name a few. Unfortunately American law regards a polluter or disturber of the environment as an innocent person, one who must be proved guilty. Thus the burden of proof rests with the injured party, who is least able to furnish resources for legal procedures. On the other hand, in Japan, the environmental damage is recognized and the polluters are assessed in a body to cover any possible damage; injured parties may apply for compensation from the assessment fund.

While working for some such compensation fund accessible to our injured citizens, we can still encourage or join in class action suits against polluters, and form ad hoc committees of injured persons to petition for environmental changes.

* *Clean up hazardous spills*—Whether these spills occur in a chemical plant, a railroad siding, or our own garage, it is the duty of the individual or corporation to see that the substances are contained or removed. This is often not an easy task, for it takes special training to do such operations properly. The contained toxic material is still present unless incinerated or chemically decomposed; thus ultimate disposal problems persist. Don't hesitate to involve fire, police, disaster, and civil defense teams in case of such accidents.

* *Reclaim disturbed ecosystems*—Besides the obvious reclamation operations in coal mining regions, there are many other disturbed areas: deforested lands, disused quarries, salted irrigation land, open-pit mineral mines, overgrazed pasturelands, garbage disposal sites, urban slums, silted riverbeds, construction sites, and many others. Pinpointing blame is a first step, and something the Office of Surface Mining actually encourages citizens to assist in doing. Where culprits cannot be found, then governmental funds are available for reclamation. All we have to do is open our eyes and start restoring—whether it be planting trees, sowing grass, or leveling off rubble.

* *Compensate for wasting resources*—When we have wasted a precious resource, maybe it can't be restored. One compensation is joining lobby groups such as Bread for the World, Impact, Common Cause, Public Citizen, or Network; donating time or money to world relief groups; volunteering to assist needy people through personal services. Citizen groups might strive to influence national resource policy in ways leading to reduced resource consumption and weapons expenditures.

SHARING RESOURCES

Our environment is an open, dynamic system. It is important that we, as participants within this environment, function within a continued atmosphere of openness and sharing with our fellow human beings. This can be done through the following ways: environmental education, information flow, research, and sharing of world resources.

Since the environment is quite complex, its understanding requires learning by citizens.

> Education in environmental matters . . . is essential in order to broaden the basis for an enlightened opinion and responsible conduct by individuals, enterprises and communities in protecting and improving the environment in its full human dimension.

> (DP #19)

We should each feel it part of our responsibility to learn about the environment. We should strive to see that part of the world's defense budget is converted to environmental education, which includes both formal programs in more advanced lands and basic literacy campaigns in the Third World countries.

A good information flow is necessary for environmental education. Quite often this flow is through our major pedagogical tool, the mass media. This vehicle of communication has at times created an atmosphere of overconsumption and ultimately environmental deterioration. On the other hand, the mass media are capable of gathering information vital to environmental protection. Openness includes publicity of appropriate and relevant information.

* *Give threatened species standing*—The question of extending ecojustice procedures to plants and animals is controversial (see Appendix II for the animal "rights" issue). However, our court system requires that the offended parties be the ones bringing suit. They must have "standing" or a cause for initiating legal action. In many wilderness areas, human beings are not to be found who have this interest. Give standing to such threatened plants and animals.

* *Make technical malfunctions known*—Sheer technical complexity is no excuse for withholding information, yet quite often weaknesses in nuclear power technology have been concealed for long periods. Citizens have a right to know what risk is involved and cannot afford to leave decisions to the technical elite. Every effort therefore must be made to ensure that stockholders require release of informa-

tion about their own industries. Attend such stockholder meetings and raise questions from the floor if necessary. It is even good long-range business sense. Use state and federal freedom of information procedures to find out what is happening.

* *Share resource and energy information*—Citizens should know what can be done in heating and use of energy resources. Pressure utility companies to develop energy conservation informational packets for all customers, as is now required by law. Have the U. S. Forest Service or state extension services survey woodlands for suggesting how to improve the land, and remove useless wood for fuel. Develop fuel cooperatives.

* *Require proper chemical labeling*—Citizens must endure chemical risks, but there are pressures that they can impose on both industry and government to see that chemicals are safely used. Read labels and see whether the directions can be safely followed (many can't). Send a faulty label directly to the Consumer Product Safety Commission or to the Federal Trade Commission. Citizen complaints to the producer also count. It is even more imperative that workers who produce, package, or ship chemicals know what safety measures are to be taken, and just how dangerous the chemical is. Another important action is to require instructions on chemical safety and toxicity in all college and university chemical programs.

* *Disseminate environmental information*—Almost anyone can become an expert on part of our environment. But this acquired information should be shared through talks, writings, discussions, workshops, conferences, and classes. Magazines like *Environment* and *Environmental Action* deserve support, along with those on energy use and alternatives such as *RAIN*.

> The free flow of up-to-date scientific information and experience must be supported and assisted to facilitate the solution of environmental problems. . . .

(DP #20)

* *Share resources*—Sharing knowledge, information, and research is only part of the picture. If we conceive of ourselves as stewards, then we sense the need to champion the environmental and resource commons. This can be done both individually (by sharing appliances and tools that are seldom used) or in community (by assembling a resource listing of technical people willing to help solve certain local environmental problems). Help workers obtain stocks and begin owning their industry or business.

PRUDENT USE

Prudence lies at the heart of ethics, including environmental ethics. Such imprudent acts as endangering plants and animals; wasting energy, water, mineral, and forestry resources; and depleting land fertility are evidently unethical. How to counter misuse and overuse of resources is not so evident. Some suggestions follow:

* *Do not endanger through commercial use*—Do not buy endangered or exotic wild animals for pets. They are among the few who survived the pillage of the jungles. Remember, baby chimps are often obtained by shooting their mothers out of trees, with the hope that the young will cling and not be hurt by the fall.[1] Business interests and the U. S. Chamber of Commerce are constantly lobbying Congress to weaken present wildlife laws. Arouse citizen support to counter commercial interests. Don't buy exotic furs, ivory, or skin products; refrain from purchase of products from remotely threatened species such as otter, lynx, and bobcat.

* *Reduce nuclear wastes*—Nuclear waste generation occurs at numerous institutions (hospitals, universities, research facilities) as well as at power plants. The largest waste generator is the weapons program. Since it is impossible to stop all of this nuclear waste generation at the moment, prudence tells us to apply pressures to reduce it as much as possible. Unite peace groups with environmental groups on this question. Find out where wastes are being transported in your locality and alert local authorities to the need for transportation ordinances, modeled after that of New York City. Demonstrate your concern at temporary waste disposal sites—

they are all presently unsafe. For other strategies and actions, contact:

Critical Mass, P.O. Box 1538, Washington, DC 20013.

Nuclear Transportation Project (AFSC), P.O. Box 2234, High Point, NC 27261.

Nuclear Information and Resource Service, 1536 Sixteenth Street N.W., Washington, DC 20036.

* *Use nonrenewable resources wisely*
The nonrenewable resources of the earth must be employed in such a way as to guard against the danger of their future exhaustion and to insure that benefits . . . are shared by all. . . .

(DP #5)

A host of actions are available that seek correct use and conservation of electricity—the area where most waste of nonrenewable fossil and uranium fuels occurs. These include: converting from electric space and water heating to solar systems; installment of windmills for local use; return to small-scale community hydroelectric systems; use of co-generation units. Some practices place new emphasis on biomass (wood and other organic matter) fuel conversion for augmenting the total fuel consumption picture; these are limited to certain areas of the country and to places where competing food and material demands are less. Methane generation from agricultural and household waste offers a clean fuel alternative with maximum use of by-products. Because renewable energy conversion involves finite resources (finances, equipment, and so on), curbing use of extravagant home appliances and lighting will always be required.

* *Never overuse chemicals*—Be cautious about the use of new chemicals even when they are believed to be environmentally safe. Refrain from using ones known to be highly toxic altogether. With moderately toxic ones, seriously question their necessity, and when they are needed proceed with careful planning, proper expertise in application, protective garments and equipment, and common sense. Even with chemicals considered slightly toxic or of unknown toxicity, care should always be observed, but especially when children are near. For all chemicals: never overuse them, and be even more cautious when using more than one at the same time, for synergistic effects may prove quite harmful.

* *Make things last*—Environmental prudence takes a variety of forms, including budgeting resources; replenishing forest reserves; and recycling clothes, furniture, and building materials. Build structures and dwellings that will endure, and refurbish older ones; exercise soil and water conservation measures and encourage crop rotation. Recycle metal, paper, and textile products, and purchase appliances and vehicles with lifetime costs in mind.

* *Change ownership practices*—Prudent use of resources is conditioned by "needs" of future and present generations. Our neighbor's essential needs hold prior claim on resources that the powerful at times think they "possess." Determine who owns land in the locality and whether it is properly taxed. Find out whether your community has ordinances to handle solar rights. Are there land trusts available to assist the landless? Join groups that seek to work for more equitable taxation. Point out the absurdity of privately owned mineral rights. Work to save the small farmers from being driven from their land. Encourage collectives in housing, farming, and food distribution.

MAKING A HUMANE ENVIRONMENT

An environmentally conscious person is one who is spiritually adjusted, historically grounded, socially and politically alive, and ecologically in harmony with the earth. This person sees value in nature, landscape, and artistic creativity. Such a person lives in a natural world, but is not afraid to give it a human touch and human value, all the time recognizing there are many ways of expressing that humanness.

> . . . it will be essential in all classes to consider the systems of values prevailing in each country, and the extent of the applicability of standards which are valid for the most advanced countries but which may be inappro-

priate and of unwarranted social cost for the developing countries.

(DP #23)

* *See each part of the ecosystem as valuable*—All created things are good and worth saving. But a species need not have a commercial or human-directed value to be worth preserving. It is assumed that each species has an "ecological" value that it contributes to the ecosystem, even when human beings do not recognize it. Encourage people to take hikes, field trips, and vacations to enjoy the wilderness and natural beauty. Keep notebooks of such experiences. Encourage painting and photography. Learn about plants and birds, and teach the young to do the same.

* *Make technology humane*—Technology should be suited to people and not harmful to the environment. Assist in adapting appropriate technology methods to communities. Require assessments of environmental impact before any new development occurs in the community. Participate in discussion of power plant siting and coal conversion plants. Make sure that all sides are heard, especially citizen complaints and concerns.

* *Recognize that landscape has aesthetic value*—Environmental treatments must include aesthetics. While beauty may be in the eye of the beholder, ugliness does have certain objective qualities found in the disarray of litter, erosion of land, and presence of highwalls. Land-use planning must consider the total aesthetic value of the setting and natural components. We must therefore include land-use planning in any development project, and each community should have strict ordinances on land use. Make an effort to preserve the natural beauty of wild rivers, mountains, and seashores. Support efforts to enhance land conservancy, especially for areas most threatened by urbanization.

* *Preserve human health*—Health risks must always be minimized. When these are environmental risks, the entire community might be involved. One area where we must concentrate is the residential zone surrounding chemical plants, refineries, power plants, and other pollution sources. Keep a citizens' committee alerted to the need for monitoring emissions, detecting health complaints, and finding out what chemicals are used in the vicinity. Bring in local health officials and technical resource people to help with these operations if necessary.

* *Defend human rights*—A balanced physical environment requires a balanced social one. One of the most glaring imbalances in our day is in the field of human rights. Environmentalists should be very concerned about supporting human-rights causes, for a sensitivity among people of others' rights will undoubtedly extend to the entire earth.

* *Enhance life for all*—People deserve more than bare essentials: they also need meaningful work; basic security in home, workplace, community, and national life; and ample leisure time for developing cultural and artistic skills. When holding environmental workshops and conferences, make sure to include the artistic component.

BUILDING COMMUNITY

Applying some of the characteristics and qualities of lifestyle to the community is very important. But this community reaches beyond town and village and includes the entire physical environment.

* *Where possible, leave plants and animals in natural habitats*—Captivity is a last resort for endangered species; otherwise it should be used for species that are not psychologically hurt by it. Surroundings should resemble natural habitats: find out whether zoological gardens are sensitive to this. Discourage people from having pets that need natural surroundings. Learn to appreciate wildlife where it is. A plant in its natural setting is far more beautiful than when plucked and brought home. Teach others to be satisfied with seeing and photographing and let natural things stay where they are.

* *Prefer appropriate technology*—As Isao Fujimoto says, technology, "despite claims that it is value free, neutral, benefits everyone and has no politics to it—always carries a burden with it."[2] The burden includes prior assumptions about the progress and efficiency technology is striving to introduce. Highly complex and centralized forms of energy

production are beyond what is needed to do the particular job. They are insensitive to people and controlled from a distance. Form an appropriate-technology committee in your town and plug into networks now being formed on solar energy, gardening, food cooperatives, and home industries and crafts.

* *Opt for renewable energy*—Follow this scheme: use recyclable and renewable resources where possible; if not possible, reduce waste of existing nonrenewable use practices; when not available, use nonrenewable resources only for efficient and nonluxurious practices on a temporary basis; when renewable resource substitution is possible, substitute promptly. When there is competition for resource use, essential life services always take precedence over nonessential ones.

* *Prefer natural substances and practices to synthetic and artificial ones*—Extend this preference to a variety of consumer goods: natural versus processed foods; biological versus chemical pest controls; organic versus synthetic fertilizers; mulching and composting versus municipal garbage disposal; firewood versus electricity; natural fibers versus synthetic ones (all other things being equal). Natural practices include: natural birth control and birth practices; breastfeeding; native arts, crafts, and community participatory sports; home entertainment; houses made from native materials; home care for the aged and infirm; simple weddings, celebrations, and funerals.

* *Support community participatory decision-making*—Democracy can thrive if the community can deliberate on developments influencing the lives of its members. Any form of community development imposed from the outside really works against that democratic spirit. Thus it is important to get the right people on "area development district" boards as well as into public office. Participate in town meetings and encourage citizen hearings before any new development projects are started.

* *Encourage a multiplicity of lifestyle expressions*—As long as lifestyles are within the bounds of sound ecological principles and respect the rights of others, they should be allowed to take a variety of forms and shapes. Encourage variety in

foods, crafts and hobbies, and decoration. Learn about local artists and craftspeople and support their efforts. Where necessary, find outlets for their works. Encourage architectural variety in buildings. Support complementary modes of public and private transportation. Help increase numerous recreational opportunities for citizens. See that the libraries have sufficient books on lifestyle practices.

ENVIRONMENTAL DEVELOPMENT

While examples of local and regional environmental improvement are numerous, it is only recently that we have become aware of what must be done on a global basis. Furthermore, a global program must include the total elevation of the human quality of life.

> Economic and social development is essential for insuring a favorable living and working environment for man and for creating conditions on earth that are necessary for the improvement of the quality of life.
>
> (DP #8)

Inevitably this development on a global basis will require large amounts of energy, mineral, water, and financial resources. We cannot expect the many poor people of this earth to enter into such improvement while hungry and lacking the essentials of life. Nor will those lacking proper garbage and waste-disposal systems dispose of garbage properly. The only sure way to initiate and continue global environmental improvement is through the redistribution of wealth and available resources (see DP #9), such as by the stabilization of prices and adequate earnings for primary commodities and raw materials (DP #10). Environmental improvement policies must complement the development potentials of so-called developing nations (DP #11 and 12).

> In order to achieve a more rational management of resources and thus improve the environment, states should adopt an integrated and coordinated approach to their development planning so as to insure that development

is compatible with the need to protect and improve the human environment for the benefit of their population.

(DP #13)

Cooperative efforts are needed for environmental improvement, as will be apparent to any person attempting to recycle materials. The local collection center becomes a junk pile if there is no integrated system of removing the waste materials and delivering them to reprocessing plants. In turn, such a backup system will not function if there is no market for the recycled materials. Improvement is more than individual good will; it must be part of a sophisticated economic system making use of a large number of organizations.

International matters concerning the protection and improvement of the environment should be handled in a cooperative spirit by all countries, big or small, on an equal footing.

(DP #24)

States shall insure that international organizations play a coordinated, efficient and dynamic role for the protection and improvement of the environment.

(DP #25)

The larger structures should not lose sight of the need for local participation and planning. Health of the more global system rests in the vitality of the local cells, which includes coordination with national and international organizations.

The Declaration of Principles states that "rational planning constitutes an essential tool for reconciling any conflict between the needs of development and the need to protect and improve the environment" (DP #14). It specifically mentions human settlement and urbanization planning (DP #15) and demographic policies (DP #16). It says that "appropriate national institutions must be entrusted with the task of planning, managing or controlling" resources (DP

#17), and that part of the task rests with science and technology (DP #18).

From what has been said, a number of actions might be listed that will aid in global environmental improvement. Many of these cannot be taken by individuals as such, but citizens are able to influence decision-makers by voting, lobbying, or letter-writing campaigns.

* *Improve the condition of wildlife*—Environmental development cannot be at the expense of wildlife. Often development has meant the destruction of natural habitats. While many naturalists view any form of environmental intervention as a threat to wildlife, it need not be destructive with proper planning. Join groups to protect the whales from commercial exploitation. Become interested in the plight of endangered species in other countries, especially in developing lands, where environmental regulations may be harder to devise and enforce.

* *Evaluate technology used for development*—Development is foremost in the minds of leaders in the Third World. Part of the assistance must come from the United States. See that A.I.D., the World Bank, and other international support groups develop guidelines for applying appropriate technology programs. Lobby to stop the sale of nuclear power plants to such countries. Work with groups in Western Europe to make sure that such bans on sales are not made useless by another country's selling.

* *Improve world energy sources*—Many Third World lands face major energy crises from increasing shortages of fuel wood. Encourage VITA (Volunteers in Technical Assistance) and numerous religious and secular groups to offer technical assistance in these countries to develop solar cookers, windmills, and passive solar heating systems.

* *Seek global toxic substance controls*—Chemicals are a world problem that needs international cooperation for its solution. Support conferences among nations on such problems as "escape industries," which are running from tighter environmental regulations. Make sure that materials banned in the United States are not exported in turn to less regulated

countries. Back development of international monitoring programs using U.S. satellites.

* *Better the lot of the least well off*—The physical environment can be improved when the social one is. Priorities must be given to those who are among the world's poorest. Very cheap housing schemes exist to remove some of the shanty towns which form the suburban slums of Lima, Rio, and numerous Third World lands. Support technical assistance programs which deal with housing and self-improvement.

* *Make environmental improvement a global concern*— Support World Environment Day on June fifth each year.

These environmental actions are not meant to be a comprehensive blueprint for some sort of utopia; they set down some of the things we must consider, and they outline a way of approaching other important environmental issues that may arise in the coming years. The agenda is unfinished, and the action outlines are perhaps far too sketchy for some. It is not meant to be a "how-to-do-it" from a technical or political standpoint, but rather an ethical "how-to-do-it." Its best measure of success is whether it has excited any citizens to work for an improved environment.

REFERENCES

1. M. Satchell, "How the Smuggling Trade Is Wiping Out Wildlife," *Parade* (Dec. 3, 1978), p. 13.
2. I. Fujimoto, "The Values of Appropriate Technology and Visions for a Saner World" (Butte: National Center for Appropriate Technology, 1977), p. 2.

PEST CONTROL

The battle to preserve endangered species is perhaps the converse of a struggle to eradicate pests. Both the methods used (mainly chemical ones such as DDT and parathion) and the ultimate definition of pests are often questioned by environmentalists. Pests and weeds are animals and plants considered unwanted and a hindrance to people. A case in point is the starlings of Kentucky.[1] They have caused great discomfort to the local inhabitants as millions congregate in the fall and winter in certain rural localities. Their droppings have created a nuisance to farmers, and a fear of the airborne lung/nervous system disease histoplasmosis has become widespread. The Department of the Army spent much time and effort spraying the birds with a chemical (Tergitol) that removed the protective oil from the starlings' feathers, and the cold weather was to do the rest. The effectiveness of the eradication campaign was, however, quite questionable. Only one starling was counted among 200,000 dead birds, the rest being blackbirds and grackles. Has the pest been properly defined, and is the method a valid one if it has?

Many other cases exist, such as use of poisonous thallium salts to kill coyotes in the West that were blamed for killing sheep and other livestock. Many of the poisons remain around to do widespread environmental damage. A still more universal issue is such programs as the spraying of vast areas of town and countryside with DDT and other organic chemical pesticides. On the benefit side, millions of lives were saved or made more healthy. On the debit side, many predators were harmed by high accumulations of persistent pesticides in their bodies; furthermore, these chemical methods have defects. They do not kill all target insects but leave immune individuals that reproduce and require still more lethal chemicals in this ever-escalating chemical warfare.

Some principles are needed with respect to pesticide use and pest definition. When wild species exceed the carrying capacity of a locality or when the species threatens the health and safety of human beings or of animals necessary to humans, then destruction is justified, provided other less drastic methods are not able to work. When creatures do only occasional damage to crops or animals, they should not be exterminated, and some form of just compensation should be made to the person damaged by society. Human health comes before the right of existence of disease-bearing insects and animals.

Methods of eradication should be used that do not cause the pest long and painful suffering before death. The method should be proportional to the potential or actual damage done. Many organic chemical pesticides act like sledge-hammers driving tacks. They are overkillers; they last a long time in the ecosystem; they may harm other animals and human beings. Where possible, physical or biological means are to be used instead of chemical ones. Where chemical methods must be used, those less persistent or toxic to human beings should have first choice. Where stronger chemicals must be used, citizens must be warned of the eradication program and of steps they can take to protect themselves from possible harm. Only licensed applicators should use the chemical pesticides. The materials should not be used in greater quantities or for greater lengths of time than necessary.

REFERENCE

1. J. R. Stevens, "Down to Earth," Louisville *Courier-Journal*, Sept. 4, 1977.

APPENDIX II

ANIMAL AND PLANT "RIGHTS"

Any treatment of ecological justice will sooner or later be faced with the "rights" of plants and animals, or at least the legal standing of species when confronted with ecological threats. Those reflecting on the subject know that every right bears a responsibility. True possessors of rights are those having corresponding duties and responsibilities that require free and rational choices and decisions. Such definitions place rights squarely within the human sphere. Dishwashers have rights to fair wages and good working conditions, and also duties to clean the dishes properly. We don't speak of a dish's right to be clean, only of the consumer's right to a clean dish when purchasing a meal.

Plants and animals stand somewhere between inanimate dishes and human beings. Animals have feelings and experience sensation; they are born, live, and die, and express certain basic needs. Plants need growing space and nutrients. But do these animals and plants have rights? Do they, or at least some of them, have legal standing?

Extension of respect and dignity to animals and plants does not deny traditional human rights, or that the attainment of these rights is an ongoing process. Perhaps the extension of concern about justice issues to animals and plants might even hasten the attainment of human rights. For, ecologically, we realize all things are interrelated. With St. Francis we say "brother fox" and "sister flower." Human beings have evolutionary roots in the same world as other creatures. We are part of a cosmic community dedicated to human service (see Chapter VII), so part of the duty of being possessors of rights is to *share* these rights with other creatures so that they may flourish.

The quality of human life rests in the degree of commitment of service both to our neighbors and to our world. Extending ourselves, sharing and forming community, is part of our social and human nature. Our human right to life extends to the poor, insane, crippled, and aged, and to fetuses, and even beyond the human, for our very well-being depends on the lives of other beings. Our right to life is a shared right. What threatens and endangers animals or plants also in an extended sense threatens us. When viewing ourselves as sole possessors of the earth, we soon isolate ourselves from other creatures' struggles and neglect problems that might soon become human ones.

Once we accept the quality of interrelatedness in the struggle for life, the sharing of rights means, not a demotion, but an emerging understanding of our role as servants and protectors of the creatures of the earth. With this awareness we are more reluctant to *use* animals and plants beyond our basic needs; we see that the standing of these creatures is part of our ecological rights, and a defense of that standing is an enhancement of the entire ecosystem, to which we are vitally linked for our well-being. We might add the rule: when an action is selfish and egocentric, omit it; when it is oriented toward service to others (including other, nonhuman, creatures), do it.

What about eating meat, or, as extreme vegetarians say, eating parts of plants that involves killing them (roots or stems as opposed to berries, fruits, nuts, grains, and leaves)? To model our conduct after nature's laws is dangerous. Carnivorous beings eat others (fish eat insects; birds, fish; cats, birds). Where do human beings fit on the food chain? May others eat us? Nature protects the hunted in a number of ways; those killed are generally killed only to satisfy hunger, but this is not always the case, such as killing to protect habitat or territory.

Sharing our right to life might make us reexamine our use of meat. We certainly must be humane; we can't allow the animal to suffer; we must not waste animal and plant life; when we need to live and be of greater service, meat should not be denied. But are there other arguments, including the symbolism of respect for life and conserving resources through less consumption of or complete abstinence from the use of meat?

APPENDIX III

TRIAGE THEORY

Garrett Hardin, in his seminal article "The Tragedy of the Commons," accurately notes the human proclivity to abuse the part of the environment accessible to all as a common heritage, the *commons*. Individuals, businesses, or certain segments of humanity benefit from exploiting these commons as if they were private preserves. Such short-sighted utilization ignores the limited capacity of the environment to satisfy human wants and comes at the expense of both the social and the physical environment. Since the well-being of all aspects of the environment is interdependent, the denial of the communal nature of the commons causes all to suffer. The tragedy of the commons is readily apparent in resource depletion and pollution—both firmly rooted consumption practices. Wanton consumption of one part of our heritage often causes irreparable harm to another.

For Hardin, the potential danger of untrammeled growth is especially alarming with respect to human population. To couple the "freedom to breed" with the right of everyone to the commons is to lock the world into a tragic course of action. While unregulated use of the commons may have been acceptable at a period of lower population density, it is not so now when growing populations demand more resources. Hardin suggests that one of humanity's highest freedoms is to act in response to a recognized necessity. In conflicts between an ever-increasing population and a finite, fragile environment, he concludes the fulfillment of freedom today means abandoning the "commons in breeding." Continued breeding at present rates will drag both humanity and the larger environment into ruin.

An explicit outgrowth of this train of thought is the triage theory. It is based on the emergency French military practice of dividing the wounded into three groups: the most critically wounded, who are allowed to expire; an intermediate group cared for as resources permit; and, finally, those most likely to live, who will receive the first priority. An analogous apportionment of the world according to gross national product finds three camps: those whose prosperity ensures salvation; a marginal group that will be sustained if resources permit; and the dispossessed, who will not be helped but allowed to expire.

Triage accepts Western lifestyle, consumption, and production—and wastes—as reasonable criteria for survival. Rather than calling into question the exorbitant consumption of the upper third, triage would do away with the lower third (on the economic ladder) whose mute presence arouses guilt in the privileged. Triage ignores the threat to the commons by the overconsumers, which is far greater than that from the destitute. It is unrealistic in expecting the starving masses to pass away quietly. It is shortsighted in failing to see more humane ways of solving the problem. It is immoral in relying on the demise of the least consumers to buy time for continued material indulgences of those doing the most environmental damage.

As Table I indicates, triage is one thing more: it is *racist*, for triagelike categories follow not only economic but racial lines as well. The upper economic third is composed mainly of the white race, the middle one of the yellow, and the bottom of the brown and black. Triage guarantees continued overconsumption of resources at the cost of both ecocide and racism: *ecocide* through widespread and irreparable damage due to production, consumption, and disposal of goods beyond the carrying capacity of the environment; *racism* through cutting away from those in need—who just happen to belong to other races. Are these methods really protection for the commons?

Hardin's underlying assumption is the continued dominance of Western lifestyles, institutions, and political structures, and especially concentration of economic power in the hands of a few. The "colonized" are becoming aware that their own lives have been disrupted by the "wheels of progress"; they know that modern control of land ownership and modes of employment have unsettled many aspects of their existence, including patterns of population growth. They regard these oppressive institutions as far more an immediate threat to the continuity of life than unchecked population; and some of their more radical members are ready to strike out wherever possible.

Hardin's assertion that the commons are finite is certainly accurate. But to bestow a caretaker status on one portion of the population is to deny others the right to self-determination. To allow some to die is to murder them. To require others to become dependent on a paternalistic dole is to deny the basic ethical values elaborated in this book. Charity is not what is needed: justice is. And this justice is recognized by reaffirming the importance of both the human and the nonhuman environment. Unjust institutions that threaten the continuity of life must be confronted and altered. Perhaps the most important ingredient of a just solution to the tragedy of the misuse of the commons is a radical decentralization of control and access to natural resources. Such decentralization fosters self-determination for all, not merely the privileged. This self-determination is a vital prerequisite for a balanced human society where population and material growth rates are stabilized within the confines of limited resources.

Hardin claims the essence of tragedy resides in the solemnity of the remorseless working of things: that is, the inevitability of destiny. Is the world's destiny in the hands of a privileged few who have squandered resources in an unprecedented fashion? *Quis custodiet ipsos custodes?* Who will watch the watchers? Who will question latent ecocide and racism? Rather, should not our destiny be the common lot of all—both human beings and the surrounding environment? Should it not be a cooperation characterized by respect for interdependence, decentralized control of nat-

ural resources, and local self-reliance? Such characteristics—
once seen to be emerging in our tired world—will keep the
temptation to triage subdued.

TABLE I-1 RACIAL COMPOSITION AND ECONOMIC STATUS OF NATIONS

Category Countries	Racial Estimates in Millions of People		
	White	Yellow	Brown/Black
Top Third ($1,100 plus per capita)			
United States and Canada	211	2	28
Europe (excluding Albania and USSR)	472	1	4
USSR (Europe and Asia)	249	10	—
Japan	—	114	—
Australia, New Zealand, and some of Oceania	17	—	1
South Africa	5	—	23
Argentina, Uruguay, Brazil, Surinam, Panama, Bahamas, Puerto Rico, Venezuela, Trinidad	100	1	60
Israel, Cyprus	4	—	—
Taiwan, Hong Kong, Singapore	—	23	—
Saudi Arabia, Iraq, Iran, Qatar, Kuwait, Egypt, Libya, Oman, Gabon	48	—	17
	1,106	150	133

TOTAL: 1,389

TABLE I-2 RACIAL COMPOSITION AND ECONOMIC STATUS OF NATIONS (cont.)

Category Countries	Racial Estimates in Millions of People		
	White	Yellow	Brown/Black
Middle Third ($400–1,100 per capita)			
China	–	865	–
Korea (North and South), Vietnam, Philippines, Malaysia, Mongolia, Papua	3	153	8
Albania	3	–	–
Jordan, Syria, Turkey, Lebanon	52	–	3
Mexico, Chile, Central America (except Panama and Honduras), Colombia, Guyana, Ecuador, Peru, Dominican Republic, Paraguay, Jamaica, Cuba	51	–	108
Algeria, Rhodesia, Botswana, Congo, Swaziland, Zambia, Ghana, Liberia, Ivory Coast, Tunisia	1	–	56
	110	1,018	175

TOTAL: 1,303

TABLE I-3 RACIAL COMPOSITION AND
ECONOMIC STATUS OF NATIONS (cont.)

Category Countries	Racial Estimates in Millions of People		
	White	Yellow	Brown/Black
Lower Third (below $400 per capita)			
Remaining nations of Africa	1	—	335
India	—	—	622
Pakistan, Sri Lanka, Laos, Cambodia, Burma, Thailand	20	88	104
Bangladesh	—	—	81
Yemen and South Yemen	—	—	9
Indonesia	—	72	71
Haiti, Honduras, Bolivia	2	—	12
	23	160	1,234
		TOTAL:	1,417

NOTES

Population estimates and racial composition (where available) were taken from *Information Please Almanac* (New York, 1978), pp. 102–266. Indonesians were assumed to be half yellow and half brown. Iranians, Turks, many of the Asian USSR inhabitants, and Syrians were assumed all white.

In the "Top Third" category are included all the highest gross-national-product nations (Europe, USA, USSR, Japan, Canada, Australia, and New Zealand). All major oil-exporting nations except Indonesia and Nigeria (with very large populations) were included, along with certain strategic nations (Panama) and small industrial nations outside Europe (e.g., Hong Kong). The "Bottom Third" includes the poorest countries of the world. The remainder constitute the "Middle Third" category.

REFERENCES

Hammond Contemporary World Atlas (Garden City, N.Y.: Doubleday & Company, 1974).

G. Hardin, "The Tragedy of the Commons," *Science* 162 (Dec. 13, 1968), reprinted in R. R. Campbell and J. L. Wade, *Society and the Environment: The Coming Collusion* (Boston: Allyn and Bacon, 1972).

E. F. Schumacher, *Small Is Beautiful: Economics as if People Mattered* (New York: Harper and Row, 1975).

DECLARATION OF PRINCIPLES

United Nations Conference on the Environment, Stockholm,
1972

(1) Man has the fundamental right to freedom, equality and adequate conditions of life, in an environment of a quality which permits a life of dignity and well-being, and bears a solemn responsibility to protect and improve the environment for present and future generations. In this respect, policies promoting or perpetuating apartheid, racial segregation, discrimination, colonial and other forms of oppression and foreign domination stand condemned and must be eliminated.

(2) The natural resources of the earth including the air, water, land, flora and fauna and especially representative samples of natural ecosystems must be safeguarded for the benefit of present and future generations through careful planning or management as appropriate.

(3) The capacity of the earth to produce vital renewable resources must be maintained and wherever practicable restored and improved.

(4) Man has a special responsibility to safeguard and wisely manage the heritage of wildlife and its habitat which are now gravely imperiled by a combination of adverse factors. Nature conservation including wildlife must therefore receive importance in planning for economic developments.

(5) The nonrenewable resources of the earth must be employed in such a way as to guard against the danger of their

future exhaustion and to insure that benefits from such employment are shared by all mankind.

(6) The discharge of toxic substances or of other substances and the release of heat, in such quantities or concentrations as to exceed the capacity of the environment to render them harmless, must be halted in order to insure that serious or irreversible damage is not inflicted upon ecosystems. The just struggle of the peoples of all countries against pollution should be supported.

(7) States shall take all possible steps to prevent pollution of the seas by substances that are liable to create hazards to human health, to harm living resources and marine life, to damage amenities or to interfere with other legitimate uses of the sea.

(8) Economic and social development is essential for insuring a favorable living and working environment for man and for creating conditions on earth that are necessary for the improvement of the quality of life.

(9) Environmental deficiencies generated by the conditions of underdevelopment and the natural disasters pose grave problems and can be remedied by accelerated development through the transfer of substantial assistance as a supplement to the domestic effort of the developing countries and such timely assistance as may be required.

(10) For the developing countries, stability of prices and adequate earnings for primary commodities and raw materials are essential to environment management since economic factors as well as ecological processes must be taken into account.

(11) The environmental policies of all states should enhance and not adversely affect the present or future development potential of developing countries, nor should they hamper the attainment of better living conditions for all, and appropriate steps should be taken by states and international organizations with a view to reaching agreement on meeting the possible national and international economic consequences resulting from the application of environmental measures.

(12) Resources should be made available to preserve and improve the environment, taking into account the circum-

stances and particular requirements of developing countries and any costs which may emanate from their incorporating environmental safeguards into their development planning and the need for making available to them, upon their request, additional international technical and financial assistance for this purpose.

(13) In order to achieve a more rational management of resources and thus to improve the environment, states should adopt an integrated and coordinated approach to their development planning so as to insure that development is compatible with the need to protect and improve the human environment for the benefit of their population.

(14) Rational planning constitutes an essential tool for reconciling any conflict between the needs of development and the need to protect and improve the environment.

(15) Planning must be applied to human settlements and urbanization with a view to avoiding adverse effects on the environment and obtaining maximum social, economic and environmental benefits for all. In this respect projects which are designed for colonialist and racist domination must be abandoned.

(16) Demographic policies which are without prejudice to basic human rights, and which are deemed appropriate by governments concerned, should be applied in those regions where the rate of population growth or excessive population concentrations are likely to have adverse effects in the environment or development, or where low population density may prevent improvement of the human environment and impede development.

(17) Appropriate national institutions must be entrusted with the task of planning, managing or controlling the environmental resources of states with the view to enhancing environmental quality.

(18) Science and technology, as part of their contribution to economic and social development, must be applied to the identification, avoidance and control of environmental risks and the solution of environmental problems and for the common good of mankind.

(19) Education in environmental matters, for the younger generation as well as adults, giving due consideration to the

underprivileged, is essential in order to broaden the basis for an enlightened opinion and responsible conduct by individuals, enterprises and communities in protecting and improving the environment in its full human dimension. It is essential that mass media of communications avoid contributing to the deterioration of the environment, but, on the contrary, disseminate information of an educational nature on the need to protect and improve the environment in order to enable man to develop in every respect.

(20) Scientific research and development in the context of environmental problems, both national and multinational, must be promoted in all countries, especially the developing countries. In this connection, the free flow of up-to-date scientific information and experience must be supported and assisted, to facilitate the solution of environmental problems: environmental technologies should be made available to developing countries on terms which would encourage their wide dissemination without constituting an economic burden on the developing countries.

(21) States have, in accordance with the Charter of the United Nations and the principles of international law, the sovereign right to exploit their own resources pursuant to their own environmental policies, and the responsibility to insure that activities within their jurisdiction or control do not cause damage to the environment of other states or of areas beyond the limits of national jurisdiction.

(22) States shall cooperate to develop further the international law regarding liability and compensation for the victim of pollution and other environmental damage caused by activities within the jurisdiction or control of such states to areas beyond their jurisdiction.

(23) Without prejudice to such general principles as may be agreed upon by the international community, or to the criteria and minimum levels which will have to be determined nationally, it will be essential in all classes to consider the systems of values prevailing in each country, and the extent of the applicability of standards which are valid for the most advanced countries but which may be inappropriate and of unwarranted social cost for the developing countries.

(24) International matters concerning the protection and

improvement of the environment should be handled in a cooperative spirit by all countries, big or small, on an equal footing. Cooperation through multilateral or bilateral arrangements or other appropriate means is essential to prevent, eliminate or reduce and effectively control adverse environmental effects resulting from activities conducted in all spheres, in such a way that due account is taken of the sovereignty and interests of all states.

(25) States shall insure that international organizations play a coordinated, efficient and dynamic role for the protection and improvement of the environment.

(26) Man and his environment must be spared the effects of nuclear weapons and all other means of mass destruction. States must strive to reach prompt agreement, in the relevant international organs, on the elimination and complete destruction of such weapons.

INDEX

Pine marten, 29

Plains Indians, 26

Plant species, extinction of, 15. *See also* Endangered species

Plutonium, 66, 67, 76, 77–78; reprocessing, 79–80

Pneumoconiosis, 108

Polonium, 55–56

Polychlorinated biphenyls (PCB's), 130, 134, 137, 213

Pope, R. M., 35, 36

Population limitation, qualitative growth and, 185–86

Potassium, radioactive, 58

Preservation movement, 16–25, 37–45; citizen action, 44–45; commercial value and, 39–40; development versus preservation cases, 43–44; ecological value and, 37; ethics of, 37–41; game, recreational, and observational values, 41; gene pools, 42–43; justifiable extinctions, 44; planning and land management, 41–42; policy implications, 41–45; rationale for, 17–25; scientific and medical value, 39; species uniqueness and, 38–39

President's Council on Wage and Price Stability, 112

Prine, John, 95

Pronghorn antelope, 22

Propanil (pesticide), 137

Prophecy, conservation consciousness and, as reason for simple lifestyle, 218

Prudence, defined, 8

Public Citizen (lobby group), 264

Pupfish: desert, 21, 36, 39; Devil's Hole, 19, 21

"Purchase time" strategy, 188–89

Qualitative growth, 9, 169–98; AT techniques, 192–94; evolving strategies, 185–89; guidelines, 194–97; historical and cultural background of, 172–79; material growth pains, 179–85; preferred strategy, 189–97; steady-state economy, 190–92; stewardship concept and, 250–51; visions of the future, 189–90. *See also* Lifestyle choices

Quality of life, meaning of, 202–3

Quinine, 21

Radiation, 53–75; exposure from nuclear facilities, 69–75; ionizing, health hazards of, 53–75; low-level doses (recent developments), 65–68; low-level hazards (early estimates), 56–60; nuclear reactor safety, 72–75; routine emissions, 69–70;